MW00787649

Zen and the White Whale

Zen and the White Whale

A Buddhist Rendering of *Moby-Dick*

Daniel Herman

LEHIGH UNIVERSITY PRESS
Bethlehem

Published by Lehigh University Press
Copublished with Rowman & Littlefield
4501 Forbes Boulevard, Suite 200, Lanham, Maryland 20706
www.rowman.com

10 Thornbury Road, Plymouth PL6 7PP, United Kingdom

Copyright © 2014 by Daniel Herman

All rights reserved. No part of this book may be reproduced in any form or by any
electronic or mechanical means, including information storage and retrieval systems,
without written permission from the publisher, except by a reviewer who may quote
passages in a review.

British Library Cataloguing in Publication Information Available

Library of Congress Cataloging-in-Publication Data

Herman, Daniel, 1980-
Zen and the White Whale : a Buddhist Rendering of Moby-Dick / Daniel Herman.
pages cm
Includes bibliographical references and index.
ISBN 978-1-61146-156-5 (cloth : alk. paper) -- ISBN 978-1-61146-157-2 (electronic)
) 1. Melville, Herman, 1819-1891. Moby Dick. 2. Melville, Herman, 1819-1891--Philosophy. 3. Zen
Buddhism in literature. I. Title.
PS2384.M62H375 2014
813'.3--dc23
2014007741

∞™ The paper used in this publication meets the minimum requirements of American
National Standard for Information Sciences Permanence of Paper for Printed Library
Materials, ANSI/NISO Z39.48-1992.

Printed in the United States of America

"There's another rendering now;
but still one text."
—Stubb

Contents

Introduction

Herman Melville's *Moby-Dick* and the teachings of Zen Buddhism share a central premise: that the ultimate truths of the universe cannot be distilled by conventional understanding, and that our "intellectual and spiritual exasperations"[1] arise from a desperate need for concrete answers to these ungraspable truths. The two are similarly unambiguous regarding the inevitable result of such philosophical endeavors. The canonical Zen Buddhist text *Hsin Hsin Ming* warns, "The more you talk and think about it, the further astray you wander from the truth."[2] Melville is even more severe, warning us that the consequence of chasing said truths (or their cetological manifestation) is "being eternally stove and sunk by him. Wherefore, it seems to me you had best not be too fastidious in your curiosity touching this Leviathan."[3]

Despite dispensing advice to the contrary, Herman Melville, by all historical accounts, was himself unable to resist chasing the White Whale, and engaged in a lifelong pursuit of these ultimate truths. One place this quest led him, as has become more clear in recent years, was toward an interest in the teachings of what we now know as "Buddhism," which had become much more widely known in the United States during the second half of the nineteenth century. Melville was a voracious reader, and knew of the historical Buddha through William Rounseville Alger's *The Solitudes of Nature and of Man* (1867) and, in particular, the widely-read volume *The Light of Asia* by Sir Edwin Arnold (1879).[4] Melville's apparent enthusiasm for Buddhism was such that in his final decade he wrote a short poem called "Buddha," began his epic poem *Clarel* by mentioning Buddha (within a declaration on "the intersympathy of creeds"),[5] and may even have had the Enlightened One in mind when lending his last doomed protagonist "Billy" the surname "Budd."[6]

But one cannot ignore that the short poem suggests a rather simplistic (and heavily Christianized) understanding of Buddhist soteriology, *Clarel* spends 18,000 lines desperate for the Levant's desert to slake his spiritual thirst, and surely the traditionally Christian imagery and allegory is more central to *Billy Budd* than any ostensible Buddhist influence. So why wonder about Melville's exposure to what was, at the time, a strange esoteric faith? Because decades earlier, I will argue, a much younger, intellectually adventurous Herman Melville demonstrated a profoundly sophisticated understanding of Buddhist philosophy in *Moby-Dick*. Such regression from a sophisticated understanding of Buddhism to a simplistic one is on the face of it unlikely, and part of my study of Melville's interest in Buddhism will be to explain why it may have happened.

Not long before he died, Shunryu Suzuki Roshi, a twentieth-century Japanese Zen master pivotal in bringing Buddhist practice to the West, told his students, "Life is like stepping onto a boat that is about to sail out to sea and sink."[7] Incidentally, so is *Moby-Dick*. It is the story of a young man who joins a whaleboat, the Captain of which is on a vengeful quest for a certain sperm whale. After chasing the whale around the world, they finally find him, at which point the whale rams the ship and the ship sinks.

It is a relatively simple premise, but for decades, scholars have struggled to affix definitive meanings to this kaleidoscopic book, and the eponymous white whale at its elusive center. In both its central narrative and tangential meanderings, *Moby-Dick* allows for myriad interpretations, from a Freudian focus on unconscious desires and sexual repression to a political scientist's study of manipulative leadership and dictatorial power. Although these interpretations differ markedly from one another, the questions with which they concern themselves are the same ones that human beings ask of God, or the universe: What does it all mean? Where did it come from? How are we supposed to understand this life? What are we supposed to do with it? Herman Melville, again, struggled with these questions his entire life—indeed, it is this inquiring impulse that would have led him to explore Eastern religions.

In this respect he is not unlike Captain Ahab, whose inability to abide with uncertainty drives the course of the narrative. As Nathaniel Hawthorne wrote of Melville, "[He] will never rest until he gets hold of a definite belief."[8] What sets Melville apart from Captain Ahab is that the sea captain does indeed have a definite belief, and his quest is to test—that is, prove or disprove—that belief. But Melville, again to quote Hawthorne, could "neither believe, nor be comfortable in his unbelief; and he is too honest and courageous not to try to do one or the other." This brings him close to Ishmael, the only character in *Moby-Dick* who is entirely without a distinct set of beliefs to which he is attached. Melville was able to instill his narrator with the equanimity that he himself never found in his own life—aligning, as it were, his objective with that of ninth-century Chinese Zen master Dong-shan (807–869), who said, "My idea is to have no particular idea."[9]

So perhaps it is appropriate that the very notion of the "White Whale" has become colloquial shorthand for something that is unattainable, but will nevertheless be steadfastly pursued. Japanese Zen traditions have a proclivity toward unattainable, seemingly paradoxical vows—suggesting that although a task may be impossible, there is merit in the attempt. Melville himself warns us that the whale "must remain unpainted to the last"[10] (a warning that surely implies "unwritten" as well), but then spends pages and pages attempting to paint a picture of it for the reader. Make no mistake, it is a task he eagerly takes up: "Fain am I to stagger to this emprise under the weightiest words of the dictionary."[11] Zen teachings, however, are (perhaps unsurprisingly) rather more stern about such literary enterprises. Zen master Dongshan wrote, "The meaning does not reside in the words . . . Just to portray it in literary form is to stain it with defilement."[12] Any endeavor that points away from oneself, that searches for answers beyond one's own mind, is doomed to fail. With that in mind, let us meet our narrator.

Ishmael begins the story very close to ending his life. He tells us little about where he has come from (other than he used to be a schoolteacher), but he makes clear that the only thing that can save him is "to get to sea as soon as I can. This is my substitute for pistol and ball."[13] These first chapters (the so-called "land chapters") leave no doubt that there remains little resemblance between Ishmael the restless roustabout wandering around Manhattan and Ishmael the sagacious narrator recalling his former self. The most obvious difference—it almost seems as if Ishmael is caricaturing himself—is in his social interactions. He is disgruntled, unsettled, and morose; pugnacious, impatient, and verbose. His friendship with the "savage" Queequeg has an immediate and profound effect on him, to be discussed at length later on. But it is when he steps aboard the Pequod that the Ishmael of the land chapters evaporates, and, for vast sections at a time, almost ceases to exist as a personage on the whaleship. His place is taken by Ishmael the narrator, speaking backward into the past, with his avatar stowed somewhere below-deck. Within this narration, and the sundry explorations and preoccupations that occupy much of the book, Ishmael presents a comprehensive testimony regarding the means of his spiritual development from the former Ishmael to the latter.

This spiritual practice (surely it is not too much to call it that) is remarkably closely aligned with the two main branches of Buddhist meditation: tranquility (or *shamatha*) meditation, and insight (or *vipassana*) meditation. It is for this reason that, while Ishmael spends a great deal of time explaining why both water and whales are essential to his spiritual journey, not everyone on the Pequod has access to this largesse. Captain Ahab has his own unique relationship with water—and, needless to say, also with a certain white whale. But his unshakable conviction that the way to resolve his existential questions is through destroying Moby Dick is precisely the reason he does not progress toward wisdom as Ishmael does. In fact, not only does he not progress, but the unrequited hunt plainly has a detrimental, even devastating effect on Ahab, as well as on those around him. As Zen master Nanquan (748–835), one of the most important teachers of the T'ang period in China, said, "If you try to direct yourself toward it, you go away from it."[14] A thousand years later, British Zen enthusiast R.H. Blyth wrote: "It is the very search, and the excessive zeal of it, which causes the truth to disappear. In our hot grasp the truth wilts away."[15]

Things only deteriorate for Ahab—until the end of the book, where he has a series of profound insights that effect an unmistakable change in the Captain. It is at this moment, having allowed himself the space to step back and for a moment even reconsider his vengeful errand, that the White Whale immediately shows up. Linji, the founder of the Rinzai school of Zen, said, "If you seek him, he retreats farther and farther away; if you don't seek him, then he's right there before your eyes, his wondrous voice resounding in your ears."[16]

But what exactly are these men seeking? What is the White Whale? There is, again, no shortage of interpretations, both from the characters within the book and the critics without. The most common interpretation, as rather over-confidently asserted by Edward F. Edinger in 1992, is that "there can be no doubt that the White Whale symbolizes the deity."[17] But as Newton Arvin points out, Moby Dick cannot be so easily reduced: "[Moby Dick] is certainly not the God of orthodox or even of modernist Christianity. . . [I]t may symbolize both the most spiritual of things, even the Christian Deity, and also the things most appalling to mankind. It cannot . . . reassuringly and finally symbolize the Christian God."[18] Arvin's final admission, that the White Whale is "a symbol of irreducible ambiguity," is certainly closer to the mark, and speaks to the lack of a consensus both on the whaleship and in the library.

This ambiguity is what inspires Ahab's wrath: "That inscrutable thing is chiefly what I hate," he says, "and be the white whale agent, or be the white whale principal, I will wreak that hate upon him."[19] But for Ishmael the whale's inscrutable nature is an object of fascination, and even veneration. Extended digressions into the whale's anatomy and physiology, intelligence and diet serve as means to express the fundamental ungraspability of the whale. His quest is not to know the whale, but *to know that it cannot be known*. While this book will touch upon many theories about the whale, these two will be discussed at length: Ahab's view will largely be dissected to expose it as not only specious but dangerous and ineffectual, while Ishmael's view will be considered through its alignment with the fundamental tenets of

Buddhist philosophy, particularly in regarding the whale as a representation and manifestation of the Buddha's central teaching: the dependently co-arisen nature of all phenomena.

Thomas Cleary argues that the Zen school was founded on the premise of studying Buddhism "not as an object of knowledge (intellectualism) but as a means of knowledge (experientialism)."[20] This is essentially what separates Ishmael and Ahab, and their competing conceptions of the White Whale. For although the two men share a common touchstone in the idea of the whale, their motives and methods in approaching it are brought into sharp relief as contrasting examples of right conduct and wrong conduct. As we will see, Ahab's attitude of self-clinging—that is, "refusing to give up, or even examine, belief in an inherently existing self"[21]—not only pushes the White Whale ever further away, but also, as the monomaniacal pursuit takes its toll on his body and mind, pulls himself further back from the peace and serenity he claims he seeks. He is fixated on his pursuit, and cannot tolerate anything that does not directly contribute to his mission. He gives the blacksmith his razors, telling him, "Take them, man, I have no need for them; for I now neither shave, sup, nor pray" until the White Whale is dead.[22] His obsession with Moby Dick is such that, after years spent as a whaling captain, he has even lost interest in all other sperm whales. Ishmael writes, "It would be refining too much . . . to hint that his vindictiveness toward the White Whale might have possibly extended itself in some degree to all Sperm Whales."[23] He allows the crew to chase other whales solely to protect against the threat of a mutiny.

Ishmael, meanwhile, is similarly fascinated with the "Albino whale," and can even get in tune with Ahab's "fiery hunt."[24] But he is fascinated with everything! Sperm whales, right whales, whaleships—and also, judging from his dozens of esoteric allusions, history, geography, religious thought, even the fiber arts. He sees the White Whale as the "symbol" of the "immensities of the universe,"[25] but just that—a symbol. The White Whale, "by its indefiniteness . . . shadows forth" intimations of the mystery, and allows us to come close to otherwise ungraspable truths.[26] It recalls the words of Eihei Dogen Zenji (1200–1253), the founder of the Soto Zen sect in Japan, who used the reflection of the moon in water as an illustration of the way enlightenment is manifested within a person's mind. Dogen said, "Enlightenment is like the moon reflected on the water. The moon does not get wet, nor is the water broken. Although its light is wide and great, the moon is reflected even in a puddle an inch wide. The whole moon and the entire sky are reflected in dewdrops on the grass, or even in one drop of water."[27] Ishmael's steady, careful awareness shows that he recognizes this mystery is everywhere around us, at every moment. His conduct follows the advice in "Harmony of Difference and Equality" (*Sandokai*), the foundational Zen poem written by

Chinese Zen master Shitou Xiqian (Japanese: Sekito Kisen, 700–790)[28]: "I respectfully urge you who study the mystery / Do not pass your days and nights in vain."[29]

This project began as an exploration of the parallels between *Moby-Dick* and Zen Buddhist philosophy. As I conducted my research, I discovered synchronicities between *Moby-Dick* and Zen literature that tested the conceivable limits of mere coincidence. Less expected was a wealth of evidence that the period in which Melville wrote the book was a particularly auspicious time for an American author to begin incorporating Buddhist themes in his work. This has led me to push further, and attempt to argue that Buddhism—which Melville had almost certainly encountered by the time he began writing *Moby-Dick*—might actually have had an influence on its composition.

To be clear, in the mid-nineteenth century, at the time of writing *Moby-Dick,* Melville could not possibly have had any direct access to classic Zen texts, since no translations would exist in the United States for at least another forty years.[30] The Zen school would not be formally introduced to the West until the World Parliament of Religions in 1893, two years after Herman Melville's death. However, as I will show, information about Zen was indeed available through more indirect channels. I also argue that this information would have been uniquely appealing to Melville, as a mysterious collection of doctrines and practices not yet collated and labeled by Western academics (unlike Hinduism and some other Buddhist schools), to the extent that it was often only tenuously connected to the historical Buddha himself, and even the word "Zen" was completely unknown.

I am not claiming an exclusive or programmatic influence, or arguing that Melville was led to write *Moby-Dick* as a way of directly expressing his new interest in Buddhist thought. Rather, I would describe my objective in terms similar to the ones Ishmael uses to describe his own: "[I] shall be content to produce the desired impression by separate citations of items, practically or reliably known to me as a whaleman; and from these citations, I take it,—the conclusion aimed at will naturally follow of itself."[31] By providing a historical context for Melville's encounters with Buddhist thought, and then investigating specifically what texts he may have had access to, I believe a compelling case will be made for the validity and significance of the reading that follows.[32]

That said, it is my intention to avoid rigid statements about the connections suggested herein. Considering the breadth and depth of Melville scholarship, it would be outrageous to suggest this interpretation as *Moby-Dick*'s cornerstone, somehow left undisturbed by the decades of literary masonry. After all, on one level *Moby-Dick* is a cautionary tale, warning us of the dangers of stubbornly attaching oneself to one specific explanation and interpretation of reality. Ishmael's repeated references to the subjectivity of interpretation are not intended to vilify interpretation, but rather to remind us not to confuse our individual construal with objective reality. Just as every whaleman in the novel has his own unique notion regarding Moby Dick the whale, every reader has his or her own unique understanding of *Moby-Dick* the book. As Ishmael might say, it "begins to assume different aspects, according to your point of view."[33] To insist that any particular reading of the novel is somehow truer, or more worthwhile, than all others is to fall into the same trap as Captain Ahab. So rather than setting out with an underlying "hypothesis" I will struggle to prove, perhaps I can call this an approach (a "hyper-thesis," perhaps, hovering weightlessly above these pages)—a possible way of considering the novel, that I hope will be of interest.

The reader may well ask why I am limiting myself to a Zen Buddhist perspective, rather than another of the great religious traditions of the Buddhist world. The simple answer would be that, in *Moby-Dick*, I find greater resonance with Zen teachings than with any other tradition. But the full answer is rather more complicated. First, by narrowly restricting my focus, I hope to avoid the inevitable schismatic differences in philosophical doctrine that would result from having to consider conflicting dogma between rival sects. Indeed, the schools that collectively fall under the umbrella called "Zen" contain within them considerable differences in both doctrine and practice. We cannot avoid questions about the doctrinal continuity between the ancient wisdom of classical Zen texts and the contemporary commentaries and interpolations on those texts (let alone the brief and often polemical sketches in travellers' accounts and colonialist studies available to Herman Melville). Before we are able to approach those questions, I should first take a moment to clarify what I mean by "Zen."

As religious traditions spread, they are invariably filtered through the cultural contexts into which they arrive. Just as the Chinese Ch'an tradition was affected by its transplant into Japanese soil, so too has Japanese Zen undergone a transformation through its enthusiastic adoption by Western countries. This latter resettlement is a particularly thorny one, wrapped as it is in complicated issues of Western philosophical influence on the Japanese intellectuals responsible for introducing Zen to the West, and the presentation of Zen as a tradition purposely adapted to Western sensibilities. The prevailing Western conception of Zen can be traced almost exclusively to Japanese intellectual D.T. Suzuki, the man whom Buddhist scholar Robert Sharf calls the "indefatigable proselytizer" of Zen.[34] But, rather paradoxically, even as Suzuki introduced the West to the study of Zen, he simultaneously rejected its existence as an object of study. Sharf writes:

> In his voluminous writings Suzuki advanced the notion that Zen eschews all doctrine, all ritual, all institutions, and is thus, in the final analysis, not a

religion at all. Zen is pure experience itself, the experiential essence lying
behind all authentic religious teachings. . . . This view of Zen has become so
well established that many hesitate to speak of Zen at all for fear of being
censured as insufficiently experienced. [35]

Suzuki's legacy has come under fire in recent decades from Zen scholars
(Sharf and others), but there is no denying his centrality to the West's enthusiastic reception to Zen in the twentieth century. Suzuki was present at Zen's
formal arrival on the world stage, when his teacher Shaku Soen Roshi spoke
(with Suzuki serving as his translator) at the World Parliament of Religions
in 1893.[36] And in the succeeding decades, Suzuki's writings stood as the
paramount authority for the first generation of Westerners interested in Zen.
Even today, it is Suzuki's popularized—and now commodified—notion of
Zen that remains prevalent in the West.

It wasn't until the mid-twentieth century, and primarily through the writings of the Beat Generation, that Zen truly entered the American imagina-
tion. The Summer 1958 issue of the *Chicago Review* offers a neat encapsula-
tion of what "Zen" meant to the American public at the tail end of the post-
war years: writings by Allen Ginsberg, Jack Kerouac, Gary Snyder, Philip
Whalen, and others. Perhaps most emblematic is an essay by Alan Watts, the
British theologian whose prominence as a communicator of Zen ideas was
surpassed only by D.T. Suzuki himself. The essay, titled "Beat Zen, Square
Zen, and Zen," deals directly with the presumption that what Kerouac and
company were doing had anything at all to do with the ancient traditions
from China and Japan.[37] As the title roguishly suggests, Watts had his
doubts:

Beat Zen is a complex phenomenon. It ranges from a use of Zen for justifying
sheer caprice in art, literature, and life to a very forceful social criticism and
"digging of the universe" such as one may find in the poetry of Ginsberg and
Snyder, and, rather unevenly, in Kerouac. But, as I know it, it is always a
shade too self-conscious, too subjective, and too strident to have the flavor of
Zen.[38]

Elsewhere Watts is less generous, describing the lifestyle of the Beats—
which for many devotees had exemplified the Zen way of life (particularly in
Kerouac's *The Dharma Bums*)—as "the life of undisciplined whimsy."[39]

Just a few years after Watts's essay, however, the landscape of American
Zen changed dramatically. New teachers began to arrive from Asia (even as
more Western seekers began traveling to Asia to track them down), and a
proliferation of teachings and traditions resulted. Perhaps most significantly,
these teachers established practice centers where, for the first time, curious
Americans could have a direct, unmediated experience with Buddhist practice.[40]

My own introduction to Zen, forty years later, gives an idea what this process of assimilation and appropriation looks like in the early twenty-first century: I first tried sitting meditation as a discontented college student, facing the wall in my dorm room with a copy of Shunryu Suzuki's *Zen Mind, Beginner's Mind* by my side. After graduation, I drove to California and began residential practice at the temples of Suzuki Roshi's San Francisco Zen Center, immersing myself in Buddhist philosophical texts and engaging with the teachings both in formal meditation and in discussion with recognized masters in his lineage. Some years later, during a period of monastic training at Tassajara, the first Buddhist monastery in the West, I read *Moby-Dick* for the first time, and began this project shortly thereafter, as a doctoral dissertation at Victoria University in Wellington, New Zealand.

Just as my understanding of Zen is shaped by the forces described above, my reading of *Moby-Dick* is shaped by my understanding of Zen. It is surely unsurprising that, in studying the sketches and images of Zen Buddhism Melville glimpsed in the 1840s, I find much that is consonant with Western Zen teachings from the twentieth and twenty-first centuries. But this intricate brocade of influence and interpretation is not a new phenomenon—again, any tradition transplanted into a foreign culture will be shaped by the many forces surrounding its arrival. In fact, this is how Zen practitioners have always engaged with the teachings—studying the classic texts of ancient masters, while also receiving commentary and interpretation from contemporary teachers. While contemporary teachings are of course very different from the ancient wisdom from which they spring, both stand fundamentally united as unique expressions of Shakyamuni Buddha's original realization.

In my view, the popular idea of Zen—that it is a specific state or experience that one must strive to realize or attain—is an incorrect understanding of the term. Zen is not itself ineffable, as D.T. Suzuki claimed, but rather is a word used to *describe* the ineffable. Writing about Zen, in turn, is a means of pointing the reader toward the ineffable. It is in this context that I believe *Moby-Dick* can itself be legitimately referred to as a Zen text, pointing as it does toward the incalculable depths of the ocean and the mind.

One way of thinking about this reading would be to compare it to Stubb's inspection of the gold coin in the chapter "The Doubloon." Although the astrological symbols engraved around the coin's edge are visible to every sailor, only Stubb (sort of an amateur astrologer) is able to interpret them as the signs of the Zodiac. But perhaps all the "strange figures and inscriptions" on the coin are like scattered stars,[41] between which each sailor draws lines and imagines connections to fit his story about the world—just as every reader of *Moby-Dick* will isolate those aspects and images that illuminate his or her ideas about the book. The crucial question, it seems to me, is whether Melville would recognize the constellations we describe.

In the spirit of Ishmael's cetological caveat—"I promise nothing complete; because any human thing supposed to be complete must for that very reason be faulty"[42]—I should set some parameters for the pages to follow. My objective is to provide a framework within which this reading of *Moby-Dick* can be placed—first by providing a very brief sketch of the trajectory of Western attitudes toward Buddhism leading up to 1851, then by attempting to focus specifically on those works that have the most resonance with Melville's *Moby-Dick* (most especially the ones he is either known to have read, or at least where a strong likelihood exists). I will then turn to the reading itself.

It is my intention that this book should be accessible to anyone with a familiarity with *Moby-Dick*. Buddhist concepts are explained as concisely and thoroughly as possible, often citing the teachings at the root of the historical Zen lineage—particularly Shakyamuni Buddha and the philosophers of the Madhyamaka school. In addition, I hope my use of contemporary Western texts as sources of Buddhist doctrine will aid comprehension to the novice reader. My goal is to present these teachings as I have received them from my teachers—and, more specifically, how I interpret them in relation to Melville's inspiring, devastating masterpiece. I hope that the pages that follow will remain true to this intention.

Finally, a few stylistic notes: I follow Melville's precedent of writing the name of the novel with a hyphen (*Moby-Dick*), while writing the name of the White Whale without a hyphen (Moby Dick). Similarly, I have retained Melville's variable capitalization of "Sperm Whale" when quoting passages from the book, but otherwise leave it lowercase. "White Whale," when used as a proper noun, will be capitalized. I follow Melville's use of the word "harpooneer" instead of the modern "harpooner." On the Buddhist side of things, Chinese, Japanese, Pali, and Sanskrit words are rendered phonetically, and without diacritical marks. As is customary, I have retained Japanese titles of respect for Zen teachers, such as Sensei, Roshi, and Zenji.

I

Melville's Encounters with Buddhism

Chapter One

The Prologue to Buddhist Studies

In January of 1844, an excerpt from the *Lotus Sutra*—the first translation of a Buddhist text into English—appeared in Boston's Transcendentalist literary journal *The Dial*, under the title "The Preaching of Buddha." Four months later, also in Boston, Professor Edward Salisbury delivered a series of lectures to the American Oriental Society that constituted perhaps the first cohesive, sophisticated representation of Buddhist history in the West. These two events alone are considered so significant, 1844 has been described as the year Buddhism entered the public consciousness in America—the year when Western understanding of Buddhism, which had undergone a gradual process of refinement between the thirteenth and eighteenth centuries, entered what was, at the time, its most auspicious era of study and understanding.

In December of that same year—again in Boston, as "those stage managers, the Fates"[1] would have it—the USS United States arrived at port, and Herman Melville returned to shore after four years at sea.

It is difficult today to appreciate the challenges an eighteenth- or nineteenth-century American would have faced in trying to locate any information about Asian systems of thought. As Thomas Tweed writes in *The American Encounter with Buddhism*,

> Almost every American interpreter drew the map of the religious world this way: There were 1. Christians, 2. Jews, 3. "Mohametans," 4. "heathens" or "pagans." . . . These spiritual cartographers usually lumped together Confucianism, Taoism, Buddhism, Shinto, Hinduism, and all other South and East Asian traditions [under the fourth heading].[2]

For example: in 1704, Daniel DeFoe published his *A Dictionary of All Religions, Ancient and Modern, Whether Jewish, Pagan, Christian, or Mahome-*

tan. More than a hundred years later, in 1824, the publication of David Benedict's *A History of All Religions, as Divided into Paganism, Mahometanism, Judaism and Christianity*, showed that popular understanding had not developed much in the interim.

Among that small slice of the public who *were* able to differentiate between the last category, Islam, Hinduism and Confucianism were the most familiar (or perhaps more accurately, the "least unfamiliar"). Buddhism in particular was repeatedly overshadowed by even these lesser-known religions: by Confucianism in China, Hinduism in India, Shinto in Japan. These "minor" religions remained obscure for decades more, until the World's Parliament of Religions met in Chicago in 1893.

Buddhist scholarship cannot truly be said to have begun until 1837, commencing a period that constituted a quantum leap forward in Buddhist studies. In that year, Brian Hodgson, an official of the East India Company in Nepal, collected about 400 previously unknown Buddhist texts—among them some of the most important texts in the Buddhist canon, including *Prajnaparamita, Lankavatara Sutra, Bodhicaryavatra,* and *Saddharmapundarika Sutra* (aka the *Lotus Sutra*). Hodgson made some attempts at his own scholarship, writing a brief "Sketch of Buddhism, derived from the Bauddha Scriptures of Nepaul," published in 1830 in the *Transactions of the Royal Asiatic Society of Great Britain and Ireland*, in which he wrote:

> I conceived the idea of drawing up . . . a sketch of the terminology and general disposition of the external parts of Buddhism, in the belief that such a sketch, though but imperfectly executed, would be of some assistance to such of my countrymen as, with the books only before them, might be disposed to enter into a full and accurate investigation of this almost unknown subject. [3]

As Buddhist scholar Donald S. Lopez tells us, Hodgson had both "a deep interest and a disdain for the doctrines of Buddhism." [4] He described himself as "a mere collector," and in his attempts at analysis, Lopez writes, he got almost everything wrong. Stephen Batchelor contends that "Buddhist ideas were of no more significance to him than a rare species of Himalayan insect," and quotes Hodgson as saying he had "no purpose to meddle with the interminable sheer absurdities of the Bauddha religion or philosophy." [5] What we know for sure is that Hodgson was unable to do any translation himself, and so sent off copies of his manuscripts to Calcutta, London, and Paris. While copies sent to the first two locales were largely ignored, the Parisian copies were received by Eugene Burnouf, who oversaw the translation into French from Sanskrit and Tibetan. Burnouf had twenty years earlier produced the world's first grammar of Pali (the language of the historical Buddha), and now set to work on his *Introduction a l'histoire du bouddhisme indie*, relying almost entirely on material received from Hodgson (to whom he would later dedicate his translation of the *Lotus Sutra*). The 1844 work is today considered "the most influential scholarly work on Buddhism in the nineteenth century."[6]

Burnouf's work crossed the Atlantic almost immediately. His translation of the *Lotus Sutra* was excerpted in the January 1844 issue of the Transcendentalist literary journal *The Dial*, under the heading "The Preaching of Buddha," appearing along with a brief summary of the life of Shakyamuni Buddha also taken from Burnouf's book. Long attributed to Henry David Thoreau, the translation from French into English is now known to have been done by Elizabeth Palmer Peabody[7]—leading Transcendentalist, publisher and business manager of *The Dial*, and sister to Nathaniel Hawthorne's wife Sophia (who Melville saw often while writing *Moby-Dick*). Four months later, in May, Edward E. Salisbury could declare confidently in Boston:

> It may be taken for granted, that Buddhism is of Indian origin. The time has been, when from the want of sufficient materials, out of which to form a correct judgment, and from the force of ingenuity seeking to supply that want by theorizing upon fancied etymologies and the like, men of great learning could differ on the question, whether the originator of this religious system was a native of Hindustan, or of Scythia, or a negro. But there is no longer any ground for such disputation. The history of Buddhism, as it may now be gathered from books of the Buddhists themselves, not only of India, but also of China, Tibet, and Mongolia, refers to Central India as the first seat of this religious system; and its doctrines, so far as they are understood, have evidently grown out of Brahmanism.

When Herman Melville left New Bedford on the *Acushnet* in 1841, Buddhism was as little known in the United States as the native peoples of the Marquesas. Upon his return, the possibilities for exploration had expanded almost as much as his own.

Chapter Two

A Universal Absorber

In the first chapter of his 1929 biography of Herman Melville, Lewis Mumford makes an interesting, and unexpected, comparison: "Melville, like Buddha, left a happy and successful career behind him, and plunged into those cold black depths, the depths of the sunless ocean, the blackness of interstellar space."[1] The analogy is tenuous, and Mumford almost certainly did not mean to suggest any weighty connection between the two men. Nevertheless, within two decades of Mumford's book (one of a handful of works credited with initiating the so-called Melville Revival of the 1920s), attempts to discern the sources for some of Melville's freewheeling allusions led scholars to investigate his relationship with Eastern thought—beginning with Howard P. Vincent's *The Trying-Out of Moby-Dick* (1949), which identified Thomas Maurice as the source of Melville's "Vishnu" references. But while his knowledge of "Vishnu,"[2] "the caves of Elephanta,"[3] and the "Grand Lama"[4] assured scholars that Melville was indeed somewhat familiar with Eastern traditions, what level of interest lay beneath these surface allusions remained obscure.

Part of the problem lay in the indefinite parameters of "the Orient." Just as they had been to religious scholars a hundred years prior, the belief systems of India and China were of secondary concern to scholars investigating Melville's religious interests. In plumbing the depths of Melville's "Orientalism," they mostly busied themselves with the faiths of what they called the Near East: Dorothee Finklestein's *Melville's Orienda* (1961) offered an exhaustive catalogue of Melville's engagement with Islamic thought; H. Bruce Franklin's *The Wake of the Gods* (1963) confidently declared the White Whale "an Egyptian myth incarnate," while dismissing Melville's incorporation of Hindu symbols as "ridicule" (a claim contested at length in H.B.

7

Kulkarni's *Moby-Dick: A Hindu Avatar: A Study of Hindu Myth and Thought in Moby-Dick* [1971]).

Regarding Buddhism, however, a consensus of ambiguity seems to have solidified. Each of these studies mentions Melville's possible interest in Buddhism, if only in a brief aside. But content to have established some semblance of a connection, the *influence* this interest might have had on his work remained largely unexplored. As William Braswell wrote in 1973, "He had neither the knowledge of the Oriental scriptures nor the reverence for them that Alcott, Emerson, and Thoreau had; but various references show that he knew something about Hinduism, Buddhism, and the Persian religions."[5] Indeed, a thorough portrait has been painted of the relationship between Eastern thought and Melville's Transcendentalist contemporaries, if only because they wrote much more explicitly (and reverentially) of these traditions, in journals, letters, and published works. But regarding Melville's distinctive association, there is considerably less certainty—for example, in 1853, he scribbled a quotation from Confucius in the margins of his copy of *Don Quixote*, a familiarity for which we have no explanation. John M.J. Gretchko's statement in 1992 is perhaps most representative: "That Herman Melville sampled the available Orientalia of his day is a commonplace long appreciated. Some of his Oriental sources still remain elusive."[6]

The word "elusive" is certainly an apt one. Melville has a well-deserved reputation as a literary magpie—or, as he described himself, "a universal absorber."[7] *Moby-Dick* is famously filled with Shakespearean echoes and Biblical allusions, with passages adopted from his direct sources—for example, Thomas Beale's *History of the Sperm Whale*—often appearing without quotation or accreditation. Melville delighted in outlandish allusions to far-flung locales, burnishing his popular image as a man who had seen unseeable things. And as Millicent Bell sagely notes, "One of the knottiest problems in considering Melville's use of his reading will always be the question of how much he read in original sources and how much he derived at second-hand."[8] His knowledge of Vishnu (who commands a powerful place in the chapter "The Honor and the Glory of Whaling"), for example, was almost certainly gleaned from Thomas Maurice, whose works also reference "Zoroaster, Mithra, Isis and Osiris, Pythagoras and the doctrine of metempsychosis, the Cave of Elephanta"[9]—all mentioned in *Moby-Dick*. If Melville did in fact know about Buddhism at the time of writing *Moby-Dick*, why would he not flaunt it as he flaunted his other interests?

For one thing, there simply was not sufficiently tangible information about Buddhism available at the time Melville was writing *Moby-Dick*. William Potter writes that while a few nineteenth-century authors attempted to bring Buddhist ideas into their work, "it seemed to perpetually perplex and confound those who tried to write on it."[10] Transcendentalist authors who attempted to grapple with it in the same direct way they had studied Hinduism and Confucianism found themselves unable to gather the threads into a cohesive understanding. Melville, then, could not point to specific mythologies as he could with Hinduism, nor insert new doctrinal terms like *nirvana* into his writing, as he would in his later work.

Similarly, he could not be at all certain of an audience who would recognize and appreciate the subject in question. From the cetological shout-out of "William Scoresby"[11] to the viticulturists' "Heidelburgh Tun"[12] in *Moby-Dick*, he might have imagined his readers running to their copies of *The American Magazine of Useful and Entertaining Knowledge* (1834–1837) to keep up with the narrator's eclectic intellect. Even in citing "Vishnoo,"[13] Hindu scholarship had advanced far enough by 1851 that the name could be considered general knowledge in New York and Boston, if not farther afield (or, indeed, to Melville's new Pittsfield neighbors). With Buddhism, however, he could not well have assumed to be at all understood. In 1871, Reverend James Freeman Clarke (a family friend of the Melvilles) would write:

> Twenty-five years ago it was hardly possible to procure any adequate information concerning Brahmanism, Buddhism, or the religions of Confucius, Zoroaster, and Muhammad . . . About the Buddhists scarcely anything was known. But now . . . we have ample means of ascertaining the essential facts concerning most of these movements of the human soul.[14]

That "twenty-five years ago," of course, would place us squarely in 1846, just two years after the arrival of Buddhism in America and Herman Melville's arrival on the literary scene.[15]

The vast majority of Americans interested in Asian religion at this time (Thomas Jefferson among them) would have learned of those faiths through the trailblazing work of Sir William Jones—who in the late eighteenth century founded the Royal Asiatic Society, and is responsible for discovering the "Indo-European" language family (although he is perhaps most famous for, as Melville mentions in *Moby-Dick*, being able to speak thirty languages).[16] Jones's name appears in the July 1842 issue of the Transcendentalist publication *The Dial*, cited as an authority on Asian religious texts without any *curriculum vitae*—suggesting an editorial assumption that his name would be familiar to their readership.

That Melville has some surprisingly harsh words for William Jones in *Moby-Dick* suggests that he was familiar with Jones's work but found it unpalatable. Riffing on the indecipherable nature of the sperm whale's brow in "The Prairie," he sneers that "Sir William Jones, who read in thirty languages, could not read the simplest peasant's face in its profounder and more subtle meanings."[17] The implication is clear: Melville derides the scholar's compilation of information as superficial, for it cannot reach the "profounder . . . subtle meanings" of the universe that, for Melville, necessarily lie deep beneath the surface.[18]

Melville was a famously voracious reader, devouring volumes on a wide range of esoteric topics, from religion and mythology to history and archaeology. His first encounter with Buddhism (albeit a fleeting one) was probably as a young boy, reading Marco Polo's *The Travels of Marco Polo*—"that wild eastern tale," he calls it in *Mardi*.[19] Given his exposure to exotic religious practices while in the Pacific, and the spiritual restlessness found throughout his work, it perhaps goes without saying that Melville would have intentionally sought after information about Eastern religions. What specific appeal Buddhism might have had to Melville is inadvertently advocated by liberal Anglican minister Frederick Denison Maurice, whose book *The Religions of the World and their Relations to Christianity* would be published in Boston just four years before *Moby-Dick*. In a passage so Melvillean it almost seems lifted from his marginalia, the reverend feared that in Buddhism, "there is no check to the conviction that a man has risen to the state of Godhead—maybe a God . . . [making] the step toward Atheism, an easier jump than it is in Hinduism, [which] preserves the tradition of a Divinity, invests it with a reality in some sense independent of the mind and the beholder."[20]

Likewise, it is hard to believe that the insatiable bibliophile Melville would not have come across the Asiatic writings of the Transcendentalists— most likely in issues of *The Dial*—around this time as well. But with so many new faiths to contend with, there was inevitably a great deal of confusion. As late as 1845, Ralph Waldo Emerson, arguably one of the most enthusiastic and influential students of Asian religions in America, mistakenly identified the sacred Hindu text *Bhagavad Gita* in a letter to his sister as that "much renowned book of Buddhism."[21] Scholars have long noted both Emerson and Thoreau took great liberties with the Oriental literature they read, adapting them to fit their own sensibilities. Thoreau scholar William J. Wolf writes:

> Obviously Thoreau selected within the Oriental religions certain elements of which he approved and rejected many features with which he was not in sympathy. . . . Quotations were torn from their context in such a way that it almost becomes more significant for our understanding of Thoreau's attitudes to the Eastern religions to see what was deliberately cast aside than what was admitted to the new Transcendentalist canon of world scripture.[22]

Thoreau boasted to a friend, "Fifty years from now the majority of people will believe as I do now,"[23] while Emerson claimed "the Buddhist is a Transcendentalist,"[24] and Thoreau goes so far as to call him "my Buddha."[25]

Since Melville seems to have been seeking something quite different than his Transcendentalist contemporaries, we might also entertain another possibility—that perhaps he simply got his information from sources other than those of his contemporaries. Rather than being spoon-fed Sir William Jones's Hindu-centrism, Melville's understanding of the teachings (as expressed in *Moby-Dick*) may have been formed from more obscure sources. Notably, a few accounts of Buddhist thought that Melville might well have read before 1851—in his edition of Pierre Bayle's *Dictionnaire Historique et Critique*, and a book on Chinese culture by John Francis Davis—were much more fluid, uncertain, inscrutable. While Indian accounts like Jones's invariably presented the historical Buddha as a god, the East Asian literature often mentioned him only in passing, before turning to descriptions of spiritual practices and explications of Buddhist metaphysics—both of which would have been especially suited to Melville's "ontological heroics."[26]

Thirty years later, however, the climate had changed considerably. Geopolitical events centered well east of the biblical Orient (most prominently, the Anglo-Chinese Opium Wars, the forcible "opening" of Japan by Commodore Matthew C. Perry's "black ships," and the incorporation of the British Raj in India), had significantly altered the American conception of the Asian continent—drawing its collective attention continually east, and arousing a new vanguard of spiritual curiosity. The travelers' accounts of Asia that had long been a staple of popular periodicals were now joined by theological disquisitions on Buddhism in religious magazines and newsletters. By 1883, a prominent Episcopal priest in Boston would find occasion to write, "[T]hese days . . . a large part of Boston prefers to consider itself Buddhist rather than Christian."[27]

Among scholars, Buddhist studies had become much more sophisticated, enough to warrant multiple editions of Dr. Ernest J. Eitel's *Hand-Book of Chinese Buddhism, being a Sanskrit-Chinese Dictionary with Vocabularies of Buddhist Terms in Pali, Singhalese, Siamese, Burmese, Tibetan, Mongolian and Japanese* (1888). More famously, Sir Edwin Arnold's *The Light of Asia*—a romantic biography of Buddha's life written in blank verse—was published in 1879 and was, to say the least, a huge success. J.J. Clarke writes, "The poem's success was phenomenal, both in Europe and America. It sold nearly a million copies, was translated into six languages, and for thirty years was a household classic, one of the best-sellers of its day. More, it was transformed into an opera, into a Broadway play, two cantatas, and a movie!"[28]

Along with this greater prominence, there also inevitably arose an "orthodox" view of Buddhism among scholars, chiefly embodied by an almost single-minded obsession with the question of *nirvana*—specifically, whether it was or was not synonymous with "annihilation."[29] This orthodoxy is reflected in Melville's later works that deal with Buddhism directly—most

especially his short poem "Buddha," published in 1891, the last year of
Melville life:

> *"For what is your life? It is even a vapor that appeareth for a little time and*
> *then vanisheth away."*
> Swooning swim to less and less,
>   Aspirant to nothingness!
> Sobs of the world, and dole of kinds
>   That dumb endurers be—
> Nirvana! Absorb us in your skies,
>   Annul us into thee. [30]

Eleanor Tilton ridicules Melville for introducing his poem with a Bible verse
as epigraph[31]; Rollyson and Paddock argue that the poem and its preceding
verse are doctrinal equivalents.[32] Indeed, the poem could easily replace the
word "nirvana" with "heaven" and have much the same meaning. Here, and
with his obscure poem "Rammon" as well, Melville's use of Buddhist terms
betrays an attachment to the terms and concepts that had recently become
fashionable among Oriental enthusiasts. In "Rammon," he imagines the title
character's conversion to the Buddhist faith, which promises a reprieve from
"the cessation of being."[33] But in fact, Rammon's conversion can be read as
unintentionally symbolizing the opposite conversion: from an understanding
and acceptance of the ephemeral nature of existence—of "an end or what
would seem to be an end"—to a fanciful belief in "the successive transmigra-
tion of souls," which would ostensibly allow Rammon to live forever.[34]

This "regression" neatly dovetails with Melville's own portrayal of Buddhism—from a profound representation in *Moby-Dick* to a shallow depiction
in his later work. For, as we shall see, while many aspects of *Moby-Dick*
suggest that Melville did in fact possess some insight into the practical implications of Buddhist practice, his own inability (either constitutional or logis-
tical) to commit to such a practice would only have led him (now having
opened himself up to even more spiritual contradiction and confusion) to
further spiritual despair:

> [I]n comparison with Melville, most of the eminent American authors of his
> day found happy answers to their questions. Emerson and Thoreau, with their
> transcendental theories, and Longfellow, Lowell, and Holmes, with their Uni-
> tarian views, were relatively contented and optimistic. Whittier was a good
> Quaker. Whitman's worship of the universe buoyed him. Even Hawthorne,
> often morose in the problem of sin, was contented enough in his beliefs to pity
> Melville.[35]

Hawthorne's "pity" is an illuminating example. In 1856, Melville visited
Hawthorne briefly in Liverpool. Upon his departure, Hawthorne wrote the
following in his journal:

Melville . . . will never rest until he gets hold of a definite belief. It is strange how he persists—and has persisted ever since I knew him, and probably long before—in wandering to-and-fro over these deserts, as dismal and monotonous as the sand hills amid which we were sitting. He can neither believe, nor be comfortable in his unbelief; and he is too honest and courageous not to try to do one or the other. If he were a truly religious man, he would be one of the most truly religious and reverential; he has a very high and noble nature, and better worth immortality than the rest of us. [36]

Buddhist practice is arguably about precisely this—cultivating the ability to relax in the space between belief and unbelief. Zen literature abounds with paradoxical situations in which both options are forbidden: staying and going, speaking and being silent, moving and remaining motionless. [37] While, again, Ishmael profoundly demonstrates the actualization of this middle way approach, Melville was never able to stop his own internal pendulum from swinging.

I will argue that *Moby-Dick*, written when he was only thirty-one, is Melville's most complete and accurate portrayal of the Buddha's teachings. And while later in life he would make a conscious effort to write about Buddhism, the more he tried to explicitly pin down the Buddha's teachings, the farther away he got from those truths. In other words, he ended up chasing the White Whale himself.

The most extensive study to date of Melville's interest in Buddhism during the last decade of his life is William B. Dillingham's *Melville & His Circle: The Later Years* (1996). [38] Dillingham claims that Melville's enthusiasm for Buddhism primarily arose through his reading of Arthur Schopenhauer, who found Buddhism to bear great resemblance to his own philosophy. One fascinating notion, originally put forth by Walter Sutton but repeated more confidently by H. Bruce Franklin, suggests that the name "Buddha" might have served at least partly as inspiration for the surname of Melville's final protagonist, Billy Budd—pointing out that in the "Rammon" manuscript, Melville twice spells "Buddha" without the "h." [39]

Dillingham is also able to point specifically to two key volumes Melville is known to have owned, namely William Rounseville Alger's *The Solitudes of Nature and of Man* (in which there is a chapter about Buddha) and the aforementioned *The Light of Asia* by Sir Edwin Arnold. Focusing on Melville's inclusion of Buddhism in his final works, he concludes, "By the mid-1870s, Melville thus appears to have acquired some knowledge of Buddhism (indeed, enough to know that in parts of China and Mongolia, Gautama was known as Fo)." [40] This is specifically referring to Melville's epic poem *Clarel*, which includes the following verse (perhaps the only well-known verse in the poem, twelve lines out of eighteen thousand):

> From eras gone he caught the sound
> Of hordes from China's furthest moat,
> Crossing the Himalayan mound,
> To kneel at shrine or relic so
> Of Buddha, the Mongolian Fo
> Or Indian Saviour. What profound
> Impulsion makes these tribes to range?
> Stable in time's incessant change
> Now first he marks, now awed he heeds
> The intersympathy of creeds,
> Alien or hostile as they seem—
> Exalted thought or grovelling dream. [41]

This is indeed irrefutable evidence of a comprehensive familiarity with Buddhism as a great world religion, which at that time was estimated to count "three hundred millions of people among its disciples; to be, therefore, by far the most prevailing religion which does exist, or ever has existed, in the world." [42] In fact, it leads Dillingham to intimate an even greater familiarity than can be confirmed by the known sources:

> If we consider what [Melville] is known to have had in his personal library on Buddhism, what he is likely to have known about or read, and what was readily available to him on the subject, a substantial body of writing emerges. . . . The point here is that in addition to what Melville is known to have read on Buddhism, he had the easy opportunity to read much more and probably did. [43]

While we cannot know precisely what Melville knew of Buddhism, we know that during his life he owned at least 350 books—over 100 of which remain missing today, either lost when he returned from Pittsfield back to New York in 1863, or sold after his death. In addition, Melville surely came across many books during his time at sea, and borrowed and glanced at innumerable more in libraries and personal collections. We might never know precisely what Melville knew about Buddhism at the time of writing *Moby-Dick*. But, as J.W.N. Sullivan writes in his 1923 essay "Melville's Lonely Journey": "We must suppose that a rapid, almost sudden, change occurred in Melville shortly before he undertook *Moby-Dick*. . . . We cannot, of course, know in any intimate way what happened, but such sudden liberations of a man's powers are by no means unprecedented." [44] If Dillingham can take for granted unknown sources in 1881, then why can we not be similarly confident about 1851? Perhaps we can.

Melville's reference to "the grand lama of Thibet" in *Omoo* confirms that he had, at the very least, a casual acquaintance with Buddhism by early 1847. That he repeats this allusion in four of his first six books—*Omoo*,[45] *Mardi*,[46] *White-Jacket*,[47] and *Moby-Dick*[48]—lends credence to the argument that, whatever he read, it made a significant impact on his thinking. When one considers all the possible ways Melville may have heard about Buddhism, a pretty compelling picture begins to emerge.

In 1871, the Reverend James Freeman Clarke published a book entitled *Ten Great Religions*, which sought to "compare the great religions of the world with each other"—with titles such as "Mohammed and Islam,"[49] "Zoroaster and the Zend Avesta,"[50] and "Buddhism, or the Protestantism of the East."[51] Reverend Clarke was a Unitarian minister, noted abolitionist, and one of the original Transcendentalists. Not only was Herman Melville familiar with his work in comparative theology, they were also personal acquaintances— Clarke gave Communion to Melville's wife Lizzie on the couple's wedding day in 1847, and later officiated at the funeral of her stepmother. Dillingham writes that, of all the religions Reverend Clarke studied, he was extraordinarily devoted to his study of Buddhism: "Clarke found himself at times so enthusiastic about Buddhist principles and so moved by the figure of Gautama [the historical Buddha] that he felt the need to correct his perspective and to remember that he was a Christian (and a minister at that)."[52] In the preface to *Ten Great Religions*, Clarke (referring to himself in the third person) writes that "he has not come to the task without some preparation, for it is more than twenty-five years since he first made of this study a speciality."[53] Twenty-five years before 1871 (again, the year of the book's publication) would mean that Clarke was studying Buddhist thought in 1846, or right at the beginning of the courtship between newly famous author Herman Melville and Judge Lemuel Shaw's daughter Elizabeth. If it is true that Buddhism was of particular interest to Clarke, then surely it is possible that in private conversation Clarke would have been keen to discuss his nascent studies of exotic faiths with the young author who had "lived among cannibals," and perhaps suggest some texts for this young man to seek out himself.

A few years later, on a summer night in 1855, one Maunsell B. Field joined Melville and a few others at a dinner party at the residence of Oliver Wendell Holmes. As he would later write in his memoir, *Memoirs of Many Men* (1874):

> We started in a buggy to call upon Melville, intending to go from there to Dr. Holmes's, then to the hotel at Pittsfield to dine, and thence home. We found Melville, whom I had always known as the most silent man of my acquaintance, sitting on the porch in front of his door. He took us to a particular spot on his place to show us some superb trees. He told me he spent much time there *patting them on the back.* . . . At length, somehow, the conversation drifted to East India religions and mythologies, and soon there arose a discussion between Holmes and Melville, which was conducted with the most amazing skill and brilliancy on both sides. It lasted for hours, and Darley and I had nothing to do but listen. I never chanced to hear better talking in my life.[54]

Once again, we cannot specify which religions Mr. Field heard the two men speaking of that night over dinner. But one is tempted to guess.

Finally, in the Melville Room of the Berkshire Athenaeum in Pittsfield, Massachusetts, inside a glass case against the wall, there is a small porcelain figurine. The index card accompanying it reads, "Chinese God of Contentment, Belonged to Herman Melville." A brief glance through nineteenth-century ceramics manuals reveal this figure to be the Chinese deity Pu-tai (Japanese: Hotei). Many Westerners today will identify this figurine as the so-called "fat Buddha." Pu-tai (or Hotei) is known today as an important symbol of the Zen Buddhist spirit (and plays a prominent role in the *Ten Ox-Herding Pictures*, to be discussed later on):

> A fat god of laughter and happiness, he often carries a bag of treasures which he bestows on those who never worry about troubles. . . . Hotei is usually shown with a large naked stomach, bald headed and with large ear lobes (symbol of omniscience). To the Zen believers, Hotei is depicted as a happy wandering monk who represents the care-free life of one who has found peace through the study of Zen. [55]

This would appear to be the final verdict as to whether Herman Melville had contact with Zen Buddhism during his life. Unfortunately, it is not known when Melville acquired this figurine, nor from where he acquired it. A photograph in Hershel Parker's biography shows the figure holding prominent placement directly in the center of the fireplace mantle in the Chimney Room of Melville's Arrowhead home. In 1868, Melville's niece Florence would write of the strange objects on the mantle in a homework assignment entitled "My Country Home," referring to the curious figurine using the common term "joss": "The mantel [sic] which is of oak is decorated with a huge pair of antlers, swords which were wielded in the Revolution, and a pair of pistols, a tomahawk, fencing foils, two old-fashioned brass lamps and a Chinese joss." [56]

I like to imagine the figurine was a gift from Melville's younger brother Thomas, brought back as a gift from his trip to China in early 1849. I like to imagine Melville wondering about this strange "God of Contentment," and being led to further investigation of Chinese Buddhism. I like to imagine this is why Ishmael is so concerned with "contentment" in *Moby-Dick*, using the word some twenty-one times, almost half of them referring to the first person. The only thing that will "content" the restless Manhattoes is "the extremist limit of the land," [57] as if silently blessing Ishmael's departure. Queequeg is three times called content, [58] and Ishmael first describes himself as content when standing in the moored Pequod: "But I am one of those that never take on about princely fortunes, and am quite content if the world is ready to board and lodge me." [59] He almost seems to be urging himself toward a goal, repeating the word like an incantation, or a mantra: "I shall be content,"[60] "I must be content,"[61] "I must be content."[62]

Chapter Three

Bayle's *Dictionary*

On 5 April 1849, Herman Melville wrote a letter to his friend (and sometime critic) Evert Duyckinck, in which he mentioned his recent purchase of a copy of Pierre Bayle's *Dictionnaire Historique et Critique*. "I bought a set of Bayle's *Dictionary* the other day," Melville wrote, "& on my return to New York intend to lay the great old folios side by side & go to sleep on them thro' the summer."[1] It was almost exactly a year before he would begin writing *Moby-Dick*.

It isn't difficult to imagine the appeal Bayle would have had for Melville. The son of a Protestant minister, Bayle's experience as a persecuted religious minority in the France of Louis XIV made him wary of religious exceptionalism—the suggestion that any one faith is intrinsically superior to all others. As Franklin notes, "Bayle took the pagan gods only slightly less seriously than he took the Christian God."[2] The *Dictionary* was an attempt to undermine all metaphysical and religious claims to truth, in the interest of promoting ideological (and specifically religious) tolerance. Hershel Parker called Bayle's *Dictionary* "a skeptic's partisan guide to the history of philosophy and religion."[3]

Suffice it to say, Bayle's project would have been right up Melville's alley. But that is not the only thing Bayle was up to in his *Dictionary*. As Millicent Bell showed in her 1951 essay, "Pierre Bayle and *Moby-Dick*," one of Bayle's primary tasks in the book was to ridicule—more like pummel, really—the philosophy of his archrival Baruch Spinoza.[4] This philosophy, known as Substance Monism, is, in short, the belief that God is the one true substance in which all things exist. It is usually regarded as a form of Pantheism. Bayle, meanwhile, pronounces it "the most absurd and monstrous hypothesis that can be imagined, and the most contrary to the most evident notions of our mind."

What Melville thought of Spinoza is rather more ambiguous. Judging from his declaration that the noble sperm whale was "a Platonian, who might have taken up Spinoza in his latter years,"[5] one might well argue he was actually quite fond of Spinozan philosophy (especially given the sperm whale's inherent genius, described in the chapter "The Prairie"). The appearance of Spinoza's name in *Mardi*, published in New York just one week after Melville's purchase of the *Dictionary*, suggests that Melville would have been keenly interested in what Bayle had to say about his nemesis. And when he finally did open up those great old folios in the summer of 1849, and turned to read of the old Dutch philosopher, this is what he would've read:

> Baruch Spinoza—a Jew by birth, who forsook Judaism, and at last became an Atheist—was a native of Amsterdam. He was a systematical Atheist, and brought his Atheism into a new method, tho the ground of his doctrine was the same with that of several ancient and modern Philosophers, both in Europe and the Eastern countries. As for the latter, one needs only read what I have said in the remarks of the article "Japan," and what I shall say below *Concerning the Theology of a sect of the Chinese.*[6]

In other words, Bayle tells us that in order to understand Spinoza's doctrine, we need only study the theology of two obscure schools of Buddhism—one in China, the other in Japan—about which Jesuit missionaries had returned reports in the late sixteenth and early seventeenth centuries. The Chinese, Bayle calls "Foe Kiao"; the Japanese, "Amida and Xaca." Today, we know these schools as the "concentration schools" of Buddhism—in China, it's called the Ch'an school; in Japan, Zen.

And so Bayle draws a parallel between Spinozan philosophy and the teachings of Zen Buddhism. First, in a lengthy footnote within the entry on Spinoza, he begins by giving a short biographical description of the life of the historical Buddha, and then describes the scene of the Buddha's death. He writes:

> At seventy-nine years of age, being upon the point of death, he declared to his disciples, that for the space of forty years that he had preached to the world, he had not told them the truth; that he had concealed it under the vail [sic] of metaphors and figures; but that it was time now to declare it to them. *"There is nothing, said he, to be inquired after, and on which one may place one's hopes, but nothingness and a vacuum, which is the first principle of all things."*[7]

We can certainly appreciate the fascination this idea must have held for Melville—that a religious founder could, in his final moments, renounce his own faith, chastise his followers for putting their trust in him, and leave them all behind without anything to cling to. "Here is a man very different from our unbelievers," Bayle begins his next paragraph. We can imagine Melville sitting up in his chair, taking notice of this strange religion, which places "nothingness and a vacuum" as the "first principle[8] of all things."

It is in this image, of the faithful practitioner abandoned by his faith, forced to contemplate the void, that Melville may have found inspiration for the perverted humanism of Captain Ahab. Bayle's reading of the Buddhists' "first principle" as a "nothingness and a vacuum" is essentially a distorted simplification of the Buddhist doctrine of *sunyata*, or emptiness. Bayle claims that, resulting from the Buddha's supposed final declaration of atheism, after his death his disciples made the decision to divide his teachings into two disparate parts:

> [O]ne is outward, and is that which is publickly preached and taught; the other is inward, which is carefully concealed from the vulgar, and discovered only to those that are initiated. The outward doctrine . . . consists: 1. In teaching that there is a real difference between good and evil, justice and injustice: 2. That there is another life wherein men shall be punished or rewarded for what they have done in this world: 3. That . . . they shall obtain salvation after death, and shall have a new and more happy birth in another world.[9]

The inner or "secret" doctrine, as mentioned earlier, is that all things are truly composed of a "certain vacuum and real nothingness," of which all things truly consist, and to which all things return after death. Bayle portrays the outer doctrine as a form of oppressive deceit over the "vulgar" masses, who must be "kept to their duty by the fear of hell."[10]

It is here that we begin to see the resonance with Captain Ahab, who finds himself similarly oppressed, and seeks unobstructed knowledge of the "first principle." Bayle's description of the relationship between the two doctrines bears resemblance to Ahab's first extended soliloquy on the White Whale. He compares "all visible objects" to "pasteboard masks," through which the "mouldings" of the "unknown" first principle can be seen.[11] By removing (or in Ahab's case, destroying) these mouldings, one would theoretically move beyond the visible and access the first principle itself. Interestingly, this view matches Bayle's conclusion that "the outward doctrine, as the Bonzes express it, 'is only like the wooden frame on which an arch is built, and that is afterwards removed, when the building is finished.'"[12] What Ahab fails to grasp is that the "first principle," as described by Bayle, itself does not exist in the terms Ahab would like. Rather, Bayle's contention that "this principle has no thought, no power, no virtue . . . the supreme perfection of that principle in its inaction, and absolute repose"[13] comes closer to Ishmael's curious term "the Divine Inert"[14] and his struggles with the whiteness of the whale.

Bayle's other extended description of Zen Buddhist thought appears within his entry on Japan, in a subsection called "Amida and Xaca" (European renderings of the Japanese names for Amitabha Buddha and Shakyamuni

Buddha). Unfortunately, like many later Europeans who encountered the
Buddhist emphasis on tranquility meditation and the limitations of language,
Bayle misinterpreted it as a form of Quietism:

> [T]he followers of Foe teach Quietism; for they say that all those, who seek
> true happiness, ought to be so far absorbed by profound meditations, as to
> make no use of their intellect, and that they ought, through a perfect insensibil-
> ity, to sink into the repose and inaction of the first principle; which is the true
> way of being perfectly like it and partaking of happiness. [15]

Although Zen has long found itself subjected to these charges, it is a charac-
terization which Thomas Cleary acknowledges, but ultimately dismisses:

> The practice of methods of silencing the mind to see reality . . . is well known
> in Zen Buddhism. This posed a drawback, however, which is also well repre-
> sented both in Zen literature and in the writings of outside observers. From the
> external point of view, the drawback was that this exercise of quiescence gave
> the appearance of quietism, preventing understanding of the true scope of Zen
> action. Within Zen schools, emphasis on stilling the mind also led some to
> regard it as a goal, and successful stilling led some to remain fixated on
> tranquility, vitiating their capacity for further progress. In both cases the prob-
> lem was one of confusing the means with the end. [16]

But the complacency inherent in Quietism, which Bayle seeks to impress
upon Zen, is a critical misreading—or perhaps a simple mistranslation—of a
fundamental Zen concept. Writing of the practice of Japanese monks, Bayle
writes the following: "They neglect externals and apply themselves only to
meditations. They cast off all discipline that consists in words, adhering only
to the exercise, which they call SOQUXIN SOQUBUT, that is, the heart." [17]
The phrase that Bayle is looking for is almost certainly "*soku-shin-ze-butsu*,"
the Japanese translation of a phrase attributed to the Chinese Zen master
Mazu (709–788). It is translated into English as either "mind itself is Buddha," "this very mind is Buddha mind," or "mind here and now is Buddha."
But, again, the phrase is not intended to complacently advocate the invariably unblemished nature of the mind, but rather, as Gudo Nishijima emphatically argues, is an admonition that this unblemished state will not be realized
without steadfast practice: "The phrase . . . is very famous in Buddhism, but
many people have interpreted the principle to support the beliefs of natural-
ism. They say if our mind here and now is just buddha, our conduct must
always be right, and in that case, we need not make any effort to understand
or to realize Buddhism. However, this interpretation is a serious mistake." [18]
Placing this in the contextual world of *Moby-Dick*, this danger of "natural-
ism" recalls Ishmael's derision of the Pantheistic impulse that can overtake a
whaleman on the mast-head—"lulled into such an opium-like listlessness" [19]
that the man is unable to keep watch for whales. Crucially, however, the

antidote to this indolence is not to more ardently search the horizon—an idea which becomes clear when we bring in a fourth thread to this discussion, tying us back to Bayle's original article: Baruch Spinoza.

Spinoza's philosophy is often described as "Pantheistic," largely because his monism asserts God as the one true substance in which all things exist. By rejecting the "transcendent personal God," Masao Abe writes, "Spinoza's position is much closer to Buddhism in general, and to Dogen's in particular, than to orthodox Christianity."[20] However, the crucial difference is that in Spinoza, "All individuality is finally swallowed up by the universality of the One God who alone truly Is."[21] This is the mistake that the Pantheist at the mast-head makes, the man who "loses his identity" by confusing "the mystic ocean at his feet for the visible image of that deep, blue, bottomless beautiful soul, pervading man and nature."[22] In other words, he loses himself in the idea that he is a part of God, without whom he has no existence: "There is no life in thee, now, except that rocking life imparted by a gently rolling ship; by her, borrowed from the sea; by the sea, from the inscrutable ideas of God."[23]

Ishmael's condemnation of this philosophy is tied to its disregard of the palpable existence of the conventional self—"move your foot or hand an inch, slip your hold at all; and your identity comes back in horror." A recognition of both the conventional and ultimate truths brings Ishmael in line with Dogen Zenji's philosophy, which insists that "every particular thing in the universe manifests itself in its individuality."[24] The "bottomless" human soul that the whaleman imagines he sees in the deep blue ocean absorbs the universe into it, just as it is absorbed into the universe.

Thus the whaleman looks outside of himself and, seeing the universe, he loses sight of his own mind. As Bayle says of the Japanese monks, in order to realize *soku-shin-ze-butsu*, "They neglect externals and apply themselves only to meditations."[25] Appropriately, in the koan collection *Mumonkan* (*Gateless Gate*), Case 30: "This Mind is Buddha" is accompanied by the following verse, clearly evocative of Ishmael's warning to the mast-head Pantheists:

> The blue sky, the bright day,
> It is detestable to hunt around;
> If, furthermore, you asked, "What is Buddha?"
> It is like shouting your innocence while holding the loot.[26]

After all, Ishmael's rebuke of the mast-head reverie is not that the Pantheists failed to keep watch for whales. Indeed, he sheepishly admits that he himself "kept but sorry guard" at the mast-head.[27] As Mumon's commentary suggests, one need not search around—but one does need to know what resides in one's pocket! Having investigated "the problem of the universe" and his relationship to the "inscrutable tides of God,"[28] Ishmael moves on to the second half of Mazu's teaching:

> A monk asked [Mazu], "Why do you say 'Mind itself is Buddha'?"
> Mazu said, "To stop babies from crying."
> The monk said, "What do you say when they stop crying?"
> Mazu said, "No mind, no buddha."[29]

Despite his own claims, Ishmael demonstrates a keen awareness while on the mast-head,[30] evidence of his mindful attentiveness of events both internal and external. Even in "Stubb Kills a Whale," when Ishmael succumbs to a "dreamy mood losing all consciousness," he describes the progression of his mental states in precise and astute detail, and within that "forgetfulness" he reports that an "invisible, gracious agency preserved me."[31] He strikes a stable balance between seeking the whale but not grasping the whale—between whaling and not-whaling (we might call it "non-whaling")—leading to his realization that there is ultimately no sperm whale to be found. Ishmael's version of Mazu's teaching might look something like this:

> A sailor asked Ishmael: "Why do you say 'Look out for sperm whales'?"
> Ishmael said, "To stop lookouts from sleeping."
> The sailor said, "What do you say when they stop sleeping?"
> Ishmael said, "No lookout, no sperm whale."

Chapter Four

Possibilities and Probabilities

In May 1849, only one month after Melville purchased his copy of Bayle's *Dictionary*, his younger brother Tom returned from a voyage to China. That summer, Melville dedicated his fourth book, *Redburn*, to Tom, writing, "To My Younger Brother Thomas Melville, Now a Sailor on a Voyage to China, This Volume is Inscribed.[1] Later that same year, journeying by ship to London in 1849, Melville had an extended conversation with a woman who "had resided some time in China."[2] So it perhaps goes without saying that China would have been on Melville's mind in the years before *Moby-Dick*. And it perhaps goes equally without saying that the bibliophile Melville would actively have sought information about China. In the middle of the nineteenth century, travel accounts from the remote East began appearing in contemporary periodicals. The words "China" and "Chinese" occur no fewer than fourteen times in *Moby-Dick*. ("Japan" and "Japanese" occur twenty-one times.) Other Asian references in *Moby-Dick*—from his extended consideration of "Vishnu" to the casual mention of "pagodas,"[3] "oriental repose,"[4] "the grand canal in China,"[5] and in particular "the universal yellow lotus"[6]— attest to his having read some literature about the East. They are certainly tantalizing to the Buddhistically-inclined reader, but unfortunately little historical record has survived to explicate precisely from where his knowledge of these things stems.

A similar regret can be sounded regarding the Oriental artifacts that Melville and his family owned, from the "God of Contentment" mentioned earlier to a Chinese opium box, a Japanese black-lacquered box, and a Chinese marble figurine, all currently on display either in the Berkshire Athenaeum or at Arrowhead.

One possible literary source for Melville's knowledge of Chinese culture is John Francis Davis's *The Chinese: A General Description of China and its Inhabitants*. Published by Harper Brothers in 1836 (headquartered on Cliff Street in Manhattan, not far from Melville's house at that time), a copy would have been readily available to him, as Harper was his publisher from *Omoo* on. Although there is no specific record that Melville knew this book, it may have served as the source of one obscure allusion in *Moby-Dick*. In the chapter "Stubb's Supper," Ishmael writes, "For, upon the great canal of Hang-Ho, or whatever they call it, in China, four or five laborers on the foot-path will draw a bulky freighted junk at the rate of a mile an hour."[7] A similar passage is found in Davis's book:

> Through this opening or sluice, and in close contact with the bank on our left, our boats were successively dragged forward by ropes communicating with several large windlasses, which were worked upon the bank; by these means the object was slowly accomplished, without the least damage or accident. After thus effecting a passage through the sluice, we found ourselves nearly in still water; not yet, however, in the southern division of the great canal, as we had expected, but in the main stream of another large river . . . It seems evident, therefore, that the course of the navigation has been latterly altered here, either from the overflowing of the Yellow river, or some other cause. That a change has taken place seems indicated by the same 'New Salt river,' on the other side of the main stream of the Hôang-ho.[8]

This specific image—of the canal, and the men on shore dragging the boat along—does not occur in any other contemporary book on China that I have located. Between that and the approximation of the name "Hôang-ho," it seems possible that Melville may have taken the image from here.[9]

Davis's presentation of Buddhism appears quite well-aligned with Melville's sensibilities—or, more to the point, with the characteristics of Melville's budding protagonist. From the outset, Davis identifies Buddhism as an outsider's religion: "Confucianism is the orthodoxy, or state religion of China," he writes, and Buddhism and Taoism are only tolerated "as they do not come into competition with the first."[10] Indeed, Davis argues that from its very origins, Buddhism has been outcast, due to the "rancorous persecution" and "most cruel treatment" it received from the Hindus in India.[11] The Buddhists, however, "[accommodated] their system to all . . . they opened the door to every sort of converts, who might retain as many of their old prejudices as they chose."[12] Here we have three separate threads that remind one of Melville's Ishmael: his status as an outsider, his distrust of orthodoxy, and his great respect for all religious traditions—all of which, again, will be discussed in greater depth later on.

Davis's glowing praise of Buddhism continues when he turns to the biography of the Buddha, painting him as both heroic revolutionary and saintly savant:

> About one thousand years before the Christian era, an extraordinary man appeared in India, who labored with unceasing assiduity, and not without success, to reform the popular superstitions and destroy the influence of the Brahmins. This was Budha. . . . The efforts of Budha were exerted to bring back the religion of his country to its original purity. He was of royal descent, but chose an ascetic life and embraced the most abstruse system of philosophy prevalent in India. . . . Many princes . . . adopted the faith of Budha, and . . . obliterated the religion of the Brahmins and the system of castes. [13]

The word choice in this passage is striking for its gracious deference. The Buddha is an "extraordinary" being, whose "assiduity" brought him great "success," allowing him to "obliterate" a corrupt and unjust system. Not only was he "of royal descent," but "many princes adopted the faith of Budha," and now Thibet has a "spiritual sovereign" of its own. That this religion has spread "throughout Thibet, Siam, Cochinchina, Ava, Tartary, and Japan," Davis concludes, represents "the triumph of atheism"[14]—and he apparently does not have any problem with that.

He then moves on to "the practice of Budhism," which, although the word itself was apparently unknown to him, describes with some precision Zen—or, as it is known in China, Ch'an—practice. Most significant is his reference to "one of their most famous professors [who] is said to have passed nine years, with his eyes fixed upon a wall!"[15] This is Bodhidharma, the legendary founder of Zen in China, said to have brought the teachings from India into China around the first century of the Common Era.

As for the devotional practices of the Buddhists, Davis is decidedly more incredulous. He declares that both the Hoshang (Buddhist priests) of China and the *bonzes* (monks) of Japan believe that "the mysteries of religion will be the more revered the less they are understood, and the devotions of the people (performed by proxy) the more welcome in heaven for their being dressed in the garb of a foreign tongue."[16] Thus they conduct their ceremonies and speak their prayers in Pali, the traditional language of the Buddha, despite it being "to them an unintelligible language . . . a complete jargon, wherein the sound is imperfectly preserved and the meaning wholly lost."[17] This image—of holy men repeating words from a text they do not understand—is also found in *Moby-Dick*, when Queequeg carves the images tattooed on his body onto his coffin. The tattoos, "a mystical treatise on the art of attaining truth" created by "a departed prophet and seer of his island," turn Queequeg himself into "a riddle to unfold," for "[their] mysteries not even himself could read, though his own live heart beat against them."[18] Ishmael suggests that the "treatise" is all the more important precisely because it is "destined to moulder away with the living parchment whereon [it was] inscribed."[19] Thus it cannot be reduced to one specific meaning, or claimed by one system of thought, but can exist in whatever frame the believer wishes to place it, just as Davis says the Buddhists allow followers to retain "as many of their old prejudices as they chose." Davis concludes by recounting a conversation he had with a Buddhist priest regarding their employment of an unknown language: "I once asked a priest, 'What advantage can you expect to derive from merely repeating a number of words, with the sense of which you are entirely unacquainted?' his answer was, 'True, I do not know the sense—it is profound and mysterious; yet the benefit of often repeating the sounds is incalculable; it is infinite!'"[20] Ishmael might have asked Queequeg something similar, as he watches him passing the pages of a book he cannot read, and is struck by his bosom friend's lack of "civilized hypocrisies and bland deceits."[21]

There is one more book from this period we should consider as a possible source for Melville. Frederick Denison Maurice, an English theologian and Anglican minister, was an eloquent and powerful voice for tolerance among religious faiths. Potter draws parallels between his book *The Religions of the World* (1846) and Melville's *Clarel*—particularly in Melville's exaltation of "the intersympathy of creeds."[22] A brief review of the book appeared in a June 1849 issue of the literary magazine *The Living Age*,[23] which published multiple pieces on Melville and his work during his early career—including, in that year alone, an excerpt from *Mardi* and a review of *Redburn*.[24] So it's very possible Melville would have seen this description of Maurice's work, and it is once again easy to imagine how Maurice's comparative theology would resonate with Melville's spiritual contemplations. The article promises that anyone who abides in "circles of nonconformity" will appreciate his analysis of "non-Christian creeds and superstitions" and "the peculiarities of the religions which prevail *in partibus infidelium*," while "a less speculative mind might perhaps object" to the "spirit of deep and liberal sympathy, in combination with extensive learning" with which Maurice considers "the relations of Christianity to philosophical systems."[25] Most important to our purposes here, in *The Religions of the World*'s deeply sympathetic portrayal of Buddhism, we find a possible inspiration for both Ishmael and Ahab, and their wildly divergent views of the universe.

In Maurice's view, the Buddhist's conception of the Absolute is the "highest, least material idea of divinity" among all the world's faiths—he describes it as "clear light, perfect wisdom."[26] It is a faith, in other words, that follows Melville's advice to, as he wrote to Hawthorne while writing *Moby-Dick*, "take God out of the dictionary."[27] However, this does not mean, according to Maurice, that the Buddhist serenely and unequivocally believes in the infallible existence of a perfect God. On the contrary, the postulation of the Ultimate is a haunting—and often overwhelming—presence in his life:

> [T]o the Buddhist, the belief in God is the most awful, and at the same time the most real of all thoughts; one not thrust back into the corner of a mind which is occupied by everything else, but which he thinks demands the highest and most refined exercise of all the faculty that he has. It is something which is to make a change in himself, which is at once to destroy him and to perfect him. And the effect is a practical one. [28]

The Absolute is to Maurice's Buddhist what the White Whale is to Ishmael—the "thought, or rather vague, nameless horror" which in its "profoundest idealized significance" and "by its intensity completely overpowered all the rest . . . so mystical and well nigh ineffable was it." [29] And just as Maurice claims this idea of divinity demands the Buddhist's "highest and most refined" effort if it is to "change" him—a change that Maurice describes as both a destruction and a perfection—Ishmael also appreciates the effort necessary for profound change: "But how can I hope to explain myself here; and yet, in some dim, random way, explain myself I must, else all these chapters might be naught." [30]

As we will discuss at length later on, Ishmael's meditation on the whiteness of the whale represents a temporary descent into the abyss of nihilism and atheism. In this book, Maurice agrees that this is a straightforward, almost natural, philosophical shift for the Buddhist. What saves Ishmael is the realization that "mortal man" cannot reach the ultimate through discursive thought ("To analyze it, would seem impossible" [31]), and that no matter how fervent his prayer for wisdom, "this prayer never has been, never can be, answered." Rather it is only, as Maurice says, "In silence [that] he may best hope to know the Unseen Intelligence." [32]

Captain Ahab experiences a similar descent into nihilistic atheism, but it is one from which he never truly escapes. Maurice argues that even as the Buddhist grapples with atheism, he is finding a way to come to terms with the "Unseen Intelligence" that exists beyond all things. The first step is to "declare in honesty, 'I see nothing' . . . the words being the utterance of despair, not of triumph or satisfaction." [33] As an escape from this vision of nothingness, he then postulates the "One Intelligence as alone real; all outward nature he discarded, as merely apparent"—a position which recalls Ahab's cry, "Oh! how immaterial are all materials! What things real are there, but imponderable thoughts?" [34] Thus, Maurice concludes, this is not a struggle with Nothing so much as an Invisible Something. Even in that "deep hopeless void" is "implied real belief in a living Divinity." [35]

Maurice contends that although the Buddhist may conclude from this that "the Intelligence is essentially one with the world," he prefers to think of it (as does Ahab) as "entirely separated from the world," and thus "his effort to contemplate the pure Essence indicates a genuine desire to see something above the world, not merely dwelling in it and actuating it."[36] This is the crucial step for Ahab, for "as the Infinite Object fades into obscurity," the world is thus robbed of its Divine Presence.[37] Maurice's Buddhist then realizes that if God exists on some other ontological plain, then "there must be some person, and that a human person, in whom the perfect wisdom resides" here on Earth.[38] The Buddhist, according to Maurice, then allows himself to rise "to the state of Godhead—maybe a God" (a position that Ahab, of course, claims for himself).

Now apparently operating on a comparable level as the Absolute, Captain Ahab and Maurice's Buddhist may wish to communicate with the still "Unseen Intelligence." The only conduit they have, given His absence, is through interaction with the "visible objects . . . pasteboard masks" around them which God still inhabits.[39] Maurice suggests that the most common objects are animals—which react and respond to the Divine Intelligence that exists within the perceiver himself:

> And we want to feel that we are not contemplating [things] in themselves, or for their own sakes, but the living, quickening Intelligence which has stamped its form upon them. They must be changed into symbols; in that character we must approach them and revere them. They must assume shapes which are given to them by the kindred Intelligence in ourselves. Oftentimes these shapes will be animal; for how ought we to think of the creatures around us, with those half-human faculties and affections which we discover in them; with the ferocity and cunning which are surely not peculiar to them?[40]

But for Maurice's Buddhist as well as for Captain Ahab, since ultimately this "animal" is only a "symbol," the seeker inevitably and perpetually returns to the matter of the Unseen Intelligence, "pushing, and crowding, and jamming"[41] himself toward a more complete knowledge of It. Maurice would certainly empathize with Ahab, understanding that he is "obliged to question the universe, because he does not know what else he should question. He has questioned it, and to every problem which disturbs him it has returned a more confused answer."[42] Maurice even conjures two extended soliloquies for his imagined Buddhist that could very easily be attributed to Captain Ahab—for example the teleological wail in "The Symphony," where Ahab pleads: "What is it, what nameless, inscrutable, unearthly thing is it; what cozening, hidden lord and master . . . how then can this one small heart beat; this one small brain think thoughts; unless God does that beating, does that thinking, does that living, and not I."[43] Compare this to the similar struggles of Maurice's imagined Buddhist:

> "What is it that I am contemplating: I cannot see it, or hear it, or handle it; I dare not conceive it; it is altogether inconceivable, and yet I know of it only by

this mind of mine": he is likely to find himself in a strange perplexity. Or, if he puts the case thus to himself: "The end I propose to myself is to become absorbed, lost, that is to say, nothing. Can it be Something which is to work this result? Can it be Something I am contemplating?" He must say at length "No, it is Nothing. Nothing must be the ground of my life, of my being—of the being of all the things I see!"[44]

This crisis arises even in Ahab's deepest uncertainty and insecurity. But in Maurice's imaginary Buddhist's other soliloquy, the author suggests that even for the self-proclaimed God-head there is neither the contentment nor repose that he would have assumed, as the unanswerable questions continue to assail him:

He has asked, what that is within him which is higher than it, what that is which seeks a knowledge it cannot give? He is sure that he is above the world—that it was never meant to be his master—that the spirit in him must have its ground elsewhere. But where? What is this ground? Is it anything? It is nothing? Who will tell him? That which has asked the question cannot give the answer. With deepest solicitude, he cries, "Do Thou, of whom I see the footmarks in natural things, but most of all in human beings, in those who have thoughts and reasons, and wills,—in those who feel that these are not meant to be the servants of their senses or of the things with which their senses deal,— do Thou tell me who Thou art, and how I may draw nigh to Thee. . . . Tell me if there be indeed a King and High Priest of the universe—a man actually Divine. And this, too, I need to know: What that Light is which dwells in me; whether it is self-derived, or, as my inward heart tells me, derived from Thee. Whether there be any Spirit coming forth from Thee to swell in men, and bind them together—to make them gentle and gracious and wise—to be the common life of all and still the life of each. And if these things be so, tell me how these things can be reconciled, as my reason has whispered that they can be, though as yet I see not how, with that Unity—the essential condition of Thy Being—that which divides thee from all the multitude of things and persons with whom in this world we converse."[45]

What plagues both these men—that is, Captain Ahab and the imaginary Buddhist—is what Maurice insists is their continued ignorance of the great epistemological leap that Ishmael makes to bring himself peace. They insist on "the infinite capacity of the human intellect" to bear them up to their goal—to Maurice's "Unseen Intelligence,"[46] or Ahab's "cozening, hidden lord and master."[47] And as we will soon see, they are not alone in their misplaced confidence.

Chapter Five

Mardi and Other Mysteries

Scholars have long searched for a way to explain Melville's evolution from the bold adventurer responsible for *Typee* and the roiling mystic who created *Moby-Dick*—some specific turning point in his life, a moment of sudden illumination to account for this inexplicable, and perhaps even unprecedented, transformation. As mentioned earlier, J.W.N. Sullivan identified 1849 as the pivotal year, in which "a rapid, almost sudden, change occurred."[1] In that year, Melville suffered through writing *Redburn* and *White-Jacket* (which he considered "jobs," written only for a paycheck), before finally turning his attention toward a "romance of adventure, founded upon certain legends in the Southern Sperm Whale Fisheries," which would eventually grow into *Moby-Dick*.[2]

Although this year certainly seems to have presented a confluence of conditions for Melville—in both his private life and in the world around him—establishing a fixed date for his supposed spiritual awakening is problematic. Melville himself regarded his "twenty-fifth year" as a pivotal moment in his life, as he would write Hawthorne while nearing completion of *Moby-Dick*: "Until I was twenty-five, I had no development at all. From my twenty-fifth year I date my life. Three weeks have scarcely passed, at any time between then and now, that I have not unfolded within myself. But I feel that I am now come to the inmost leaf of the bulb, and that shortly the flower must fall to the mould."[3] This would place us between the Augusts of 1846 and 1847. Melville spent most of that time writing *Omoo,* and on his twenty-sixth birthday he was married—bringing him, as mentioned earlier, into contact with minister (and Buddhism enthusiast) James Freeman Clarke. Melville biographer Hershel Parker, meanwhile, identifies late 1847 as the occasion of an unknown change:

[T]he timing is not certain, but within weeks of his resuming his work on the
book [*Mardi*] . . . very possibly before Thanksgiving 1847, Melville decided to
change the basic nature of the work he was writing. Around this time, clearing
the way for his new plot, Melville wrote a scene in which the surviving, and
more or less realistic, characters encounter a large double-canoe . . . [4]

At this moment in the book, the story fundamentally shifts, from an oceanic
adventure story to a philosophical fantasy, with rambling discussions of religion and a perpetual chase after an ethereal princess. And here we find in
Mardi many of the nascent ideas that would come to fruition in *Moby-Dick*.

In *Mardi* are the first references to Indian religion, with allusions to "the
books of the Brahmins" and "the Hindoo deity Brahma."[5] Expanding upon
the ecumenical theme first addressed in *Typee*, he presents us with mystical
religion in a world where "no custom is strange; no creed is absurd."[6] He has
already latched upon the idea of the sea voyage as spiritual journey—"No
school like a ship for studying human nature"—in particular, a voyage for
"the whale, whose brain enlightens the world."[7] And there are hints of an
understanding of non-duality in his philosophers' maxims: "Whatever is not,
is. Whatever is, is not,"[8] "Things nearest are furthest off"[9] and a majestic
interdependence overarching their beliefs: "All things form but one
whole,"[10] "The universe is all of one mind."[11] But most telling is a passage
that qualifies as a mission statement in itself: "I am intent upon the essence of
things; the mystery that lieth beyond; the elements of the tear which much
laughter provoketh; that which is beneath the seeming; the precious pearl
within the shaggy oyster. I probe the circle's center; I seek to evolve the
inscrutable."[12] What newfound wisdom Melville had attained by this time, or
from whence it came, we cannot say for sure. Parker imagines him "lounged
on a sofa, reading . . . changing, growing—growing beyond *Mardi*, he was
sure."[13] In late 1849, just before beginning *Moby-Dick*, Melville took a trip
to Europe, which, Parker contends, afforded him the opportunity to reassess
his views of the universe:

He had been undergoing, by the time of this voyage and return, an accelerated
unfolding within himself which he could now begin to take stock of. The
prolonged Atlantic voyage of five and a half weeks gave Melville the time he
needed to reflect on the book that he would begin as soon as he greeted his
family and friends and settled into a late winter's work. [14]

This "late winter's work," of course, would lead him to "the mystery that
lieth beyond," and an exploration of the deepest metaphysical depths. It
would lead him to *Moby-Dick*.

There are many books scrutinizing Melville's incorporation of religious
imagery in his work. These have largely focused either on his undeniable

struggle with his mother's Calvinism (Herbert's *Moby-Dick and Calvinism*; Thompson's *Melville's Quarrel with God*), or on his superficial incorporation of Eastern "mythologies" into his work—most often focusing on Egyptian or Zoroastrian symbolisms, as in Franklin's *The Wake of the Gods*. To my knowledge there has not been a thorough investigation of the parallels with Zen philosophy that exist in *Moby-Dick*.

Melville almost certainly never in his life heard the word "Zen." But we can say with confidence that he encountered some Zen terms and concepts, in Bayle's *Dictionnaire* if nowhere else. And as I hope I have convincingly argued above, the Chinese and Japanese traditions would have been of particular interest to him, being largely devoid of the overt religiosity of the Hindu-centric reporting on Buddhism. In any case, whether the resonance in *Moby-Dick* was deliberately intended by the author, or is merely an illusion of interpretation on the part of this reader, must remain a mystery. Melville addressed this affliction of interpretation, and the difficulty in extricating one from another, in a letter to Nathaniel Hawthorne's wife Sophia, after she'd written with some thoughts about the "Spirit Spout" chapter in *Moby-Dick*:

> [Y]our allusion for example to the "Spirit Spout" first showed me that there was a subtile significance in that thing—but I did not, in that case, *mean* it. I had some vague idea while writing it, that the whole book was susceptible of an allegorical construction, & also that *parts* of it were—but the speciality of many of the particular subordinate allegories, were first revealed to me, after reading Mr. Hawthorne's letter, which, without citing any particular examples, yet intimated the part-&-parcel allegoricalness of the whole. [15]

So this study is offered as just one more glance at the doubloon, and one more story about the great White Whale. As *Mardi*'s philosopher Babbalanja says, "The mystery of mysteries is still a mystery. How this author came to be so wise, perplexes me." [16]

II

Ishmael's Way-Seeking Mind

Chapter Six

Groundlessness

In the opening paragraph of *Moby-Dick*, a young man in Manhattan, feeling dissatisfied with his life on shore, decides to set sail on a whaleship. While he tells us there is "nothing surprising about this," he also makes clear that he considers this his only option other than suicide: "This is my substitute for pistol and ball."[1] So we might despair for this young man, if not for the three words with which he begins his story, which offer a great deal of hope for his future.

"Call me Ishmael," he instructs the reader. Melville scholars have long discussed the importance of the Biblical name "Ishmael" in signifying that our narrator, like Abraham's exiled elder son, is an outcast from society. But the directive preceding it immediately contradicts this idea of solitary self-identification. Call me, he says, as I begin this new life, with this new name. It is at once an embrace of his own existence and a plea for us to join him. Call me—establishing the reader's essential role in his narrative. Call me—I cannot exist without your call. Call me.

This kind of vocal interaction is very common in ancient Zen koans. Monks are constantly calling each other out by name—for example, in the *Blue Cliff Record*, "Call once and he turns his head: Does he know the self or not?"[2]—suggesting it is only through this kind of spontaneous meeting that a monk's understanding can be verified. Further, that Ishmael requires us to join him on his cetological meditation suggests that he would be unable to attain knowledge of the whale without his reader participating in his effort. This recalls Dogen Zenji's teaching (originally from the second chapter of the *Lotus Sutra*, "Preaching") that "buddhas alone, together with other buddhas, are directly able to realize [truth]."[3] It is only through appealing to an outside source that one can "affirm that he understands clearly and fully."[4]

The etymology of the name Ishmael tells us more about our relationship with the narrator, as well as our place in the narration. Ishmael is often translated as "God hears."[5] So we might read this sentence as "Call me 'God hears.'" Or perhaps it should be "Call me the one who God hears" or "Call me the one who God has heard." This brings this opening sentence very close to the sentence that begins all Buddhist sutras: "Thus have I heard." Ostensibly spoken by Ananda, Shakyamuni Buddha's personal attendant (and cousin), the words serve to frame the Buddha's teachings, and announce their authority. Something similar is happening here with Ishmael. In the Bible, when that Ishmael's mother Hagar is cast into the wilderness, the Lord once again hears Ishmael's cries, and comes to assure her, "God has heard the voice of the boy where he is."[6] So the first sentence may also read, "Call me God has heard." Either way, it suggests this troubled young man already has a relationship with something higher than himself.

Thus, Ishmael's re-appellation places him in an unexpectedly positive place—despite his difficulties, and despite his otherwise desperate existential condition. Suzuki Roshi taught that these two things are not unrelated: that the difficulties set one on the path, and by setting out on the path one finds oneself anew: "In your very imperfections you will find the basis for your firm, Way-seeking mind . . . When you are sitting in the middle of your own problem, which is more real to you: your problem or you yourself? The awareness that you are here, right now, is the ultimate fact."[7] Ishmael's decision to join the whaleship is an unmistakable illustration of what Suzuki Roshi calls "Way-seeking mind," a phrase we can trace back to Dogen Zenji, who wrote in *Guidelines for Studying the Way*, "The thought of enlightenment has many names but they all refer to one and the same mind. Ancestor Nagarjuna said, 'The mind that fully sees into the uncertain world of birth and death is called the thought of enlightenment.' . . . Freedom from the ties of sound and form naturally accords with the essence of the Way-seeking mind."[8]

But in order to determine how Ishmael has arrived at this Way-seeking mind, we must explore what is underlying his existential crisis—what exactly it is that is leading him to the water's edge:

> Whenever I find myself growing grim about the mouth; whenever it is a damp, drizzly November in my soul; whenever I find myself involuntarily pausing before coffin warehouses, and bringing up the rear of every funeral I meet; and especially whenever my hypos get such an upper hand of me, that it requires a strong moral principle to prevent me from deliberately stepping into the street, and methodically knocking people's hats off—then, I account it high time to get to sea as soon as I can.[9]

The repeated phrase "I find myself" is key, indicating he has arrived here through introspection and self-examination. That he concludes the paragraph, "If they but knew it, all men . . . cherish nearly the same feelings toward the ocean with me" suggests that this is the natural place for one to arrive through such a process. [10] But this passage also betrays the despair Ishmael is experiencing at having found himself, after "so living or so striving," [11] still unable to control his emotions, much less understand the mysteries of existence. He remains at the mercy of his "hypos," swaying him with ambivalent adverbs: *involuntarily*, *deliberately*, *methodically*. Even those first words, "I find myself," indicate that he is not really in control of his state of mind. While his existential condition suggests a profound *lack* (for example, having "little or no money in [his] purse," and the barren trees of "damp, drizzly November" [12]), the internal battle he describes—between the macabre misanthrope and his "strong moral principle" [13]—together create the conditions for the arousal of Way-seeking mind.

Ishmael's persistent focus on his inconsistent mental states—his *concentration on concentration*, one might say—is essentially aligned with the practice of Zen Buddhism. The Japanese word *Zen* translates as "meditation," or "concentration"—that being the central practice of the Zen school (setting it apart from various other Buddhist traditions, with central practices like prayer, chanting Buddha's name, etc). It is taken from the Chinese word *Ch'an*, which in turn comes from the Sanskrit word *dhyana* and the Pali *jhana*, meaning "meditation" or "absorption." The lineage of Zen ancestors is traced from the legendary figure Bodhidharma, who is credited with single-handedly establishing the Zen school in China, having travelled there by ship (what else?) from India. Bodhidharma, as mentioned earlier, is perhaps most famous for having spent nine years in seated meditation (Japanese: *zazen*), facing a wall in a cave. He exhorted those who came to study with him to "outwardly cease all involvements, inwardly have no coughing or sighing in the mind—with your mind like a wall you can enter the Way." [14]

This teaching—echoed two generations later in Seng-Ts'an's "Live neither in the entanglements of outer things, nor in inner feelings of emptiness" [15] and then in Dogen's "Cast aside all involvements and cease all affairs" [16]—is indeed precisely how Ishmael "enters the Way." Of course he says straightaway that he has "nothing particular to interest [him] onshore," [17] and sets to sea with nothing but his "old carpet-bag." [18] In an April 1851 letter to Hawthorne, Melville called it "a carpet-bag,—that is to say, the Ego" [19]; I will call it his "sense of self."

When he attends the sermon in the Whaleman's Chapel, Ishmael is fascinated by Father Mapple's "physical isolation," and wonders if it "signifies his spiritual withdrawal . . . from all outward worldly ties and connexions." [20] He also describes the whaleman's life in terms that sound not so different from the monastic's, who has removed himself from the world, and for whom life's daily necessities are provided, so he can more easily concentrate on his spiritual practice (a topic we will return to at length later on):

> For the most part, in this tropic whaling life, a sublime uneventfulness invests you; you hear no news; read no gazettes; extras with startling accounts of commonplaces never delude you into unnecessary excitements; you hear of no domestic afflictions; bankrupt securities; fall of stocks; are never troubled with the thought of what you shall have for dinner—for all your meals for three years and more are snugly stowed in casks, and your bill of fare is immutable.[21]

In the loomings of the first chapter we find parallels to another teaching attributed to Bodhidharma: his "four all-inclusive practices."[22] First, Bodhidharma advises that, when encountering adversity, we should accept it with an open heart and without complaint. Ishmael concurs: "Well . . . however they may thump me and punch me about, I have the satisfaction of knowing that it is all right; that everybody else is one way or another served in much the same way."[23] Second, Bodhidharma says, we must adapt to our circumstances, for, as mortals, we are controlled by conditions, not by ourselves. Ishmael intuits this as well: "Though I cannot tell why it was exactly that those stage managers, the Fates, put me down for this shabby part of a whaling voyage . . . cajoling me into the delusion that it was a choice resulting from my own unbiased freewill and discriminating judgment."[24] Third, we must seek nothing. Ishmael says, "I abandon the glory and distinction of such offices to those who like them. . . . It is quite as much as I can do to take care of myself."[25] Fourth, Bodhidharma insists that having a clear understanding of the emptiness of subject and object is of the utmost importance. Ishmael expresses his insight through appealing to the story of Narcissus and his reflection in the water: "And still deeper the meaning of that story of Narcissus, who because he could not grasp the tormenting, mild image he saw in the fountain, plunged into it and was drowned. But that same image, we ourselves see in all rivers and oceans. It is the image of the ungraspable phantom of life, and this is the key to it all."[26]

We may be surprised by Ishmael's confident resolution in taking to the whaling life—especially since his emotional life seems so fragile. What reason does he have to believe that life on the sea will effect a positive change? That he pays homage to the "magnanimity of the sea" suggests that he does indeed expect to benefit from his voyage—although, needless to say, not in a financial sense, considering the miserly "lay" he receives from the Pequod's owners.[27] For Ishmael, his journey at sea entails a journey of the mind as well: "Yes, as everyone knows, meditation and water are wedded for ever."[28]

Just as the sea is "bottomless,"[29] so too does he call the human soul "deep, blue, bottomless."[30]

The sea provides a fitting metaphor for the human mind—restless and tumultuous, ideas rising and falling moment-to-moment (like the waves), emotions coming and going day-to-day (like the tides). Suzuki Roshi, speaking of meditation practice, goes so far as to refer to thoughts as "mind waves": "Many sensations come, many thoughts or images arise, but they are just waves of your own mind. Nothing comes from outside your mind. Actually water always has waves. Waves are the practice of the water. To speak of waves apart from water or water apart from waves is a delusion. Water and waves are one."[31] The ocean is the quintessence of fluidity—the perfect symbol of the impermanent nature of all phenomena. It is literally impossible to stay in one place in the ocean, for it is always shifting beneath one's feet.

Of course we are constantly changing on land as well. But our routines and commitments leave us "nailed to benches, clinched to desks,"[32] and it is often difficult to step outside ourselves (or look within ourselves) to see the ways in which we are changing every moment. The same can be said about the land itself. Looking down at the ground, it is not so easy to see how it is changing—perhaps we could sit and watch the grass grow, or kick a pebble down the road. And the air is unbounded, invisible, and so intangible as to be abstract. But the ocean is simultaneously static (in that it has identifiable boundaries) and constantly shifting within its borders. Ishmael addresses water's unique materiality in chapter 13, as he and Queequeg take the schooner from New Bedford to Nantucket. "Gaining the more open water," he writes, "How I snuffed that Tartar air!—how I spurned that turnpike earth!—that common highway all over dented with the marks of slavish heels and hoofs; and turned me to admire the magnanimity of the sea which will permit no records."[33] The air is "Tartar"—Melville's shorthand for "wild, ungovernable," as in the Turkic ethnic group that once inhabited Central Asia. Conversely, the earth is "common," "dented," "slavish"—the heavy static earth being the polar opposite of the wild spinning barbarism of the air.[34] Further, the reflective quality of the ocean—that looking into water we see ourselves—confirms Ishmael's commitment to a self-exploration that would simply not be possible on land. Thomas Cleary (author and translator of dozens of religious texts, from Buddhist to Islamic) asks: "How do we know if our perceptions and beliefs are valid? If we use our own knowledge to check our own knowledge, how can we know we are not revolving in circles?"[35]

So Ishmael senses the answer may lie in "groundlessness." Embracing the groundlessness of the sea is a way to step outside one's usual perspective, and abide in uncertainty and doubt.[36] (The land-locked equivalent might be living one's life in a perpetual earthquake.) Ishmael will use the sailor's life not only to uproot himself from his past, but to constantly dislodge himself

from anywhere he alights. As he prepares to embark, he imagines his superiors making him "jump from spar to spar, like a grasshopper in a May mead-
ow."[37] For on the open ocean, he says, "you cannot sit motionless in the heart
of these perils, because the boat is rocking like a cradle, and you are pitched
one way and the other, without the slightest warning."[38] Contrasted against
the weighted entrenchment of life on land, it is "only by a certain self-
adjusting buoyancy and simultaneousness of volition and action" that the
whaleman can survive the capricious seas. Through subjecting himself to a
constant harassment and tribulation, and forcing himself to commit constant
effort to remaining "upright"—both physically and ethically[39]—he will attain the Way.

Contrast Ishmael's intention of grounding himself in groundlessness, and
making his home in homelessness, against the Nantucketer, who aims to turn
the water *into* the land: "For the sea is his; he owns it . . . following the sea as
highwaymen the road . . . ploughing it as his own special plantation . . . as
prairie cocks in the prairie; he hides amongst the waves, he climbs them as
chamois hunters climb the Alps."[40] Captain Ahab, the exemplary Nantucketer, carries with him "a small vial of sand . . . filled with Nantucket sound-
ings," in order to keep himself always tethered to certainty and stability.[41]
But the contrary response—of turning land into water, and thus being unable
to abide anywhere—is just as disastrous, as demonstrated by the "six-inch
chapter" that is the "stoneless grave" of the oracular character Bulkington.[42]

Bulkington's heralded arrival and abrupt disappearance from the novel
are usually explained away by assuming Melville originally intended a larger
role for him in the narrative, but in the end decided against this and killed
him off. While this might very well be historically accurate, I will argue that
his unexpected—and unexplained—"ocean-perishing" makes philosophical
sense as well.[43] Bulkington is the antithesis of those "tied to counters . . .
clinched to desks"[44]—to him "the land [seems] scorching to his feet."[45] As
the "apotheosis" of landlessness, his absolute "open independence" prevents
him from enjoying "safety, comfort, hearthstone, supper, warm blankets,
friends, all that's kind to our mortalities."[46]

From Bulkington's first appearance in the Spouter-Inn, Ishmael notes
how in his eyes "floated some reminiscence that did not seem to give him
much joy."[47] And while his shipmates, for whom he was "for some reason a
huge favorite," try to include him in their reverie, he slips solemnly away
into the dark night. Philosopher Hubert Dreyfus considers Bulkington's fatal
flaw to be his utter joylessness.[48] It is "for refuge's sake" that Bulkington
"forlornly" pushes off from the "treacherous, slavish shore."[49] While Ishmael argues that going to sea is restorative, Bulkington does not seem to have
any love for the sea, only hatred of the land.

All this contrasts strikingly with Ishmael's presentation of the sea as the
locus of spiritual exploration and restoration. Just as, in a material sense,

water serves as the middle way between the land and the air, Ishmael finds a happy and pragmatic balance by taking to the "watery part of the world" between periodic returns to life on land. Bulkington has so fanatically embraced the detachment of the landless sailor that he has become attached to the detachment itself, and cannot allow himself any human comfort or solace. Ishmael may have Bulkington in mind when he later writes: "For as this appalling ocean surrounds the verdant land, so in the soul of man there lies one insular Tahiti, full of peace and joy, but encompassed by all the horrors of the half known life. God keep thee! Push not off from that isle, thou canst never return!"[50] While he celebrates Bulkington (if for nothing else than for his fortitude), the barrel-chested sailor cannot be brought back to land. Thus, his final appearance in the book arrives within scattered images of wind and air: "But in that gale . . . she must fly all hospitality . . . 'gainst the very winds that fain would blow her homeward . . . while the wildest winds of heaven and earth conspire."[51] He perishes in "the howling infinite," his grave is "stoneless," and even though he apparently perishes in the ocean, even here he cannot remain: "Bear thee grimly, demigod! Up from the spray of thy ocean-perishing—straight up, leaps thy apotheosis!"[52]

Chapter Seven

Narcissus and Dongshan

We have discussed how landlessness (or groundlessness) serves as the ultimate symbol of non-attachment, and why Ishmael considers going to sea to be the most efficacious means of investigating the cause of his existential angst. Both his fascination for the sea, and his resolve to get at the heart of his difficulties, are best expressed about halfway through the first chapter. Sermonizing about the magic and holiness of water, he seems to pause and thrust himself toward his readers, emphatically, "Surely all this is not without meaning."[1] That is, surely there is something going on here—some universal truth connecting the ancient Persians and Greeks to the Tennessee poet and Rockaway Beach pedestrians, all of whom he claims share the same aquatic preoccupation. This persistent questioning, so central to developing Way-seeking mind, is the key element of Ishmael's endeavor, and we will discuss it at length when we consider Ishmael's meditation practice. It leads him from these musings of the water's surface, "still deeper," to "the image of the ungraspable phantom of life," which is "the key to it all."[2]

The idea of "seeking"—after meaning, after Truth, after whales—is central to *Moby-Dick*. Captain Ahab is torn apart (both physically and psychologically) by his obsessive pursuit of Moby Dick. And it is Ishmael's "Way-seeking mind" that leads him to the whaleship and guides him through his spiritual journey. While it is perhaps obvious that the two men aspire toward quite different objectives, what may not be as clear is the motivation that lies behind their actions. Melville is walking a volitional tightrope here, creating two clear models of spiritual aspiration—Ishmael's, which we may truly call "seeking," and Ahab's, which is more akin to "grasping."

To take one brief example: when Ishmael asks, "Can we thus hope to light upon some chance clue to conduct us to the hidden cause we seek? Let us try,"[3] we notice the language—and therefore the intention—is very flexible.

His use of words like "hope," "chance," "try" resembles his delightful maxim "I try all things; I achieve what I can."[4] This is seeking. But when he writes, "in pursuit of those far mysteries we dream of, or in tormented chase of that demon phantom that, some time or other, swims before all human hearts; while chasing over this round globe, they either lead us on in barren mazes or midway leave us whelmed," the distinction is clear.[5] This suggests a fixed idea that exists in one's mind, and setting out to prove that the world conforms to one's idea of it. His message: the verbs "pursuit" and "chase" of the nouns "dream" and "phantom" leave us adjectives like "barren" and "whelmed."

The idea of "grasping" is exemplified by the Greek god Narcissus, whose story Ishmael recounts in the first chapter: "And still deeper the meaning of that story of Narcissus, who because he could not grasp the tormenting, mild image he saw in the fountain, plunged into it and was drowned."[6] As it appears in book 3 of Ovid's *Metamorphoses*, it is a meditation on impermanence: "But he glances down to see how the face has subtly changed / implausibly but exquisitely improved, and his heart is shattered / anew."[7] But Ishmael alters the story slightly (and crucially) from its classical rendering, having Narcissus drown instead of merely "waste away" as in the original.

This is one way of responding to a profound insight into the nature of Selfhood. But there is another model. Compare the Narcissus legend to the enlightenment story of Chinese Zen master Dongshan (807–869), founder of the Caodong (Japanese: Soto) school of Zen, and one of the principal figures of the so-called "golden age" of Zen:

> Dongshan continued to experience doubt. Later as he crossed a stream he saw his reflection in the water and was awakened. He then composed this verse:
>
> > *Avoid seeking elsewhere, for that's far from self.*
> > *Now I travel alone, everywhere I meet it.*
> > *Now it's exactly me, now I'm not it.*
> > *It must thus be understood to merge with thusness.* [8]

These two stories, of Narcissus and Dongshan and their respective reflections, correspond to the two characters in *Moby-Dick* whose views of themselves and the universe are shaped by their relationships with the image they each see in the water. But while these classical figures look into the water and see their literal reflections, Melville's characters face an abstracted reflection—or, rather, a representation of their conception of Self, as expressed by "the image of the ungraspable phantom"—that is, their idea of the White Whale, Moby Dick.[9]

Ahab, like Narcissus, is tortured not by the "mild image" he sees, but by his inability to "grasp" it. As this image of the whale is ostensibly a reflection of himself, he feels he should be able to grasp it as he believes he grasps his sense of a separate self. In this reading, Starbuck's admonition, "let Ahab beware of Ahab; beware of thyself, old man," can be taken as a warning against *Ahab's idea of himself*—"beware of thy self"—beware of the idea of Ahab as an independently existing thing.[10] Obsessed with determining whether the phantom itself conforms to the ideas of Self and Other that exist in his mind, Ahab chases that "tormenting" image around the world's oceans, and ultimately suffers a similar fate to that of Narcissus. Captain Ahab is not searching within himself for answers to the questions that plague him, but rather grasping for external validation of what he already believes.

Thus when Ahab playfully asks the carpenter, "shall I order eyes to see outwards? No, but put a sky-light on top of his head to illuminate inwards,"[11] the language seems to align with Dogen Zenji's admonition to "learn the backwards step that turns your light inward to illuminate your self."[12] But in effect, we might say simply that Ahab is "doing it wrong." As contemporary Zen teacher Steve Hagen writes: "Although we might think we're seeking Truth, we're not looking carefully at what's actually taking place. We're caught by our thinking, our desires, our wants, our fears, our sense of self. . . . Instead, we're focusing on what we think—and on what we expect to find."[13] Dogen's teaching is precisely the opposite—that by searching within ourselves, "when you practice intimately and return to where you are, it will be clear that nothing at all has unchanging self."[14] Like Narcissus, Ahab is so caught up in his ideas of a reified Self—and a reified Whale—that he cannot see beyond that underlying fallacy.

We see this also in the late chapter "Ahab and Starbuck in the Cabin," and Ahab's initial refusal to comply with Starbuck's plea to descend into the hold to check the oil barrels for leaks. Here Ahab shows he has no interest in exploring his attachments: "Let it leak! I'm all aleak myself. Aye! leaks in leaks! not only full of leaky casks, but those leaky casks are in a leaky ship. . . . Yet I don't stop to plug my leak; for who can find it in the deep-loaded hull; or how hope to plug it, even if found, in this life's howling gale?"[15] Ahab's reluctance to look deeply within himself (and that natural extension of himself, his ship), belies his allegedly introspective mind. While Ishmael is constantly examining phenomena hoping to understand things as they are, Ahab simply wants to prove what he already believes is true.[16]

Ishmael, then—experiencing doubt, travelling over water—is aligned with the story of Dongshan. Dongshan's opaque verse quoted above provides a framework that describes Ishmael's own process of discovery and realization. The first line, "Avoid seeking elsewhere, for that's far from self," clarifies the intention, and defines the scope of the search, as Ishmael first embarks. He sees the listless crowds of Manhattoes wandering without aim, and sees that "nothing will content them. . . . They must get just as nigh the water as they possibly can without falling in."[17] They don't even have a real understanding of what it is they seek; they are utterly lost: "How then is this? Are the green fields gone? What do they here?"[18] But he also recognizes the dangers, once one has aroused Way-seeking mind, of seeking outside oneself for answers, for this would be grasping—the "tormented chase" that "either lead[s] us on into barren mazes or midway leave[s] us whelmed."[19] He recognizes that he must remain focused on the reflection—that "the image . . . is the key to it all." But Dongshan's second line, "Now I travel alone, everywhere I meet it," both undermines and expands this focus, confirming that everything Ishmael comes in contact with is a reflection of his sense of self, not only the White Whale.

The third line serves as a reminder of the ungraspability of the reflection, and, even more fundamentally, a reminder not to confuse a reflection of a thing with the thing itself: "Now it's exactly me, now I'm not it." Finally Dongshan declares, "It must thus be understood to merge with thusness"—underscoring the fact that an understanding of the selflessness of phenomena is attained only through a thorough examination of the apparent nature of self—that is the reflection. Where this examination leads one is to an insight into "thusness" or "suchness"—rather clumsy English terms used to signify "reality as it is" or "the ineffable." The "thusness" of a thing is the true nature of a thing—that is, a thing as it exists beyond distinction of Self and Other. In other words, it is emphatically *not* the thing as it appears in the world, nor how we normally perceive it. So, again, it is through closely studying perception—the apparent polarity between subject and object—that we come to "merge with thusness." Ishmael, then, will study the whale (which he sees in the water and which seems so very different from himself) until he finally merges with thusness—or, as he says, until he "owns" the whale: "For unless you own the whale, you are but a provincial and sentimentalist in Truth."[20]

Chapter Eight

Searching for Ishmael

There is considerable disagreement among Melville scholars regarding the relationship between Ahab and Ishmael. Did Melville intend to contrast them against one another? Is one of them the hero? If so, which one? As usual, there is no clear indication of an answer—and thus no shortage of possible explanations. The two men are so fundamentally different, that it is almost impossible to compare them. In narrative terms, they seem to exist on separate planes of existence. But as the story progresses, although they remain ineluctably remote from one another, their philosophies inch ever closer, and at times it is no longer clear where the narrator ends and the central character in his drama begins.

Ishmael cannot be easily placed in any defined narrative mode. He is everywhere at once. Critics say he is "notorious for reporting soliloquies he cannot pretend to have witnessed,"[1] "able to report an interior life in Ahab that he cannot possibly witness,"[2] and constantly "telling us things he cannot possibly know: all over the ship sailors mutter to themselves while standing in the howling wind, yet Ishmael, wherever he is, somehow hears every word."[3] Ishmael barely interacts with anyone on the ship, but somehow knows their innermost thoughts.[4] Ishmael disappears for chapters at a time, returning with a subtle flourish (chapter 41 begins, "I, Ishmael, was one of that crew"[5])—and then furtively sneaking off once again (chapter 104 ends, "I leave you, reader"[6]). A bitter, vituperative character on land, the moment he steps on the ship this man all but dissolves, as if forsaking his existence as a static entity and becoming the novel's "central consciousness and narrative voice . . . a lyrical, poetic meditator upon whales and whaling."[7]

Even Ishmael's literary technique is mercurial: his judicious prose on land unrolls wildly on the open ocean, with portentous stage direction, arguments and soliloquies, delirious sketches of drunken revelry. Of course there is no way to distinguish between the "objective reality" of the Pequod's journey and Ishmael's subjective interpretation of those events in his retelling. But even the barriers between narrator and character (or subject and object) begin to blur—most notably when Ahab begins repeating phrases from Ishmael's narration (for example calling the sperm whale's head a "dead, blind wall").[8] Do they finally merge, when Ahab's "Oh, grassy glades" soliloquy in "The Gilder" is written without quotation marks? Some editions (beginning with the 1967 Norton Critical Edition) have begun to place quotation marks around it, to make clear to readers that it is in fact Ahab speaking. But Melville's omission may have been intentional—the language here almost seems an Ishmael-Ahab hybrid, fusing the former's incisive diction with the latter's magniloquent delivery. Perhaps we are meant to think of these three men as layers of a single narrative voice: as Ahab speaks through Ishmael, and Ishmael speaks through Melville, "fact and fancy, half-way meeting, interpenetrate, and form one seamless whole."[9]

Ishmael has been called the "false center" of the story.[10] The conventional terms we might usually give someone in his position—protagonist, hero—none of them seems to be quite appropriate. We can only say with any confidence that he is the narrator—everything we see and hear is filtered through him. Once at sea, it is impossible to pin him down—he appears and disappears at will, embodying the groundless life he has embraced. We are left with a "centerless center," our attempts to find consistency and continuity in the novel thwarted by a perspective that is continually shifting, dissolving, reassembling elsewhere. Melville exposes the reader's desire for a static reliable narrator by having Ishmael—perhaps alone among narrators—endeavor to dissuade us from looking for centers.

Perhaps the most crucial demonstration of Ishmael's centerlessness is his consistent self-identification as a *marginal* figure. In the opening sentence, he assumes the name of a man rejected by his family, cast into the wilderness.[11] This marginality is further reinforced by his aligning himself with Queequeg. Having left his island home and joined the land of "Christiandom,"[12] Queequeg is necessarily a marginal figure, being unable to assimilate with so-called "civilized" society. As befitting his outcast namesake, Ishmael describes himself as being strangely pulled toward these same margins: "I began to feel myself mysteriously drawn toward him. And those same things that would have repelled most others, they were the very magnets that thus drew me."[13] Most people, Ishmael argues, would be magnetically drawn toward the center of society. Indeed, even Queequeg seems to feel this natural pull toward assimilation—his outcast status is a result of his cultural displacement, and he vows to return to Kokovoko "as soon as he felt himself baptized again."[14] Finally, in the final scene in the book, as the whirlpool consumes the Pequod and her crew, rather than being pulled toward the center as well, Ishmael instead finds himself "floating on the margin of the ensuing scene, and in full sight of it."[15]

Thus our narrative center is by definition an outcast—living on the margins, away from center. Insofar as we cannot help identifying with our temperate guide, Melville puts the distinctly modern feeling of "'exile,' of abandonment," at the forefront of his drama.[16] Even the chapter at the philosophical core of the novel, "The Whiteness of the Whale," is itself a wild gesticulation on the horror inherent in the centerlessness of experience. And while *Moby-Dick* the book lies at both the biographical and emotional centers of Melville's literary career, "extravagant violations of generic boundaries have always rendered it virtually unclassifiable."[17]

Further complicating our attempts to clearly understand our narrator is the profound separation between the troubled young man in the opening chapters from the serene metaphysician who narrates the book. It is an astounding transformation, and narrator Ishmael recounts in detail his spiritual development on the journey, as he grows ever more tranquil, and ever more wise. Although this journey seems to have continued after the events on the Pequod (most notably in his encounter with the whale skeleton in the Arsacides) he offers us clues as to his progression along the way. When we come to answer the question why Ishmael alone survives the sinking of the Pequod (which we will discuss at length in the final chapter) we can point to precisely these awakening experiences.

But for now we will focus on the transformation itself, which begins when he meets Queequeg. Although Ishmael describes the harpooneer as "a creature in a transition state—neither caterpillar or butterfly,"[18] this definition more aptly applies to Ishmael himself, on the cusp of his great awakening to groundlessness. The evening before they end up sharing a bed, Ishmael lashes out at the Spouter-Inn landlord. He describes himself "getting into a towering rage," then briefly calming down before "flying into a passion again" (for no apparent reason, really) in his conversation with the landlord.[19] This brings into sharp relief the change Queequeg will effortlessly effect, and Melville makes sure to take note of both Ishmael's erratic behavior and his lack of inner composure. Ishmael speaks "quite calmly" in between flashes of anger, and then describes himself "as cool as Mt. Hecla in a snow storm"[20]—suggesting that regardless of his outward appearance he might nevertheless be boiling with rage within, and thus reinforcing the emotional disconnect in the novel's opening paragraph. But once in bed with Queequeg, Ishmael says he has "never slept better in [his] life."[21]

The effect that meeting Queequeg has over Ishmael is both immediate and overpowering, for in Queequeg he finds his spiritual guide: "Yes, we became very wakeful," Ishmael says of the new happy couple.[22] When he rises the following morning, Ishmael describes to us an experience from his childhood in which he felt he held hands with "the nameless, unimaginable, silent form or phantom."[23] He feels similar now, he says, waking up with Queequeg's hand in his own, but without "the awful fear" from his past.[24] While as a child he felt a terrifying "horrid spell,"[25] this experience is comforting and "affectionate."[26] And while as a child Ishmael "lost [himself] in confounding attempts to explain the mystery," here he feels assured of his identity, and can lie "only alive to the comical predicament."[27] Some have suggested that this mollifying effect is one of simple human companionship—but while Queequeg describes their relationship as friendship ("bosom friends" is a Kokovokan phrase, after all[28]), it is clear that Ishmael does not at all consider them equals. Ishmael describes his "bosom friend" in the most exalted terms. Speaking of his "calm self-collectedness," he seems transfixed; staring at his tattooed face, he marvels that "there was something almost sublime in it."[29]

Ishmael immediately recognizes the qualities in Queequeg he would like to emulate: he is "very civilized," with an "innate sense of delicacy."[30] He considers it "marvellous how essentially polite they are," those who are called savages.[31] This thought brings Ishmael to reconsider his own actions, and quickly realizes "he treated me with such civility and consideration, while I was guilty of great rudeness.[32] Minutes later, Ishmael descends to the bar-room and encounters the landlord he treated so harshly the night before. Having been subtly turned by Queequeg, Ishmael notes he "cherished no malice toward him" and greets him "very pleasantly."[33] His conversion has begun.

The idea that Melville intends Queequeg as a religious figure is perhaps most powerfully illustrated in the chapter "The Ramadan," in which Queequeg spends long hours in seated meditation practice—the only lengthy description of religious practice in the book. Ishmael bursts into their shared room to his new friend—"squatting on his hams . . . [h]e looked neither one way nor the other way, but sat like a carved image with scarce a sign of active life."[34] Having never encountered the kind of stillness now embodied by Queequeg, Ishmael lashes out in sheer panic: "'Queequeg,' said I, going up to him, 'Queequeg, what's the matter with you?'"[35]

The possibility that Queequeg is a sage or savior is lent weight by the lives he saves in the novel.[36] First he dives into the icy sea to save the drowning greenhorn (who moments earlier had insulted him).[37] Later, in the "Cistern and Buckets" chapter, when Tashtego falls into the sperm whale's head, Queequeg once again "[dives] to the rescue"—at which point there is a curious episode, in which Queequeg first succeeds at extracting Tashtego's leg, "but well knowing that that was not as it ought to be . . . thrust back the leg, and by a dextrous heave and toss" spins Tashtego around and pulls him out headfirst. Thus, thanks to Queequeg's "agile obstetrics,"[38] Tashtego is literally reborn.

But Queequeg's greatest "miracle" is his own rebirth. After a serious illness, from which it seems there will be no recovery, Queequeg suddenly decides (from "nigh to his endless end"[39]) that it is not time to die at all—that he had "recalled a little duty ashore, which he was leaving undone; and therefore had changed his mind about dying."[40] There is a similar story about Shakyamuni Buddha, who, at eighty years old, became gravely ill: "But with great self-control he suppressed the pain and overcame his sickness. It was not right for him to die . . . until he had made some practical arrangements."[41] Queequeg contends that if a man makes up his mind to live, nothing as insubstantial as illness can kill him—only a "violent, ungovernable, unintelligent destroyer" like "a whale, or a gale."[42]

In all these cases, Queequeg is the picture of equanimity. Ishmael writes, "[H]e seemed entirely at his ease; preserving the utmost serenity; content with his own companionship; always equal to himself."[43] He is uninterested in answers to metaphysical questions: although he sits in the chapel with a "wondering gaze of incredulous curiosity,"[44] he himself maintains that "Queequeg no care what god made him shark . . . wedder Fejee god or Nantucket god."[45] He is "altogether cool and self-collected,"[46] and full of "concern and compassion."[47]

Melville gives us little hint of how any of Queequeg's flock are changed by their experiences—except for Ishmael, who declares himself a convert the evening after he meets his guide. Sitting together before the fire, Ishmael experiences a profound transformation:

> As I sat there . . . I began to be sensible of strange feelings. I felt a melting in me. No more my splintered heat and maddened hand were turned against the wolfish world. This soothing savage had redeemed it. There he sat, his very indifference speaking a nature in which there lurked no civilized hypocrisies and bland deceits. Wild he was; a very sight of sights to see; yet I began to feel myself mysteriously drawn toward him. And those same things that would have repelled most others, they were the very magnets that thus drew me. I'll try a pagan friend, thought I, since Christian kindness proved but hollow courtesy.[48]

He pledges himself to whatever "fine philosophy" Queequeg holds within him: "Consequently, I must then unite with him in his; ergo, I must turn idolator. So . . . we undressed and went to bed, at peace with our own consciences and all the world."[49] This conversion represents Ishmael's utter abandonment of his former life—the things he once held dear, the value system to which he previously adhered. It accompanies a turn from suicidal hopelessness in Manhattan (the self-proclaimed "center of the world") to a vivacious embrace of a centerless life on the margins.

Chapter Nine

Whaling Life, Monastic Life

In Shakyamuni Buddha's India, the spiritual life was characterized by home-lessness. Shakyamuni said, "Household life is crowded and dusty; life gone forth is wide open. It is not easy, while living in a home, to lead the holy life."[1] Even today, ordination as a Zen monk is called *shukke tokudo*, which in Japanese literally translates as "leaving home and accomplishing the Way." In Vedic India, where mendicancy was very common, Buddhist monks were able to beg for their food, and survive through the generosity of others. Buddhist monasticism arose when the Buddha's followers temporarily gathered during the annual monsoon season, to confer on their understanding of the teachings. Unlike Catholicism, for example, where monks generally enter the monastery for their lives, from the very beginning Buddhist monastic practice was seen as a temporary training period, between peripatetic wanderings.

When Buddhism reached countries in which this culture of mendicancy was unknown, a new model was established. In China, where monastic self-sufficiency was highly valued, Ch'an (Zen) monks began growing their own food, and physical labor became one of the fundamental practices of Zen Buddhist monastic training. The great Zen master Baizhang (720–814) encapsulated this spirit when he said, "A day of no work is a day of no eating."[2] This new paradigm was intended to integrate meditation practice with everyday activities—every monk in the community, regardless of status or rank, is expected to engage in manual labors like cooking, sweeping, and cleaning toilets. Zen teachers have been known to de-emphasize abstract textual study, and instruct their students in the actualization of the practice in the immediacy of these monastic tasks.

It is in this sense that D.T. Suzuki—the Japanese intellectual largely responsible for introducing Zen to the West—described the Zen monastery as "a community of men pursuing one common object, and the spirit of mutual help and service is everywhere evident in its life."[3] And it is in this sense that we can speak of the Pequod as a "floating monastery," a spiritual training center where men can retreat from the "turnpike earth" and devote themselves to the pursuit of Truth.[4]

One first-hand account of Zen monastic life which there is a good chance of Melville having read appeared in the pages of Evert Duyckinck's weekly magazine *The Literary World* in late 1847. He would certainly at least have held this piece in his hands, for he himself was a frequent contributor—writing articles and publishing excerpts from his own work. It was in *The Literary World* that his pivotal work "Hawthorne and His Mosses" first appeared, in the 17 and 24 August 1850 issues of the magazine.[5]

This account, an excerpt from the book *Consular Cities of China* by Reverend George Smith, was by no means complimentary—far from it—but its description of life in the monastery does bear a striking resemblance to life on the whaleship:

> More than a hundred priests dwell in the temple. . . . No community of interest, no ties of social life, no objects of generous ambition, beyond the satisfying of those wants which bind them to the cloister, help to diversify the monotonous current of their daily life. Separated by a broad line of demarcation from the rest of society, and bound by vows to a life of celibacy and asceticism, they are cut off from the ordinary enjoyments of one world, without any well-founded hope of a better life.[6]

What Smith describes as "the monotonous current of their daily life" points to the strong emphasis Zen places on routine. On a practical level, through strict adherence to the monastic schedule and devoted repetition of mundane tasks, we can break through our habitual responses of likes and dislikes, and casting judgments. Dogen Zenji, for example, placed almost paramount importance on the devoted performance of monastic tasks, teaching that the correct performance of monastic routine is itself the realization of Buddha's teaching. One of his disciples, Tettsu Gikai (1219–1309), wrote after Dogen's death:

> Buddhism transmitted by our teacher is [the correct] performance of one's present monastic tasks. Even though I had heard that Buddhist ritual is Buddhism, in my heart I privately felt that true Buddhism must reside far from this. Recently, however, I have changed my views. I now know that monastic ritual and deportment themselves are that true Buddhism.[7]

Ishmael channels this spirit of steadfast effort within routine in "Stowing Down and Clearing Up," in which the crew scrubs down the ship after the lengthy and messy processing of a sperm whale:

> Oh! my friends, but this is man-killing! Yet this is life. For hardly have we mortals by long toilings extracted from this world's vast bulk its small but valuable sperm; and then, with weary patience, cleansed ourselves from its defilements, and learned to live here in clean tabernacles of the soul; hardly is this done, when—*There she blows!*—the ghost is spouted up, and away we sail to fight some other world, and so through young life's old routine again. [8]

This episode is notable particularly for its emphasis on the "singularly cleansing virtue" of the sperm oil, that through performing this routine the men will be "cleansed" of "defilements." [9] In the ceaseless tumult of the whaleship, each sailor is constantly called upon to perform certain tasks and fulfill certain roles. Ishmael describes in great detail the various positions at sea, making clear that while it is indeed a hierarchical system, every man must execute his tasks, or the entire operation will fall apart. The roles and responsibilities of the mates and the harpooneers are particularly resonant, since they are the ones most directly chasing that which is our embodiment of Truth, the sperm whale. [10] Thus if they avail themselves of the opportunity, wholehearted performance of daily activities are directly pointing them toward this realization of Truth. This points us once again toward the admonition in Zen practice to pay close attention to all one's daily activities, an ideal that arguably serves as the basis of Zen monasticism.

Reverend Smith's book (excerpted in *Literary World*) errs in assuming the monks to be "separated by a broad line of demarcation from the rest of society." As mentioned above, from its earliest incarnations, Buddhist monastic life was not conceived as a life-long pursuit. Zen scholar Taigen Dan Leighton writes:

> A major paradigm of Mahayana Buddhist monasticism has been oscillation between periods of training in the monastic enclosure and re-entry into the marketplace. Monks test their practice by returning to interact with conventional society, and also help fulfill the development function of the Buddhist order by sharing with the ordinary world whatever they have learned of self-awareness, composure, and compassion during their monastic training. [11]

This is precisely how Ishmael characterizes his episodic returns to the whaling life: "Whenever I find myself growing grim about the mouth . . . I account it high time to get to sea as soon as I can." [12] Contemporary Zen teacher Daigan Lueck describes monastic life as having originally arisen from a desire for non-attachment, for relief from the anxiety inherent in having a family to protect, property to defend, a livelihood to pursue and preserve.

While Ishmael certainly qualifies as such an existential pilgrim, it is the brief appearance of Perth, the Pequod's blacksmith, who most pitiably represents this trauma of attachment. He is a man who has lost everything he held dear: his trade, his health, his home, his wife, his children—even his ten toes to frostbite. As Ishmael himself admits, after all this, death seems the most merciful fate for the blacksmith: "Oh, Death, why canst thou not sometimes be timely? Hadst thou taken this old blacksmith to thyself ere his full ruin came upon him. . . . Death seems the only desirable sequel for a career like this."[13] But the whaling life offers an alternative. We are told that before Perth "postponedly encountered that thing in sorrow's technicals called ruin,"[14] he had never before been given reason to deep thinking about the nature of existence. But through these successive disasters, having watched as the people and things he loved were taken from him, he is left with "some interior compunctions against suicide."[15] It might be too charitable to ascribe this "compunction" to fortitude rather than fear, but Ishmael insists it is from this willingness to continue that the ocean "spread forth his . . . wonderful, new-life adventures . . . and from the hearts of infinite Pacifics, the thousand mermaids sing" to him:

> "Come hither, broken-hearted; here is another life without the guilt of intermediate death; here are wonders supernatural, without dying for them. Come hither! bury thyself in a life which, to your now equally abhorred and abhorring, landed world, is more oblivious than death. Come hither! put up *thy* grave-stone, too, within the churchyard, and come hither, till we marry thee!"[16]

Perth, the "begrimed, blistered old blacksmith,"[17] hears the mermaids' call: "Hearkening to these voices, East and West, by early sun-rise, and by fall of eve, the blacksmith's soul responded. Aye, I come! And so Perth went a-whaling."[18] This suggests, in no uncertain terms, that whaling offers a chance at rebirth—being reborn into a world "more oblivious than death,"[19] or *beyond* birth and death. Reverend Smith acknowledges this possibility of salvation:

> It is probable that some of these [monks] have been driven to seek a solace in this retreat from the sorrows of life, or from the anguish of remorse. By means of self-righteous asceticism, they hope to be delivered from the grosser elements from which form the compound being, man, and to be assimilated to, and at length finally absorbed into, the immaterial substance of the holy Budh. . . . [once] the requisite amount of purity and merit has been gained, and the more devout are enabled to revel in the imaginary paradise of absorption, or, in other words, of annihilation. This is the grand hope of Budhism: this is the only stimulus to present exertion which it offers.[20]

But what remains hidden from Smith is the means of deliverance, the practice that turns the monk (and the whaleman) toward the proverbial light.

This is what is most remarkable about the blacksmith—that the man who appears in this chapter is not the pitiful vagabond described in Ishmael's short history. Though he toils away, as if "the heavy beating of his hammer [were] the heavy beating of his heart,"[21] he appears content: "No murmur, no impatience, no petulance did come from him."[22] The blacksmith is "incessantly invoked" by the sailors, "surrounded by an eager circle, all waiting to be served."[23] Captain Ahab, for one, cannot understand how, having suffered losses far beyond anything he himself has experienced, the blacksmith can remain "calmly, sanely woeful."[24] Ahab encourages him to go mad: "[W]hy dost thou not go mad? How can'st thou endure without being mad?"[25] But Perth is "silent, slow and solemn," with a "patient hammer wielded by a patient arm."[26] Through whole-hearted devotion to his role as blacksmith—to monastic tasks—Perth has achieved some semblance of peace in his heavy heart. As Master Hongzhi said, "Accept your function and be wholly satisfied."[27]

We find another example of this "work practice" in the carpenter, the blacksmith's brother in craftsmanship, who is proficient in "numerous trades and callings collateral to his own."[28] But while Ishmael does not question the carpenter's mastery of his trade, it is his demeanor that Ishmael finds so fascinating, and commendable. He rattles off a few disparate tasks that the carpenter might be asked to perform: he "concocts a soothing lotion" for an oarsman's sprained wrist, "makes a pagoda-looking cage" (note the architectural choice) for a "lost land-bird of strange plumage," paints "vermillion stars" onto Stubb's oars, drills holes in the ears of a sailor fond of "shark-bone earrings," and even extracts a sailor's tooth.[29] In all of these charges the carpenter is "unhesitatingly expert,"[30] and for Ishmael, this is what sets him apart from the world's "mob of unnecessary duplicates":

> Thus, this carpenter was prepared at all points, and alike indifferent and without respect. Teeth he accounted bits of ivory; heads he deemed by top-blocks; men themselves he lightly held for capstans. . . . He was a stript abstract; an unfractioned integral; uncompromised as a new-born babe; living without premeditated reference to this world or the next. . . . [H]e did not seem to work so much by reason or by instinct, or simply because he had been tutored to it, or by any intermixture of all these, even or uneven; but merely by a kind of deaf and dumb, spontaneous literal process.[31]

On the surface, this does match Reverend Smith's sneering portrayal of the Chinese monks as "wretched men [who] saunter about with an idiotic smile and vacant look, and appear little removed in intellect above the animal creation. Only a few seemed raised by mental culture about the generality, and exhibit a refinement of mind and manner."[32] But looking deeper, what makes the carpenter so unusual is his refusal (or inability) to build up stories around those tasks to which he is assigned. He does not complain or expect praise; he neither accepts nor deflects attention. Ishmael cannot ascribe to him summary adjectives of bravery or cowardice, joy or sadness, as he has with the rest of the crew. The carpenter defies all categorization: "For nothing was this man more remarkable, than for a certain impersonal stolidity as it were; impersonal, I say; for it so shaded off into the surrounding infinite of things, that it seemed one with the general stolidity discernible in the whole visible world."[33] One might say that the carpenter exists only through his activity—as an instrument, or manifestation, of carpentry. But he is "no mere machine of an automaton"[34]—rather he has cultivated this state of being through his devotion to his charge, so much so that "his brain, if he had ever had one, must have early oozed along into the muscles of his fingers."[35]

D.T. Suzuki writes that Zen monks are "disciplined to take up whatever work that is assigned to them without a murmur and to do it in the best possible manner.[36] From the blacksmith "no murmur . . . did come"[37]; the carpenter tells Ahab, "I don't mean anything, sir. I do as I do."[38] Dogen advises, "The essential point is deeply to arouse genuine mind and respectful mind without making judgments."[39] We can equate "making judgments" with creating stories, or being caught up in self-centered thinking:

> Was it that this old carpenter had been a life-long wanderer, whose much rolling, to and fro, not only had gathered no moss; but what is more, had rubbed off whatever small outward clingings might have originally pertained to him? . . . If he did not have a common soul in him, he had a subtle something that somehow anomalously did its duty. What that was, whether essence of quicksilver, or a few drops of hartshorn, there is no telling. But there it was; and there it had abided for now sixty years or more.[40]

Ishmael learns firsthand the importance of concentrating on one's work. "Fantasies are fatal to Zen," D.T. Suzuki said,[41] and in "The Mast-Head," almost falling to his death, Ishmael nearly finds those words literally true. And by contrasting these assiduous craftsmen with Ahab and his anguished rants, Melville suggests they might be able to help the Captain in the same way. As it happens, their industriousness does indeed shift from fashioning the instruments of his mania (the harpoon, his boat) to literally piecing him back together again (fitting him with a new leg). Finally he asks them "to forge a pair of steel shoulder-blades" to alleviate the weighty burden of his afflictions and attachments: "there's a pedlar aboard with a crushing pack."[42]

Another part of Ishmael's portrayal of the whaleship that recalls Zen monasticism is his initiation into the whaling life. In Japan, it is traditional for a student requesting admission into a monastery to be ritualistically refused entry, at which point the student's role is to ignore this ignominious welcome, and begin sitting meditation outside the temple, for an unspecified amount of time, until he is granted entry. In Japanese this is called *tanga-zume*, literally "staying in the guest room"; in the Western Buddhist world the word *tangaryo* is more common, which means "guest room," or "waiting room."

Edward Salisbury's 1844 lecture *Memoir on the History of Buddhism* reports on the origins of this tradition, which can be traced back to the time of Shakyamuni Buddha:

> The noviciate had first to choose some one among the brotherhood as his instructor . . . [and] was then introduced to the whole body, and charged to answer truly, whether he was free from disease, of the male sex, having his own free will, clear of debt, not owing military service. . . . After this interrogation, he was to ask admission three times, and again he was questioned as before. [43]

Stepping onto the Pequod for the first time, Ishmael is clearly asked three times by Captain Peleg whether he is sure he wants to ship as a whaleman:

> "I have given thee a hint of what whaling is; do ye yet feel inclined for it?"
> "I do, sir."
> "Very good. Now, art thou the man to pitch a harpoon down a live whale's throat, and then jump after it? Answer, quick!"
> "I am, sir, it should be positively indispensable to do so; not to be got rid of, that is; which I don't take to be the fact."
> "Good again."
> "Well, what dost thou think then of seeing the world? Do ye wish to go round Cape Horn to see any more of it, eh? Can't ye see the world where you stand?"
> I was a little staggered, but go a-whaling I must, and I would; and the Pequod was as good a ship as any—I thought the best—and all this I now repeated to Peleg. Seeing me so determined, he expressed his willingness to ship me. [44]

This momentary hesitation is precisely the reason for asking three times, and the attempt at dissuasion. In Japanese tradition, it was not uncommon for those requesting entry to be verbally berated, or even physically abused (for example, throwing buckets of cold water on monks sitting in the dead of winter), to test their mettle. Ishmael must wholeheartedly commit to the practice of whaling before embarking.

It should be mentioned that by no means is monasticism the only path toward enlightenment. Shakyamuni Buddha taught laywomen and laymen, alongside monks and nuns. The *Vimilakirti Sutra*, one of the most important texts in Mahayana Buddhism, tells the story of a wise layman who defeats some of the Buddha's greatest disciples in doctrinal debate. The Middle Way is a wide path, and accommodates as many interpretations as there are practitioners. The monastic model is simply put forth as the way of life most conducive to awakening—for by entering the monastery, or in this case the whaleship, we can single-mindedly pursue our ultimate goal. Dogen addresses this point in his fascicle *Shukke Kokudo*, "The Merits of Leaving Family Life":

> Although both [laypeople and monks] can attain salvation, still there is difficulty and ease. Laypeople's livelihoods have all sorts of jobs and duties; if they want to concentrate their minds on the truth and the Dharma, their trade will deteriorate; and if they concentrate on practicing their trade, matters pertaining to the truth will deteriorate. They should be able to practice the Dharma without selecting and without abandoning [one or the other], which is called "difficult." If we leave family life and part from secular society, to eradicate miscellaneous irritations and disturbances, and to concentrate the mind solely on practice of the truth, is called "easy." Further, family life, being disorderly and noisy, with many jobs and many duties, is the root of hindrances and the seat of many sins. It is called "very difficult." If we leave family life, we are like, for example, a person going off to stay in a deserted place, among empty fields, and making the mind whole so that there is no mind and no concern: we are already rid of inner thoughts, and external matters also have departed. [45]

It is not a matter of "right and wrong," but rather "easy and difficult." Nevertheless, for most of us, "difficult" as it may be, the path of the householder (with its many blessed distractions) is the right one. And despite these superficial distinctions between the monastic and secular worlds, both eventually arrive at the same insight—something Ishmael addresses in the chapter "A Squeeze of the Hand": "For now, since by many prolonged, repeated experiences, I have perceived that in all cases man must eventually lower, or at least shift, his conceit of attainable felicity; not placing it anywhere in the intellect or the fancy; but in the wife, the heart, the bed, the table, the saddle, the fire-side, the country."[46] Indeed, it is through accepting the wide variance in spiritual paths that one becomes capable of realizing Truth. Ishmael, again, walks the spiritual path with a great degree of latitude, with the assurance that all points lead to the same destination. As he says, "Take almost any path you please, and ten to one it carries you down in a dale, and leaves you there by a pool in the stream."[47]

Ishmael finds this "felicity" in squeezing the globules of spermaceti with his shipmates—which, with its overt homoeroticism, suggests a brief "return to the marketplace" after having cloistered himself away (from the reader, and apparently from his fellow sailors as well) for most of the novel:

> Squeeze! Squeeze! Squeeze! all the morning long; I squeezed that sperm till I myself almost melted into it; I squeezed that sperm till a strange sort of insanity came over me; and I found myself unwittingly squeezing my co-laborers' hands in it, mistaking their hands for the gentle globules. Such an abounding,

affectionate, friendly, loving feeling did this avocation beget; that at last I was continually squeezing their hands and looking up in their eyes sentimentally; as much as to say,—Oh! my dear fellow beings, why should we longer cherish any social acerbities, or know the slightest ill-humor or envy![48]

More important, however, than the sensuality of the scene is the activity itself—squeezing the solidified lumps of spermaceti. Throughout the book, Ishmael champions variety and flexibility in spiritual pursuits, and here he is exalting in fluidity—rather, a literal *liquidity* in the substance that is the essence of the whaleman's spiritual journey. And in that liquidity—in turning what was solid into something fluid—he finds great delight and sympathetic joy (Sanskrit: *mudita*).

So once again Ishmael points us back toward groundlessness and fluidity. He has embraced the whaling life—presented here as analogous to the monastic life—specifically because it allows him to move freely between the "many prolonged, repeated experiences" through which he accumulates wisdom. He finds no contradiction between the orgiastic (as seen here) and the almost catatonic (on the mast-head in "Stubb Kills a Whale"). Each directs him to the whale, and to Truth.

Chapter Ten

Ishmael's Meditation

Most readers of *Moby-Dick* will agree that Ishmael is not only keenly aware of the world around him, but in possession of surprising insights into the nature of reality. But the question remains, how does he arrive there? What is it that turns Ishmael from the suicidal schoolteacher, lashing out at landlords, to the wise old whaler narrating this tale? I will argue it is his meditation practice—not literally suggesting his having stealthily adopted some ancient system of religious discipline that has somehow escaped all readers and scholars, but rather that his philosophical and cetological ruminations in the book are precisely aligned with the ideas of what Buddhists call tranquility (*shamatha*) and insight (*vipassana*) meditation, regarded as the two factors necessary for enlightenment. Tranquillity practice is, as it suggests, a practice of calming the mind, of eliminating discursive thought and simply being aware, without judgment, of mental and bodily processes as they arise and cease. Insight practice *uses* discursive thought to penetrate the nature of phenomena, to see through the way things *seem* into the way things *are*.

The Sanskrit term *shamatha* literally means "dwelling in tranquility." Ishmael's profound sensitivity is evident throughout the book, beginning with his aforementioned conversion experience with Queequeg: "As I sat there . . . I began to be sensible of strange feelings. I felt a melting in me. No more my splintered heart and maddened hand were turned against the wolfish world."[1] One immediate effect of this experience is a move toward silence and stillness. As he prepares to embark on his journey, Ishmael writes, "I said nothing, and tried to think nothing"[2]—echoing both Dogen's "How do you think of not thinking? Non-thinking"[3] and Seng-Ts'an's "Stop talking and thinking, and there is nothing you will not be able to know."[4]

Tranquility is not some dreamy attempt to remove oneself from the world that surrounds us, but a state of keen awareness of sense faculties and mental consciousness. Ishmael explores this awareness in fascinating detail—particularly from the Queequeg chapters onward, as he begins to explore his new psychological sensitivities, documenting both the ephemeral nature of thought and his increasing compassion toward the world:

> As I walked away, I was full of thoughtfulness; what had been incidentally revealed to me of Captain Ahab, filled me with a certain wild vagueness of painfulness concerning him. And somehow, at the time, I felt a sympathy and sorrow for him, but for I don't know what, unless it was the cruel loss of his leg. And yet I also felt a strange awe of him; but that sort of awe, which I cannot at all describe, was not exactly awe; I do not know what it was. [5]

As the restless quest progresses, and Ishmael does indeed come to know Ahab, he nonetheless remains serene, imperturbable, "divinely free of ill-will," [6] amidst the furious tumult everywhere surrounding him. Ishmael is himself the "enchanted calm which they say lurks at the heart of every commotion." [7] The only other figures described in similar terms are, again, Queequeg, and also the sperm whales, who swim with "a gentle joyousness—a mighty mildness of repose in swiftness . . . that great majesty . . . this serenity . . . that quietude . . . calm, enticing calm . . . serene tranquilities . . . exceeding rapture." [8]

So, once again, what is it that allows Ishmael to maintain such a state of mind? It is his willingness to abide in whatever situation presents itself, his adaptability to the reality of what is happening *now*. Ishmael echoes Dogen Zenji's teaching, "When you find your place where you are, practice occurs, actualizing the fundamental point" [9]—saying that, on the Pequod, "For one, I gave myself up to the abandonment of the time and the place." [10] He takes Ahab's oath alongside the rest of the crew, and even while he shouts, he remains keenly aware of his mind, as a "wild, mystical, sympathetic feeling" momentarily envelops him. [11] He does not restrain himself from negative or even wicked states of mind, for he knows them to be ephemeral: "Wrapped, for that interval, in darkness myself, I but the better saw the redness, the madness, the ghastliness of others." [12] *Hsin Hsin Ming* expresses this point nicely: "Just let things be in their own way . . . the burdensome practice of judging brings annoyance and weariness. What benefit can be derived from distinctions and separations?" [13]

Ishmael offers us a warning in this same vein—that one must dwell in neither positive nor negative thoughts. For the person who attaches to darkness will remain in darkness, while for Ishmael "[t]omorrow, in the natural sun, the skies will be bright; those who glared like devils in the forking flames, the morn will show in far other, at least gentler, relief." [14] Ishmael argues that clinging to positive thoughts is similarly unhelpful, for the one who "dodges hospitals and jails, and walks fast crossing grave-yards, and would rather talk of opera than hell . . . not that man is fitted to sit down on tombstones, and break the green damp mould with unfathomably wondrous Solomon."[15] Ishmael offers the image of a "Catskill eagle," and we might imagine him as the ideal symbol:

> And there is a Catskill eagle in some souls that can alike dive down into the blackest gorges, and soar out of them again and become invisible in the sunny spaces. And even if he for ever flies within the gorge, that gorge is in the mountains; so that even in his lowest swoop the mountain eagle is still higher than other birds upon the plain, even though they soar.[16]

He allows himself to get into various moods, in the same way that, as he says, "to and fro I idly swayed in what seemed an enchanted air."[17] When he is feeling one way, he calls out Pantheists with derision in "The Mast-Head"; soon after, feeling another way, he imagines that the ocean's "vast tides were a conscience; and the great mundane soul were in anguish and remorse for the long sin and suffering it had bred,"[18] which sure sounds a lot like Pantheism. He later goes even further, sensing in the sea's "gentle awful stirrings . . . some hidden soul beneath"—finally admitting that "lifted by those eternal swells, you needs must own the seductive god, bowing your head to Pan."[19] Ishmael has no home, and thus he can be at home everywhere. Even regarding the White Whale he claims no consistent belief; he can only tell how us how he feels about it "at times."[20]

A key expression of Ishmael's non-judging mind comes in the very first chapter, as Ishmael the narrator states, "Not ignoring what is good, I am quick to perceive a horror, and could still be social with it—would they let me—since it is but well to be on friendly terms with all the inmates of the place one lodges in."[21] The key phrase, of course, is "would they let me"— that the world of appearances is based upon strict delineations of right and wrong, and does not take kindly to those who test these boundaries. Chinese Zen master Huanglong (1002–1069) wrote, "Once poison is gone from your heart, even serpents and tigers are your friends."[22] Ishmael, friends with Christian and cannibal, the mindless and the monomaniacal, is able to flourish in whatever circumstances he finds himself—unlike Starbuck, for example, whose refusal to adapt to changing conditions causes him nothing but strife. Nor does Ishmael fault others for their "so striving and so grasping," being content with his own contentment, and "the privilege of making my own summer with my own coals."[23]

The most prominent example of Ishmael's infinite compatibility is his attitude toward religion. He seems to adhere to the words of *Hsin Hsin Ming*: "Do not search for the truth; only cease to cherish opinions."[24] Whatever one wishes to call it—pluralism, ecumenicism, ironic relativism—it is clear that he is not as interested in what one believes in (or even whether or not one believes in anything at all) as he is in whether one remains open to the possibility of alternative perspectives. He alone understands that beliefs are as malleable and mutable as opinions and prejudices: "Be it said, that though I had felt such a strong repugnance to his smoking in the bed the night before, yet see how elastic our stiff prejudices grow when love once comes to bend them. For now I liked nothing better than to have Queequeg smoking by me, even in bed, because he seemed to be full of such serene household joy then."[25] Furthermore, in saying, "Methinks that in looking at things spiritual, we are too much like oysters observing the sun through the water, and thinking that thick water the thinnest of air,"[26] Ishmael implies that, whatever we believe, the reality of even our most tightly-held truths remains well outside the realm of rational thought. His interest is not in the systems of belief themselves, but rather what those practices are directed toward. He suggests that, as F.D. Maurice advised, we should not "merely look to find a meaning in the dry records of other people's notions or practices, but compare them with what we have felt and experienced in our own lives."[27]

In Zen terms, our religions are merely different ways of pointing at the moon, and must not be taken for the moon itself—as Hongzhi writes, "It is said that the various kinds [of belief] are not equal, but beyond each of them is the path."[28] Ishmael says this even more simply—"All truth is profound"[29]—and he praises that place where all these narrow faiths meet:

> "I mean, sir, the same ancient Catholic Church to which you and I, and Captain Peleg there, and Queequeg here, and all of us, and every mother's son and soul of us belong; the great and everlasting First Congregation of this whole worshipping world; we all belong to that; only some of us cherish some queer crotchets noways touching the grand belief; in *that* we all join hands."[30]

Ishmael addresses this point at length in "The Ramadan," having just come up against one such "queer crotchet"—namely Queequeg's extended "fasting, humiliation, and prayer."[31]

> [F]or I cherish the greatest respect toward everybody's religious obligations, never mind how comical, and could not find it in my heart to undervalue even a congregation of ants worshipping a toad-stool; or those other creatures in certain parts of our earth, who with a degree of footmanism quite unprecedented in other planets, bow down before the torso of a deceased landed proprietor merely on account of the inordinate possessions yet owned and rented in his name.
>
> I say, we good Presbyterian Christians should be charitable in these things, and not fancy ourselves so vastly superior to other mortals, pagans and what not, because of their half-crazy conceits on these subjects. There was Queequeg, now, certainly entertaining the most absurd notions about Yojo and his

Ramadan;—but what of that? Queequeg thought he knew what he was about, I suppose; he seemed to be content; and there let him rest. All our arguing with him would not avail; let him be, I say; and Heaven have mercy on us all— Presbyterians and Pagans alike—for we are all somehow dreadfully cracked about the head, and sadly need mending.[32]

Ishmael scoffs both at the arbitrary distinctions between piety and heresy ("But what is worship?—to do the will of God—*that* is worship. And what is the will of God?—to do to my fellow man what I would have my fellow man do to me—*that* is the will of God"[33]) as well as the idea that our narrow ideas about faith and worship are satisfying or fulfilling some divine devotion quotient. Instead he emphasizes "the general stolidity of the whole visible world," arguing that "the surrounding infinite of things . . . which while pauselessly active in uncounted modes, still eternally holds its peace, and ignores you, though you dig foundations for cathedrals."[34]

Insofar as our beliefs are only to be judged by whether they contribute to our ability to, as Ishmael says, "do to my fellow man what I would have my fellow man do to me," even belief and disbelief cannot be so easily distinguished. Though both "can hypothesize . . . [they] cannot prove and establish," he says in "The Fountain."[35] Recognition of this fact "makes neither believer nor infidel, but makes a man who regards them both with equal eye."[36] Ishmael is therefore able to either "dabble" in a number of faiths serially, or "[bolt] down all events, all creeds, and beliefs, and persuasions" en masse.[37] In both cases, the crucial element—and what sets him apart from everyone else in the book—is his ability to hold these belief systems lightly (an ability he has been cultivating since first shaking off all attachment to ego and identity on a wharf in downtown Manhattan). For in this way, holding them all equally in his mind, the variety of distinctive belief systems line up like colors of the rainbow, and create the clear light of "the grand belief."[38] If a man were to really *believe* in his belief, so to speak, his perspective could not be so easily shed. In this case, the colors of the rainbow would not work so much as wavelengths of light happily shading into one another and adding up to bright whiteness, but rather as colors of paint, which, when combined one on top of one another, add up to a deep black, which might be nihilism, spiritual materialism, or just deep befuddlement.

Ishmael seems constitutionally unable to wear any particular guise that might weigh him down too heavily. When he momentarily cloaks himself in Queequeg's poncho, he feels immediately and intolerably constricted: "I put it on, to try it, and it weighed me down like a hamper . . . I tore myself out of it in such a hurry that I gave myself a kink in the neck."[39] In this way, Ishmael is alone in his ability to declare, "My original opinion remains unchanged; but it is only an opinion."[40] This prepares him to leap to take the final step—a leap beyond all views, beyond belief and disbelief, into non-belief.

Ishmael returns again and again to this idea of subjectivity, most notably with the doubloon and the White Whale itself. But it is there from the very beginning—even in the competing views of whales and whaling in the Extracts, and the views of the sea from Manhattan. Things really get moving in the Spouter-Inn, when he spies the oil painting hanging on the far wall, and begins to examine its "unaccountable masses of shades and shadows."[41] When his eye falls on the "long, limber, portentous, black mass of something hovering in the center of the picture," he watches as his mind instantly whirls into overdrive, hoping to attach an identity, and a *meaning*, to this "indefinite, half-attainable, unimaginable" thing: "It's the Black Sea in a midnight gale.—It's the unnatural combat of the four primal elements.—It's a blasted hearth.—It's a Hyperborean winter scene.—It's the breaking-up of the ice-bound stream of Time. But at last all these fancies yielded to that one portentous something in the picture's midst."[42] As he remarks later, not only is there no single objective identity (let alone meaning) to anything, but our subjective interpretations are determined by what is happening in our minds. Again and again he patiently describes reactions to phenomena—for example, a squid: "If to Starbuck the apparition of the Squid was a thing of portents, to Queequeg it was quite a different object."[43] Dogen Zenji's "Mountains and Rivers Sutra" expands on this idea, to rather fantastical effect:

> All beings do not see mountains and waters in the same way. Some beings see water as a jeweled ornament, but they do not regard jeweled ornaments as water. Some beings see water as wondrous blossoms, but they do not use blossoms as water. Hungry ghosts see water as raging fire or pus and blood. Dragons see water as a palace or a pavilion. Some beings see water as the seven treasures of a wish-granting jewel. Some beings see water as a forest or a wall. . . . Human beings see water as water. Thus the views of all beings are not the same. You should question this matter now. Are there many ways to see one thing? Or is it a mistake to see many forms as one thing? You should pursue this beyond the limit of pursuit.[44]

This is where Ishmael is aiming—"beyond pursuit." As he meditates on whiteness, and immerses himself in the emptiness of all phenomena, he may be able to, as he says, "own the whale."[45] Thomas Cleary writes, "The practice of relinquishing views, stopping mental talk, and detaching from mental patterns is an exercise employed to gain the objectivity whereby opinion is distinguished from fact."[46] Again I am reminded of Dongshan: "My idea is to have no particular idea."

But it must be repeated that it is not simply Ishmael's adaptability that makes him special. For we all play many different roles at different times in our lives, and are thrown around by different moods and conditions. What sets Ishmael apart is that, throughout it all, he maintains this clear tranquil awareness—or, as he might put it, "interior spaciousness"[47]—no matter what the universe throws at him.[48] Indeed, Ishmael himself uses cosmological imagery to describe his imperturbability: "But even so, amid the tornadoed Atlantic of my being, do I myself still for ever centrally disport in mute calm; and while ponderous planets of unwaning woe revolve round me, deep down and deep inland there I still bathe me in eternal mildness of joy."[49] He has attained Bodhidharma's ideal of "inwardly [having] no coughing or sighing in the mind—with your mind like a wall you can enter the Way."[50]

Ishmael is truly like his beloved whale, "enabled to keep himself comfortable in all weathers, in all seas, times and tides."[51] He implores us all:

> It does seem to me, that herein we see the rare virtue of a strong individual vitality, and the rare virtue of thick walls, and the rare virtue of interior spaciousness. Oh, man! admire and model thyself after the whale! Do thou, too, remain warm among ice. Do thou, too, live in this world without being of it. Be cool at the equator; keep thy blood fluid at the Pole. Like the great dome of St. Peter's, and like the great whale, retain, O man! in all seasons a temperature of thine own.[52]

Once again, Ishmael's experience at sea is representative of his ability to endure adversity. And once again it illuminates the importance of flexibility and playfulness in the face of fickle uncertainty. Returning to the profound instability of the open ocean, he describes the experience of crashing through powerful waves in an overmatched whale-boat:

> It is worse; for you cannot sit motionless in the heart of these perils, because the boat is rocking like a cradle, and you are pitched one way and the other, without the slightest warning; and only by a certain self-adjusting buoyancy and simultaneousness of volition and action, can you escape being made a Mazeppa of, and run away with where the all-seeing sun himself could never pierce you out.[53]

As alluded to earlier, it requires constant effort to remain upright in such an unstable environment. The pairing of "self-adjusting buoyancy" with "simultaneousness of volition and action" is particularly interesting, because it emphasizes the importance of balancing buoyancy (holding one's preferences and aspirations lightly) with maintaining consistent virtue. That Ishmael describes this buoyancy as "self-adjusting" suggests that it is not something one can control oneself, but instead is spontaneously manifested through close attention to volition and action. We find this same pairing in the words of Seng-Ts'an, who taught, "The Great Way is without difficulty for those who have no preferences."[54] The virtue can arise only through buoyancy, but the buoyancy can easily make one lose sight of said virtue. Thus one must maintain vigilance in continuously aligning volition (Sanskrit: *cetana*) with action (Sanskrit: *karma*)—which brings us to the other aspect of Ishmael's meditation.

Insight meditation, *vipassana*, is often described as "analytical." Once tranquility meditation has sufficiently calmed the mind, we can employ insight meditation to scrutinize the world around us. Ishmael's phrase "profound mathematical meditation" may amount to much the same thing. [55] But it is only through practicing tranquility meditation that one's mind becomes prepared for insight meditation. In Ishmael's case, it is only once he has detached himself from old patterns by taking to the whaleship, and calmed his mind through "thinking nothing," that he can devote his energies to what he variously calls "the problem of the universe revolving in [him]," [56] "the universal problem of all things," [57] and "an inequality in the deeper analysis of the thing." [58] For we each have the impression that we are a substantial entity, that our consciousness is speaking on behalf of something, namely the self. But when we subject that idea to close scrutiny, that fallacy is dispelled. As Dogen's maxim states, "To study the Buddha Way is to study the self. To study the self is to forget the self. To forget the self is to be actualized by myriad things." [59]

Ishmael consistently returns to this idea of subjecting all experience to careful analysis. Describing the painting in the Spouter-Inn, he uses terms applicable to his spiritual endeavor, saying "it was only through diligent study . . . and careful inquiry . . . that you could any way arrive at an understanding." [60] This practice of paying close attention to phenomena is continued in "The Fountain." He notably grounds himself first in the present moment, "down to this blessed minute (fifteen and a quarter minutes past one o'clock P.M. of this sixteenth day of December, A.D. 1850)," then entreats us to join him in looking more closely at the nature of the sperm whale's spout: "Let us, then, look at this matter, along with some interesting items contingent." [61] What he finds supports his general view that there is indeed an Order to the Universe—as he might say, "a fine boisterous something about everything." [62] In this case, he notes that each sperm whale breathes in a very specific—and entirely unique—pattern:

> This is what I mean. If unmolested, upon rising to the surface, the Sperm Whale will continue there for a period of time exactly uniform with all his other unmolested risings. Say he stays eleven minutes, and jets seventy times, that is, respires seventy breaths; then whenever he rises again, he will be sure to have his seventy breaths over again, to a minute. [63]

As this passage makes clear, it is only in paying close attention to the activities of the whale (which, in turn, is only possible when one has a focused mind capable of such activity) that one will notice the sublime rhythm of its life at sea.[64] But we are immediately reminded that it is only "when unmolested" that such wonders appear: "Besides, if you regard him very closely, and time him with your watch, you will find that when unmolested, there is an undeviating rhythm between the periods of his jets and the ordinary periods of respiration."[65] Just pay close attention to what is happening, Ishmael instructs, without burdening things with our explanations and delineations.

One final place we find evidence of this watchful eye is the non-dualistic language spread throughout the book. Ishmael addresses aspects of duality with a playfulness that often surpasses even what we find in the teachings of Zen masters. While Seng-Ts'an warns in *Hsin Hsin Ming*, "Do not remain in the dualistic state, avoid such pursuits carefully," Ishmael keenly immerses himself in it—throwing the reader off-balance with seemingly incompatible phrases, bringing together opposites in "young life's old routine,"[66] "a careful disorderliness,"[67] "a humorously perilous business,"[68] "evangelical pagan piety,"[69] Queequeg "hopelessly holding up hope,"[70] and moving toward his "endless end."[71]

Melville also calls these distinctions into question by assuming the equatorial ground between the poles. Peleg says of Ahab, "he ain't sick; but no, he isn't well either,"[72] and as the crew prepares to leave the harbor, Bildad looks "everywhere and nowhere."[73] The ocean is presented as a place where these distinctions cannot even exist: the ship is "both chasing and being chased,"[74] and "air and sea were hardly separable in that all-pervading azure."[75] While for Ishmael "fact and fancy, half-way meeting, interpenetrate, and form one seamless whole,"[76] Ahab simply smashes them flat: "alike, joy and sorrow, hope and fear, seemed ground to dust, and powdered, for the time, in the cramped mortar of Ahab's iron soul."[77] He boasts, "In the midst of the personified impersonal, a personality stands here"—notable in that he acknowledges the non-dual nature of existence, but then reaffirms his own existence somewhere beyond that non-duality.[78]

Finally, having paired opposites and split the difference between them, Melville begins to question the basis on which we make these distinctions to begin with. Fleece throws the first punch in his sermon to the sharks: "An angel is not'ing more dan de shark well goberned,"[79] a theme continued in Ishmael's consideration (or perhaps Ishmael's contention that Ahab is considering) that "the most poisonous reptile of the marsh perpetuates his kind as inevitably as the sweetest songster of the grove."[80] Faced with a world in which a coffin can be transformed into a life-buoy, Ahab exclaims, "How immaterial are all materials!"[81] Ultimately, Ishmael comes to ridicule our haughty insistence in demanding that things be either one or the other: "My dear sir, in this world it is not so easy to settle these plain things. I have ever found your plain things to be the knottiest of all. And as for this whale spout, you might almost stand in it, and yet be undecided as to what it is precisely."[82] Pip's near-drowning—"a significant event" that befalls "the most insignificant" of the crew[83]—shows that our assessments of people and things are entirely subjective, and with a change in conditions something can even become its opposite. "Man's insanity is Heaven's sense," we are told, and so Pip may be "called a coward here, hailed a hero there [in Heaven]."[84]

Zen master Huang Po (d. 850) said: "When the time has come for a Buddhist to discipline his mind so as to rise above duality, he enters a stage where the notions of both good and evil must be transcended like any other form of duality." It is by looking closely at these seeming dualities that Ishmael sees through their apparent dissimilarity. As the carpenter notes, "That is hard which should be soft, and that is soft which should be hard."[85] Not only are these dualities mutually inclusive, they are mutually dependent. And nowhere is this teaching more important to recognize than regarding the doctrine of the Middle Way between existence and non-existence. On the one hand, there is the conventional truth of existence, which refers to our everyday, common sense understanding of the existence of things: people exist, things exist, there is good and bad, right and wrong. The ultimate truth, generally speaking, is the notion that there is nobody separate from anybody, that there is not one single thing that exists by itself. In other words, things are conventionally many, but ultimately one.

However, our usual way of thinking is to believe that things exist independently from one another—that people and things have essences, that they have inherent existence. That is not the conventional truth—that is simply not true. As Ishmael himself says, "there is no quality in this world that is not what it is merely by contrast. Nothing exists in itself."[86] Though people and things do indeed exist, they exist dependently—they are dependently arisen, in dependence on conditions. Phenomena come into existence when certain causes and conditions arise, and when those conditions cease to exist, the phenomena cease to exist as well. Thus Buddhists regard all things as "empty"—that is, empty of inherent existence, or essence.

One easy way to think about this is with the example of a car—it's pretty uncontroversial to point at a Honda Civic and assign it the label *car*. But let's say we started taking it apart, piece by piece: the hubcaps, the steering wheel, the engine block, the fuel tank, until we have completely disassembled it. Where has the car gone? In which of these pieces does the essence "car-ness" reside? And at what point did it cease to be a car? When it is no longer functional? Or when it no longer looks like a car? Ultimately, the designation lies entirely within each of our minds—its existence as a car is entirely dependent on perceivers who will come along and give it the label *car*. After all, it is really just an assemblage of plastic, rubber and steel. And those materials are themselves assemblages of individual molecules, with nothing remotely resembling "car-ness" within them. Eventually this Honda Civic will be impounded, sold into scraps, the steel melted down, the materials returned to the earth. Its existence *as a car* is fleeting, and entirely dependent on the label applied to it from without.

We will return to this tricky subject, the "essencelessness" of phenomena, in the final chapter, when we discuss the coffin life-buoy, and its crucial importance in the narrative.

Chapter Eleven

Impermanence and Interdependence

By the time of shipping on the Pequod, Ishmael has arrived at a far more optimistic view of humanity than the one that begins "Loomings." In the chapter "His Mark," his short sermon on "the grand belief" and the "great and everlasting First Congregation of this whole worshipping world" moves Peleg to declare, "Young man, you'd better ship for a missionary, instead of a fore-mast hand; I never heard a better sermon."[1] In "The Hyena," Ishmael stands drenched and shivering on the deck, his boat having been smashed during a whale-chase, he himself the last man retrieved from the water. The situation is not so dissimilar to what will soon befall poor Pip. But while Pip is entirely unprepared for the experience (as we will discuss at length later on), Ishmael's spiritual development allows him to arrive back on deck and proclaim, "I survived myself"[2]—a phrase which, like Starbuck's warning to Ahab mentioned earlier, may be read as I survived "my self," or even "my sense of self." As in "The Mast-Head," a near-death experience brings up a strong sense of identity, of existence. Not coincidentally, as this experience rouses Ishmael's sense of himself as a human being living on planet earth, "The Hyena" includes the one and only time Ishmael engages in conversation with anyone on the Pequod other than Queequeg (a very short dialogue with Stubb and Flask).

But Ishmael has already attained some understanding of the impermanence of all phenomena, including himself. So the terror that most of us would feel, he has risen above:

> And as for small difficulties and worryings, prospects of sudden disaster, peril of life and limb; all these, and death itself, seem to [me] only sly, good-natured hits, and jolly punches in the side bestowed by the unseen and unaccountable old joker. That odd sort of wayward mood I am speaking of, comes over a man only in some time of extreme tribulation; it comes in the very midst of his

earnestness, so that what just before might have seemed to him a thing most momentous, now seems but a part of the general joke. There is nothing like the perils of whaling to breed this free and easy sort of genial, desperado philosophy; and with it I now regarded this whole voyage of the Pequod, and the great White Whale its object.[3]

An appreciation of impermanence inevitably leads him to a meditation on mortality as well, and as he drafts his last will and testament for the "fourth time in [his] nautical life," he is further removing himself from an attachment to self: "After the ceremony was concluded upon the present occasion, I felt all the easier; a stone was rolled away from my heart. . . . I survived myself; my death and burial were locked up in my chest. I looked round me tranquilly and contentedly, like a quiet ghost with a clean conscience sitting inside the bars of a snug family vault."[4] Bodhidharma says, "Once you stop clinging and let things be, you'll be free, even of birth and death. . . . You'll be free wherever you are."[5] Ishmael finds himself similarly unrestrained, and prepared for whatever comes next: "Now, then, thought I, unconsciously rolling up the sleeves of my frock, here goes a cool, collected dive at death and destruction, and the devil fetch the hindmost."[6]

Any discussion of impermanence carries with it a consideration of interdependence as well. They are truly two sides of the same coin. Because things are dependent on the conditions that allow them to exist, they are impermanent; because they are impermanent, they cannot have any abiding essence, and therefore are reliant on conditions. Melville alludes to them both in a November 1851 letter to Hawthorne:

> The world goes round, and the other side comes up. So now I can't write what I felt. But I felt pantheistic then—your heart beat in my ribs and mine in yours, and both in God's. . . . This is a long letter, but you are not at all bound to answer it. Possibly, if you do answer it, and direct it to Herman Melville, you will missend it—for the very fingers that now guide this pen are not precisely the same that just took it up and put it on this paper. Lord, when shall we be done changing?[7]

Ishmael unexpectedly—and rather off-handedly—addresses these concepts early in the book, in the chapter "Nightgown." As he lies in bed beside his new bosom friend Queequeg he muses, "The more so, I say, because truly to enjoy bodily warmth, some small part of you must be cold, for there is no quality in this world that is not what it is merely by contrast. Nothing exists in itself. If you flatter yourself that you are all over comfortable, and have been so a long time, then you cannot be said to be comfortable any more."[8] Things are what they are "merely by contrast," and as that contrast is constantly shifting, things are "what they are" for not very long at all. Ishmael goes on to say that he always keeps his eyes closed when lying in bed. But this idea ("I have a way of always keeping my eyes shut"[9]—that is, even when they are open) seems a fitting description of his meditation practice— of, as Dogen says, learning "the backward step that turns your light inward."[10] And so Ishmael continues looking inwardly—to discern whether "by any possibility, there be any as yet undiscovered prime thing in me"[11] or if, finally, a man "can't amount to much in his totality."[12]

Ishmael addresses interdependence at length in the chapters "The Mat-Maker" and "The Monkey-Rope," first on a cosmic level, and then on an interpersonal level. The introductory paragraph of "The Mat-Maker" even reads like a description of a meditation hall, with each sailor "vacantly gazing over into the lead-colored waters. . . . So still and subdued and yet somehow preluding was all the scene, and such an incantation of revery lurked in the air, that each silent sailor seems resolved into his own invisible self."[13] We might take "invisible self" to mean searching for this elusive idea of self. It cannot be said what the other sailors discover out in those "lead-colored waters," but Ishmael, as ever, looks for himself, and stumbles upon the entire universe.

More than any other, this chapter has an almost parabolic resonance, as Ishmael (in the tradition of all great spiritual teachers) uses a tangible example to illustrate his idea of how one's life is dependently co-originated with every single thing in the universe. He rejects as erroneous dogmatic theories of determinism, accidentalism, and libertarianism, instead advocating a middle-way philosophy that describes all three as "interweavingly working together":

> I say so strange a dreaminess did there then reign all over the ship and all over the sea . . . that it seemed as if this were the Loom of Time, and I myself were a shuttle mechanically weaving and weaving away at the Fates. There lay the fixed threads of the warp subject to but one single, ever returning, unchanging vibration, and that vibration merely enough to admit of the crosswise interblending of other threads with its own. This warp seemed necessity; and here, thought I, with my own hand I ply my own shuttle and weave my own destiny into these unalterable threads. Meantime, Queequeg's impulsive, indifferent sword, sometimes hitting the woof slantingly, or crookedly, or weakly, as the case might be; and by this difference in the concluding blow producing a corresponding contrast in the final aspect of the completed fabric; this savage's sword, thought I, which thus finally shapes and fashions both warp and woof; this easy, indifferent sword must be chance—aye, chance, free will, and necessity—no wise incompatible—all interweavingly working together. The straight warp of necessity, not to be swerved from its ultimate course—its every alternating vibration, indeed, only tending to that; free will still free to ply her shuttle between given threads; and chance, though restraint in its play within the right lines of necessity, and sideways in its motions modified by

free will, though thus prescribed to be both, chance by turns rules either, and has the last featuring blow at events. [14]

Call it the Parable of the Loom. The warp is the universe as it exists at any one moment, its threads vibrating with all the energies of everything that has occurred (and has not occurred) since beginningless time. Ishmael calls this "necessity"; I would call it "cause and effect." This vibration operates in the same way as Newton's third law of motion, endlessly resonating energies between everything that has ever existed in the universe—thus it is "ever returning" and "unchanging." This is the template within which we live our lives, the ontological ground on which we stand.

So, again, while there is volitional action—we do have "will"—it is most certainly not "free." Ishmael says as much in his very first chapter, as he attempts to pin down just what it was that led him to join "the shabby part of a whaling voyage": "[N]ow that I recall all the circumstances, I think I can see a little into the springs and motives which being cunningly presented to me under various disguises, induced me to set about performing the part I did, besides cajoling me into the delusion that it was a choice resulting from my own unbiased freewill and discriminating judgment." [15] This energetic process is endlessly resonating, and we ourselves are operating in the universe with the same "material" as the "unalterable threads" of cause and effect. Every one of our actions of body, speech and mind "interblend" with the vertical threads and directly affect the circumstances of our personal "loom."

I would argue that what Ishmael refers to as "chance" might otherwise be called "everything that is not personal volition." Ishmael has a certain plan for his weaving, creating his story by moving his shuttle horizontally through the existing vertical template. But operating simultaneously with that process is Queequeg's "impulsive, indifferent" sword. [16] The sword—representing circumstances outside our control—has a direct impact on the choices we make in our lives, as Ishmael makes clear. For example, Starbuck's shuttle is no match for Ahab's sword; nor is Ahab's shuttle to the White Whale's sword. (Starbuck closes his eyes and hopes the sword will disappear; Ahab, obstinately refusing to stop weaving, gets repeatedly and resoundingly whacked.) The fact that all of our shuttles and swords are intertwined is brought into terrible relief in the final chapter, as otherwise-innocent men are sent to their deaths not only through Ahab's monomaniacal fury, but from each of their being unwilling and/or unable to stop him—most notably Mr. Starbuck.

However, Ishmael suggests that we are "still free to ply [our] shuttle." If we pay close attention to both our actions (the shuttle) and the actions of others (the sword), we can respond appropriately to fickle chance, and weave a different pattern, undo past mistakes, be a more skillful mat-maker. It is an image of what might be called "theological synergy"[17]—that just as the shuttle, the sword and the loom all work synergistically to create the mat, each of us works together with all beings and the universe to create our world.

From the cosmic vision of "The Mat-Maker," we move to a more personalized experience of interdependence in "The Monkey-Rope." Ishmael returns to the scene of Stubb's having killed their first whale, to describe in greater detail the process of "cutting-in," or stripping the flesh from the whale. Queequeg is assigned the task of descending to the whale and attaching a hook through its blubber, and then remaining standing atop the half-submerged sperm whale, surrounded by sharks, the carcass continually rolling as the blubber is stripped off, until the stripping process is complete. This is obviously a dreadfully perilous task, and so the whale-spinner is attached to a man onboard the ship by what is called a "monkey-rope." In this case, the men in question are Queequeg and, no surprise, Ishmael.

Ishmael describes the rope as "fast at both ends"—if anything should befall Queequeg, Ishmael would be necessarily pulled down after him. They are thus both "wedded" and "inseparable twin brother[s]."[18]

> So strongly and metaphysically did I conceive of my situation then, that while earnestly watching his motions, I seemed distinctly to perceive that my own individuality was now merged in a joint stock company of two; that my free will had received a mortal wound; and that another's mistake or misfortune might plunge innocent me into unmerited disaster and death. Therefore, I saw that here was a sort of interregnum in Providence; for its even-handed equity never could have sanctioned so gross an injustice. . . . I saw that this situation of mine was the precise situation of every mortal that breathes; only, in most cases he, one way or other, has this Siamese connexion with a plurality of other mortals. If your banker breaks, you snap; if your apothecary by mistake sends you poison in your pills, you die.[19]

The monkey-rope is essentially a convenient starting point, as it illustrates interdependence in its most immediate and literal sense. But Ishmael broadens this view, saying that although it is not as viscerally obvious, all of us are, at every moment, in similar relationships with "a plurality of other mortals." Here the role of the "plurality" is acted out by the sharks nipping at Queequeg's heels, and "suspended over the side . . . Tashtego and Daggoo,"[20] who (not unlike the sword of chance mentioned above) stab at the sharks below with "keen whale-spades,"[21] but often in "their hasty zeal . . . would come nearer [to] amputating a leg than a tail."[22]

Melville's most insightful comment on the interconnectivity of the human condition appears in the chapter's lone footnote:

> The monkey-rope is found in all whalers; but it was only in the Pequod that the monkey and his holder were ever tied together. This improvement upon the original usage was introduced by no less a man than Stubb, in order to afford to the imperilled harpooner the strongest possible guarantee for the faithfulness and vigilance of his monkey-rope holder. [23]

Most of us have an easier time with the interdependence of *things* than that of our *selves*. We have little trouble processing the idea that things are dependent on *us*, but the idea that *we* are dependent on *things* is troubling news indeed. Ahab is the most grotesque example of this defensive reflex, smashing the ship's quadrant and spurning its sails. With "The Monkey-Rope" footnote, Melville admits having amended the authenticity of his monkey-rope to most expressly suit his metaphysical stance: that not only are other beings and things dependent on us, but we are correspondingly dependent on those beings and things as well. Tenshin Reb Anderson writes:

> This is Buddha's main teaching. It's called dependent co-arising: that everything comes forth from all directions in the universe to make each thing, and that this coming forth is what gives each thing authority. Everything has authority because everything is the arrival of everything else. Everything is a realization of the rest of the world. . . . Everything. This is Zen. [24]

How, Ishmael asks here, can all these factions be so (benevolently, malevolently) intermingling? Were we not bestowed free will by an "even-handed" Deity? Well, no. What Ishmael calls an "interregnum in Providence" translates to an idea similar to that in "The Mat-Maker"—of no one (or One) being in charge, and of this idea of "theological synergy." Our actions are ineluctably tied up (in this case, literally) with the actions of all other beings in the universe—and ultimately these competing factions are not separate at all.

Chapter Twelve

Philosophy, Koans, and Silence

I've argued that Ishmael is wary of religious dogmatism, and of the scientific method. Given his proclivity to metaphysical rumination, we might expect him to be rather more friendly toward philosophical inquiry. But on the contrary, from the novel's opening paragraph, he seeks to draw a sharp contrast between himself and his vision of a haughty philosopher: "With a philosophical flourish Cato throws himself upon his sword; I quietly take to the ship."[1] He later recommends that, when the whaleship (that is, the mind) is burdened with Locke's head on one side, and Kant's on the other, one should "throw all these thunder-heads overboard, and then [one] will float light and right."[2] In these two comments alone, he contrasts philosophy against quietude (or silence), suggests a connection between philosophy and suicide (whaling being the antidote to both), and argues that whaling is necessarily anti-philosophical. In the chapter "The Mast-Head" he "movingly admonish[es]" all Nantucket shipowners to "beware enlisting . . . any lad . . . given to unseasonable meditativeness."[3] These "absent-minded young philosophers," Ishmael suggests, arrive on board not only with their idealized views of whaling—"seeking sentiment in tar and blubber"[4]—but also idealized views of Reality itself, which renders them impotent in a world that does not conform to their preconceived ideas: "those young Platonists . . . are short-sighted: what use, then, to strain the visual nerve? They have left their opera-glasses at home."[5]

This seems to leave little room for misconstrual. But then, elsewhere in the novel, he suggests that a "metaphysical professor" would be a suitable guide for a caravan seeking water in "the great American desert"[6]—that is, in a nation athirst for real meaning, lost in the desert of delusion. And, in a remarkable passage in "The Line," he suggests that philosophers are endowed with both awareness and equanimity:

> All are born with halters round their necks; but it is only when caught in the
> swift, sudden turn of death, that mortals realize the silent, subtle, ever-present
> perils of life. And if you be a philosopher, though seated in the whale-boat,
> you would not at heart feel one whit more of terror, than though seated before
> your evening fire with a poker, and not a harpoon, by your side.[7]

The explanation to this seeming contradiction may lie in a comment he
makes about "true philosophers": "[T]o be true philosophers," Ishmael
writes, "we mortals should not be conscious of so living or so striving."[8]
Melville finds fault with philosophers who distance themselves from reality,
seeking idealized explanations to the universe: Cato cannot accept his defeat
in battle and throws himself on the sword; the young Platonists discount their
new circumstances (i.e., experiences) because they do not align with the
lessons (i.e., forms) they have learned on land. It is a crucial difference, in
both intention and perspective—suggested by Dogen Zenji's teaching, "To
carry the self forward and illuminate myriad things is delusion. That myriad
things come forth and illuminate the self is awakening."[9]

The serene philosopher in the whale-boat, meanwhile, sits composed. He
has an intimate understanding of life and death, Ishmael argues, and so he
feels no more threatened than he would at his fireside. This idea of introspection is, again, introduced in the book's opening lines. For the metaphysical
professor, in order to be of any help in the desert, must first be "plunged into
his deepest reveries"—then, just "set his feet a-going, and he will infallibly
lead you to water."[10]

Ishmael's apparent ambivalence toward philosophy, then, is really not
ambivalence at all. Rather, he is speaking of two completely different attitudes toward metaphysical questions—seeking outwardly and looking inwardly—both of which he confoundingly calls "philosophy." Clinging to
views, Kant and Locke sway the ship right and left; Cato and the Platonists
stop the ship dead in the water. Bodhidharma says, "Doctrines are only for
pointing to the mind. Once you see your mind, why pay attention to doctrines?" The whale-boat philosopher is enticed by neither of these extreme
views—he watches his own mind, and is imperturbable.

Bodhidharma's "four statements of the Zen school," with which the Zen
school is often said to have begun, are particularly applicable to the text, for
they advocate precisely this spirit of "true philosophy." Bodhidharma taught:

> No dependence on words or letters
> A special transmission outside the Scriptures
> Direct pointing to the soul of man
> Seeing into one's nature and the attainment of Buddhahood.[11]

Ishmael points again and again to the inadequacy of both the written and spoken word— while his fascination with hieroglyphics indicates an acknowledgment of truths that are beyond description.

With regard to words, Ishmael the narrator pokes fun at his former tendency toward excessive verbosity. He was once the kind of man who, when told to "Answer, quick!" found it reasonable to reply, "I am, sir, if it should be positively indispensable to do so; not to be got rid of, that is; which I don't take to be the fact."[12] Again and again, this loquaciousness is met with derision:

> The Spouter-Inn landlord: "Wall," said the landlord, fetching a long breath, "that's a purty long sarmon."[13]
> Captain Peleg: "Talk not that lingo to me . . . thou dost not talk shark a bit."[14]
> Flask: "Can't you twist that any smaller?"[15]

Looking back at his former self, Ishmael contrasts silence, and silent things, against dependence on words and letters. Ishmael marvels at the "profound silence" of the whalemen he watches in "The Spouter-Inn"; in "The Ramadan" his raving hysterics are sharply contrasted against Queequeg's quiet serenity.[16]

But chief among silent things is the sperm whale, who "has no voice."[17] Ishmael claims that "the Sperm Whale has no tongue, or at least it is so exceedingly small, as to be incapable of protrusion." But more to the point, he says, "Has the Sperm Whale ever written a book, spoken a speech? No, his great genius is declared in his doing nothing particular to prove it. It is moreover declared in his pyramidical silence."[18]

The Zen practice of studying koans, which arose about four centuries after Bodhidharma's arrival in China, is meant to expose precisely these limits of language. Well-known koans include "What is the sound of one hand clapping?" and "What was your face before your parents were born?" Answers to the koan "What is Zen?" include such vertigo-inducing responses as "Three pounds of flax," "The cypress tree in the garden," and "See the eastern mountains moving over the waves!" These answers intend to disrupt our habitual reliance on intellectual reasoning, while also serving as prickly reminders that the ineffable cannot be expressed in words. That is, they point to Zen. The enlightenment stories described are not always gentle—Gisei cuts off a boy's finger, Nanquan kills a cat, lots of people get smacked—but in most every case, the student experiences profound realization. As we will discuss later on, a number of events that occur in *Moby-Dick*, particularly in the "omens" that arise scattered through Ahab's quest, provide similar occasions for enlightenment experiences.

The efficacy of koan practice—pushing beyond conventional discursive thought—is grounded in the understanding that attempts to verbally express ineffable concepts inevitably miss the mark. Seng-Ts'an says, "The more you talk and think about it, the further astray you wander from truth."[19] In *Moby-Dick*, Ishmael describes his "confounding attempts to explain the mystery,"[20] and deplores his "inability to express" anything about the whale's tail.[21] He laments, "Seldom have I known any profound being that had anything to say to this world, unless forced to stammer out something by way of getting a living. Oh! happy that the world is such an excellent listener."[22] His shipmate Pip tries to articulate his harrowing experience in the chapter "The Castaway," "and therefore his shipmates called him mad."[23] As Pip discovers, it is not only the insufficiency of speech that is at issue here—it is the matter of being understood as well. Ishmael appreciates the paradox inherent in language—that although the ultimate reality is "ineffable," we are linguistic beings, who cannot communicate without referring to objects with words that do not come close to expressing what those things truly are. So he praises the audience—thanking us, with a wink, that we are "excellent listeners"—having invited our direct participation in the creation of the text from his very first sentence.

Ishmael recognizes the charges of hypocrisy he faces in putting his story to paper, for he considers books to be perhaps even more dangerous than speech. The written word can all too easily be taken as fixed and final Truth—that is, as scripture. For Ishmael, one of the most crucial characteristics of the sea is that it "will permit no records."[24] To this end, he is constantly undermining his own medium, reminding us of the inherent unreliability of any description of reality: "For whatever is truly wondrous and fearful in man, never yet was put into words or books."[25] He insists that "of real knowledge there be little, yet of books there are plenty"—and having "swam through libraries," he playfully divides his examination of Cetology into "Folios" and "Books" and "Chapters."[26] The second mate Stubb speaks even more bluntly: "Book! you lie there; the fact is, you books must know your places. You'll do to give us the bare words and facts, but we come in to supply the thoughts."[27] (The word "lie," of course, having the wonderful double meaning of "sitting idly" and "not telling the truth.")

Thus Ishmael spends a great deal of time describing the attempts that human beings have made to depict the whale in pictorial form—and inarguably empathizes with the motivation of these cetological artists. It might be a case of apophenia that has Ishmael seeing whales everywhere, catching "passing glimpses of the profiles of whales defined along the undulating ridges" of mountains (as Melville did Mount Greylock, which he thought resembled a white whale from the vantage afforded from his study), but make no mistake: "you must be a thorough whaleman to see these sights."[28]

He recognizes that the drive to depict the whale is not too far from the drive to sail with him on the open ocean, but emphatically affirms that the Leviathan "must remain unpainted to the last."[29] For we can only paint what something *looks like*, not what it *is*. As Hongzhi states so beautifully, "All [things] are innately amazing beyond all description. . . . This marvel is beyond the vast thousands of classical texts, so where could you hold on to the shadowy world?"[30] And for Melville, of course, it is the "shadowy world"—or, in his case, the "watery part of the world"—that interests him most.

This position is similar to Dogen Zenji's teaching in the fascicle "A Painting of a Rice Cake." The rice cake serves as a symbol of something serving no useful purpose—for, needless to say, one cannot eat a painting of a rice cake. But Dogen suggests that the painting is still important, for it represents the conceptual side of the universe—or, as Melville's sub-sub-librarian might have it, our ideas about rice cakes throughout history. Gudo Nishijima writes:

> A painted rice cake—theories and concepts—cannot satisfy hunger, but they can be utilized to understand and explain the truth. Master Dogen insists that all existence has both a physical, material side and a conceptual, mental side, and that these two aspects are inseparable in reality. Thus without a picture of a rice cake—that is, the concept "rice cake"—we can never find the real existence of rice cakes.[31]

Ishmael is confronted with this contradiction in the chapter "The Whiteness of the Whale," writing: "I almost despair of putting it into a comprehensible form . . . But how can I hope to explain myself here; and yet, in some dim, random way, explain myself I must, else all these chapters might be naught."[32] The understanding that a painting of a rice cake is not a rice cake allows him to remain free of the illusion of objectivity. And though his literary endeavor is but "a story of a rice cake," bearing the heaviness of language, in the end he happily announces that "when Leviathan is the text, the case is altered. Fain am I to stagger to this emprise under the weightiest words of the dictionary.[33]

I would argue that the sheer enormity, the unspeakable vastness of his subject, that makes him "faint with [its] outreaching comprehensiveness,"[34] actually relieves him of his burden, and allows him to feel "fain" (that is, "pleased or willing") to write about the whale: "One often hears of writers that rise and swell with their subject, though it may seem but an ordinary one. How, then, with me, writing of this Leviathan? Unconsciously my chirography expands into placard capitals. Give me a condor's quill! Give me Vesuvius' crater for an inkstand! Friends, hold my arms!"[35] If the whale "must remain unpainted to the last," surely it must remain unwritten to the last as well.[36] If Ishmael were, as he says, writing a book about a flea, surely he would be expected to succeed in composing a fixed and complete Truth of the Flea. And no matter how long he went on about how "any human thing supposed to be complete, must for that very reason infallibly be faulty,"[37] and tried to explain that "this whole book is but a draught—nay, but the draught of a draught,"[38] for surely his readers cannot have an accurate idea about Fleas, "and the only way to have even a tolerable idea" is to go "a-fleaing"[39] themselves—no one would believe him.

He finally compares his own cetological endeavor to a religious activity, which he will leave unfinished, "even as the great Cathedral of Cologne was left, with the crane still standing upon the top of the uncompleted tower."[40] Just as the topmost tower merely points to the highest heavens, in constructing his own cathedral, Ishmael reaches a point beyond which nothing can truly be said. One might propose that *Moby-Dick* is his own unfinished cathedral, but as he says, "My object here is simply to project the draught of a systematization of cetology. I am the architect, not the builder."[41] *Moby-Dick* is a blueprint, for each of us to build our own cathedral.

The whale, as I have said and will return to at length, cannot be fully expressed in words. And this allows Ishmael to straddle the fence, so to speak: he can speak without the illusion of objectivity, on his own part or by his audience. For it is not language itself that is the problem—it is our perpetual assumption that what we say about a thing is a complete description of that thing. This idea is best represented by Ishmael's fascination with what he calls "hieroglyphics"—linguistic symbols that he is unable to decipher.

It is no accident that the two main places Ishmael finds hieroglyphics are on the two things he holds in the highest regard: Queequeg and the sperm whale. Queequeg's tattoos are, from the first time he spies them from under the covers in the Spouter-Inn, a source of continual fascination to Ishmael. (As opposed to Ahab, who, since he does not have a clear idea of the tattoos, wants nothing to do with them, and calls them a "devilish tantalization of the gods."[42]) Ishmael explains:

> And this tattooing, had been the work of a departed prophet and seer of his island, who, by those hieroglyphic marks, had written out on his body a complete theory of the heavens and the earth, and a mystical treatise on the art of attaining truth; so that Queequeg in his own proper person was a riddle to unfold; a wondrous work in one volume; but whose mysteries not even himself could read, though his own live heart beat against them; and these mysteries were therefore destined in the end to moulder away with the living parchment whereon they were inscribed, and so be unsolved to the last.[43]

It is no doubt significant that Queequeg, as Ishmael's spiritual guide, would have allowed himself to be tattooed with a "treatise on the art of attaining truth" without asking the island prophet for a translation. This is Ishmael's—and Bodhidharma's—ideal. Scriptures (for that is precisely what these tattoos are) can indeed point the way toward "attaining truth," but, if we take the treatise on Truth to be Truth itself, we can just as easily be led astray. The island prophet's marks are a "theory" of the heavens and the earth, and represent his own understanding of reality. But each of us must find the way him or herself. After all, he writes his scripture on "living parchment"—on that most potent symbol of impermanence, human skin, "destined in the end to moulder away"—showing that even the most profound scripture is ephemeral and enigmatic.

So Queequeg embodies this profound riddle of human existence. But he *enacts* it as well—as when he stands before the weighty symbols on the doubloon, "comparing notes; looking at his thigh bone,"[44] and later carves the hieroglyphics into the lid of his coffin, spending "many spare hours" copying out the figures, completely untroubled that he knows not what they mean.[45] Queequeg's buoyant attitude toward words is evident in the delightful scene in the Spouter-Inn where we find him counting the pages of a book, not at all interested by what might be written therein—just leafing through, and every so often "giving utterance to a long-drawn gurgling whistle of astonishment" that someone could possibly have thought it worth the trouble of writing down so very many words.[46]

This non-grasping attitude (we might call it Queequeg's "negative capability"), Ishmael argues, is unknown "among the polite society of a civilized town."[47] The reaction of a "good Presbyterian"[48] seeing these tattoos—though the symbols are indecipherable—would be to ascribe some meaning to the text, even if only to classify Queequeg as a "savage," as an "other." Ishmael initially has this same reflexive reaction, admitting that he considers the tattoos "hideous—at least to my taste"—but he immediately steps beyond that reflex, and finds in Queequeg's face "something in it which was by no means disagreeable. You cannot hide the soul." He recognizes that although he has been taught that these symbols mean one thing (hideousness), they may represent something else entirely: "Through all his unearthly tattooings, I thought I saw the traces of a simple honest heart."[49] Ishmael has not yet attained Queequeg's abilities of non-discrimination—and he will not until he has extensively meditated on the whale—but he is making progress.

Sperm whales are marked by hieroglyphics of their own, being "obliquely crossed and re-crossed . . . upon the body itself . . . with linear marks."[50] Ishmael recalls one particular sperm whale he once saw, whose "hieroglyphical . . . cyphers" reminded him of the "famous hieroglyphical palisades" of a Mississippian Native American tribe.[51] "Like those mystic rocks," Ishmael writes, "too, the mystic-marked whale remains undecipherable."[52] Note his careful language—he is not saying the marks themselves are undecipherable, but rather the object on which they are written! This is pretty strange, since there is no reason why rocks should be undecipherable, for we usually have a very clear idea about them. Perhaps he is suggesting that, when placed beneath these mysterious markings, things become newly unknown to us. We cannot well call them rocks anymore—they have now been given new names, or even turned into new objects altogether. Thus one more way the whale is mysterious to us, and in which the whale's skin remains "unvexed" by our ideas about it. [53]

The great power embedded in this mysteriousness, the freedom that arises from this sort of relationship with language, is most eloquently expressed in Ishmael's vision of the "weaver-god":

> Speak, weaver!—stay thy hand!—but one single word with thee! Nay—the shuttle flies—the figures float from forth the loom. . . . The weaver-god, he weaves; and by that weaving is he deafened, that he hears no mortal voice; and by that humming, we too, who look on the loom are deafened; and only when we escape it shall we hear the thousand voices that speak through it. For even so it is in all material factories. The spoken words that are inaudible among the flying spindles; those same words are plainly heard without the walls, bursting from the opened casements. [54]

It has an almost mythological resonance, this vision, wherein the silent ones are silent because they are close to God, and thus neither hear nor are heard; only the ones who are separate from God remain troubled with speech, "bursting from the opened casements."

The contrary position—reliance on words and letters, and labels and things—is epitomized by Captain Ahab. (And in an ironic twist, there is far less to say than there is in describing silence.) Ahab speaks largely in monologues, muttering to himself and shouting to the heavens. Once Ishmael has stepped off stage, exhorting us to "silently worship," [55] it is these soliloquies that consume much of the action on the ship. But Ahab not infrequently accosts those around him, demanding that they themselves speak as well. Whereas Ishmael leaves no doubt that words cannot possibly express the mysteries of the universe, Ahab confronts the decapitated head of the sperm whale hanging from the ship, demanding answers: "Speak, thou vast and venerable head . . . speak, mighty head, and tell us the secret thing that is in thee. Of all divers, though hast dived the deepest . . . O head! thou hast seen enough to split the planets and make an infidel of Abraham, and not one syllable is thine." [56] In the chapter "The Sphynx," Ishmael connects Ahab to silence in such a way that the Captain seems to carry noise and speech within his very person, eradicating silence wherever he stands: "Silence reigned over the before tumultuous but now deserted deck. An intense copper calm, like a universal yellow lotus, was more and more unfolding its noiseless measureless leaves upon the sea. . . . A short space elapsed, and up into this noiselessness came Ahab alone from his cabin."[57] On another occasion, Ahab orders Starbuck as well, "Speak, but speak!—Aye, aye!" and when the first mate refuses, Ahab declares, "Thy silence then, *that* voices thee."[58] In a sharp contrast to the "profound silence" of the whalemen, Ahab hears a silence which still remains speech.

And Ahab is as dependent on the written word as he is dependent on speech. Every evening he descends into his cabin, to consult his "sea charts [and] piles of old log-books . . . wherein were set down the seasons and places in which, on various former voyages of various ships, sperm whales had been captured or seen,"[59] confident that they will direct him to his goal. (In Zen this would be considered "slurping the dregs," copying the successes of the old masters under the assumption that those same paths will lead us to truth as well.) For Captain Ahab, his reliance on texts begins to turn his own body into a text: "while he himself was marking out lines and courses on the wrinkled charts, some invisible pencil was also tracing lines and courses upon the deeply marked chart of his forehead."[60] Thus while Queequeg and the sperm whale are covered in unknowable enigmatic symbols, Ahab is carved with the latent instructions which he believes will deliver him to Moby Dick.

III

Moby Dick's Inscrutable Selflessness

Chapter Thirteen

Sarcastic Science

In Captain Ahab's first extended soliloquy, he presents his case against Moby Dick to a skeptical Starbuck—allowing his first mate a glimpse into what lies at the heart of his obsession with the White Whale. As readers, in sharp contrast to Ishmael's equanimity in "not-knowing,"[1] we are introduced to Captain Ahab's raging intolerance of the unknown:

> "All visible objects, man, are but as pasteboard masks. But in each event—in the living act, the undoubted deed—there, some unknown but still reasoning thing puts forth the mouldings of its features from behind the unreasoning mask. If man will strike, strike through the mask! How can the prisoner reach outside except by thrusting through the wall? To me, the white whale is that wall, shoved near to me. Sometimes I think there's naught beyond. But 'tis enough. He tasks me; he heaps me; I see in him outrageous strength, with an inscrutable malice sinewing it. That inscrutable thing is chiefly what I hate; and be the white whale agent, or be the white whale principal, I will wreak that hate upon him."[2]

Here Ahab claims God is "unknown," and unknowable. But He can be known through "all visible objects," through which "the mouldings of [His] features" are projected. Ahab sees the White Whale as not merely another mask, but a wall—an obstacle behind which he knows not what lies, or if anything lies there at all. This wall—which keeps him separate, and keeps him from having any knowledge of the Almighty—must be broken through.

The White Whale is therefore (in this instance at least) merely a convenient surrogate, a "visible object" Ahab can easily define and, hence, that he can "wreak that hate upon." What Ahab sees in the sperm whale—indefiniteness, or "that inscrutable thing"—is, for Ahab as well as Ishmael, the very stamp of the Almighty, and precisely what lends the whale its Divine mien.

Ishmael tells us, "But in the great Sperm Whale, this high and mighty god-like dignity inherent in the brow is so immensely amplified, that gazing on it, in the full front view, you feel the Deity and the dread power more forcibly than in beholding any other object in living nature. For you see no one point precisely; not one distinct feature is revealed."[3] He says of the sperm whale's head, "It signifies—'God: done this day by my hand.'"[4] Further, his remark that this head contains a "most buoyant thing within . . . a mass of tremendous life"—which it both protects and is "unerringly impell[ed]" by—suggests that he too considers the sperm whale to be a means of attaining "clear Truth."[5] And Ishmael and Ahab both describe the head as "a dead, blind wall."[6] But it will come as no surprise that, regarding the nature of this wall, as with the whale itself, Ishmael and Ahab are irretrievably divided. Ahab considers the "inscrutable thing"—that is, the ultimate mouldings framing his conventional foe—an aberration, a pustule fouling this otherwise graspable "visible object."[7] By "thrusting through the wall," he will reach the "unknown . . . thing" that lies beyond.[8]

This struggle with "the wall" is also a potent symbol in the Zen school, stemming from Bodhidharma's aforementioned nine years of seated meditation facing a wall in a cave. Obsessed with the wall itself, while simultaneously worrying that there might be "naught beyond,"[9] Ahab is thus entrapped by despair. Ishmael's intuitive leap is first to prove that Ahab's supposed means of accessing the Divine is absolutely "impregnable, uninjurable,"[10] and cannot possibly be overcome—and ultimately to dismantle the wall, and prove it to be "a total delusion."[11] This aligns him with the Zen understanding that it is not simply staring at the wall—what is essential is becoming a wall oneself. Ishmael declares himself ready to renounce "all ignorant incredulity. . . . For unless you own the whale, you are but a provincialist and sentimentalist in Truth."[12]

For Ishmael, not only is the sperm whale as unknowable as its Maker—it is the very symbol of the ungraspability of all phenomena. So throughout the book, Ishmael is deconstructing—and eventually literally dissecting—the whale, to demonstrate that the symbol of the ungraspable *is itself ungraspable*. He approaches this "ungraspable ungraspable" from every possible angle—historical, zoological, sociological, epistemological. Indeed, through the narrative events themselves—chasing, sighting, killing, boiling, even eating whales—the text itself becomes like a thousand little whale pieces, which do not lend themselves to simple explanations. While it sometimes seems as if Ishmael hopes to assemble a complete understanding of the whale, he knows that to be impossible: "Dissect him how I may, then, I but go skin deep; I know him not, and never will."[13] Thus while elaborating on his own sundry theories concerning the whale, he is simultaneously dismantling Ahab's erroneous view.

The White Whale serves as Ishmael's primary example that objects are empty of any and all interpretations laid on them from without—an idea he brings into sharp focus by offering us a multitude of perspectives on the White Whale, incompatible and often outright contradictory to one another. Ahab believes the whale has a "malicious intelligence"[14]; Starbuck insists he is "a dumb brute . . . that simply smote thee from blindest instinct."[15] In "The Town-Ho's Story," Moby Dick kills the story's villain, so is then considered an instrument of Divine Retribution; on the Rachel, he kills the captain's twelve-year-old boy, so he is seen as iniquitous. The captain of the Pequod loses a leg and devotes his life to vengeance; the captain of the Samuel Enderby loses an arm and decides, "No more White Whales for me; I've lowered for him once, and that has satisfied me."[16] The whale remains untouched by any of these "subtle deceits . . . laid on from without."[17] It remains "white."

These competing views of the whale are representative of the myriad theories and beliefs about God and the order of the universe held by human beings on planet earth. But it is absolutely crucial to recognize that the sperm whale is in no way essentially different from other phenomena. Like every other thing in the universe, the sperm whale is dependently co-originated, and thus both impermanent and interdependent. The labels we have for objects serve as only approximate descriptions so that we can speak intelligibly about them, but they cannot encapsulate the boundless ontological dimensions of any one thing.

Ishmael is pointing to this same truth when he wonders "where lie the nameless things of which the mystic sign gives forth such hints."[18] The ultimate reality of any one thing is beyond comprehension (and certainly beyond simple language) and is therefore truly nameless. We do have some information about individual objects, and these "hints" we share with other human beings, and can thus communicate ideas about them. But, again, these "signs" are merely that: signs pointing at the signless. What makes the sperm whale unique is that, while most things we come in contact with are easily apprehended, readily definable, and appear to be inherently existing, the sperm whale exists entirely outside our conscious capacities of perception and cognition. Melville (through Ishmael) brings us a subject that is remarkably well-suited to expressing these profound realities of existence. However, it must be repeated, there is nothing fundamentally different about the sperm whale, or even the White Whale, from other phenomena. Rather, just as Ishmael places "dried bits" of an "infinitely thin, transparent substance" scraped off a dead sperm whale's skin over the pages of his whalebooks— fancying it exerts "a magnifying influence" on the text[19]—so too does scrutinizing phenomena through a cetological lens wonderfully embody the ungraspability at the center of Ishmael's worldview.

Little is known about the sperm whale—even the name used to refer to it is "philologically absurd."[20] Its eating habits are shrouded in mystery: "though other species of whales find their food above water, and may be seen by man in the act of feeding, the spermaceti whale obtains his whole food in unknown zones below the surface."[21] Some believe that the sperm whale survives on squid, "yet very few of them have any but the most vague ideas concerning [the squid's] true nature and form; notwithstanding, they believe it to furnish to the Sperm Whale his only food."[22] References to its habitat— the "unfathomable waters,"[23] the "bottomless profundities"[24]—are unmistakably linked with spiritual and existential inquiry.

Our direct perception betrays us when we approach the whale. "Physiognomically regarded, the Sperm Whale is an anomalous creature," Ishmael tells us, "For you see no one point precisely; not one distinct feature is revealed."[25] The head, containing the vast reservoir of precious oil, should be the specific focus of the whaleman's passion. But the head cannot be distinguished from the body, for "the whale has nothing that can properly be called a neck" and the place where they seem to join "is the thickest part of him."[26] Furthermore, the head is protected by thick armour, "as though [it] were paved with horses' hoofs."[27] Thus the ultimate source of the whaleman's quest is, as mentioned above, absolutely impenetrable: "the severest pointed harpoon, the sharpest lance darted by the strongest human arm, impotently rebounds from it."[28]

Here Ishmael is discussing the deceptive nature of cognition, and our human proclivity toward making distinctions: "Physiognomy," he writes, "like every other human science, is but a passing fable."[29] We want the whale to exist independently of the sea, and the pieces of the whale to exist independently of one another. But the whale's head "is an entire delusion."[30] His brain "is hidden away behind its vast outworks . . . you can then see no indications of it."[31] "The digestive organs of the whale are . . . inscrutably constructed."[32] Most famous is Ishmael's "celebration" of the sperm whale's tail:

> The more I consider this mighty tail, the more do I deplore my inability to express it. . . . Dissect him how I may, then, I but go skin deep; I know him not, and never will. But if I know not even the tail of this whale, how understand his head? Much more, how comprehend his face, when face he has none? Thou shalt see my back parts, my tail, he seems to say, but my face shall not be seen. But I cannot completely make out his back parts; and hint what he will about his face, I say again he has no face.[33]

This points us back at the two truths: the conventional truth of phenomena existing within a place called the universe; and the ultimate truth that the universe and everything in it are indivisible—or perhaps "undifferentiatable." But of course, neither of these truths is the way we interact with things in our daily lives. Instead, we habitually impute inherent existence to phenomena (most importantly ourselves), and thus turn them into individually labeled and independently existent *things*. This third way of interaction is an absolute and utter fallacy. And Ishmael venerates the sperm whale's capacity to render us incapable of perpetuating this fallacious view. He even taunts our attempts to do so: "I but put that brow before you. Read it if you can."[34]

Ishmael's investigation of the whale is proof of the impossibility of such a task: "Dissect him how I may," he says, "I but go skin deep."[35] But how deep is skin deep? Twenty chapters earlier, he had a different question altogether: "The question, is, what and where is the skin of the whale?"[36] Now he even finds an "infinitely thin, isinglass substance," which he contends might be "the skin of the skin."[37] Ultimately, he finds it impossible to say where the skin ends and the blubber begins. Any attempt to break down the sperm whale into components like "blubber" and "skin" and "isinglass" is an exercise in futility.

Concurrent with his more abstract musings on the traits and habits of the sperm whale, Ishmael progresses through an exhaustive "scientific" examination of the sperm whale, expressly to demonstrate how such endeavors are doomed to fail: "To analyze it, would seem impossible."[38] This process begins with the Extracts, an introductory section which scholars often describe as Melville's attempt to ground his readers in the world of whales and whaling. But considering the "sub-sub-librarian" begins by warning us against taking his offering as "veritable gospel cetology," and insists it is but a "glancing bird's eye view" of the subject,[39] Melville's objective seems to be something a bit more mischievous.

The uncredited quotes that introduce the sarcastic science of the "Cetology" chapter offer a hint of Melville's intention, assuring us there is an "Impenetrable veil covering our knowledge of the cetacea" and that "All these incomplete indications but serve to torture us naturalists."[40] Ishmael begins his examination of the sperm whale by first cataloguing the different species in the scientific order Cetacea—comparing the task to "the classification of the constituents of a chaos."[41] By then immersing us in that chaos, Melville, it seems, is trying to unsettle his readers—exposing us to the groundlessness his narrator embraces in taking to the whaleship—while also parodying the attempts of science, religion, and philosophy to unlock the mysteries of the universe through classification and theorization. Ishmael specifically rejects the presumption that science will one day give us a complete explanation of the universe, saying "I promise nothing complete; because any human thing supposed to be complete, must for that very reason infallibly be faulty."[42] Thus, we find Ishmael's would-be definitive text riddled with half-measures: the Algerine Porpoise is only found in the Pacific, "I think."[43] The Narwhale is an example of "Unicornism."[44] He does not know much about the Razor

Back, so "let him go."[45] He calls his task "ponderous,"[46] the area of study "uncertain, unsettled,"[47] its questions "moot"[48]—and then infamously declares "for all time to come" that the whale be labeled "a spouting fish with a horizontal tail"[49]—leaving unexplained the evidence that whales have "lungs and warm blood" while "all other fish are lungless and cold blooded."[50] He also definitively proclaims the sperm whale "without doubt, the largest inhabitant of the globe"[51]—later including the Blue Whale in his list of "half-fabulous whales,"[52] calling them "uncertain whales,"[53] and anyway "altogether obsolete."[54]

The irreverence he shows for his subject aims to undermine the entire scientific enterprise. For the scientific method seeks to pin things down, arrange them methodically on a page, give them a name and a story. Ishmael makes clear that by seeking endless explanations, we deprive ourselves of the full majesty of a thing's existence: "How wonderful it is then—except after explanation—that this great monster . . . should be found at home, immersed to his lips for life in those Arctic waters!"[55] He describes science's "endless subdivisions" as "inconclusive" and, more tellingly, "repellingly intricate"[56]—later adding, "Physiognomy, like every other human science, is but a passing fable."[57] While "such a nomenclature" (that is, assigning names and labels) "may be convenient in facilitating allusions," he concludes, "yet it is in vain to attempt a clear classification of the Leviathan."[58]

Chapter Fourteen

The First Principle of All Things

Looking closely at Ishmael's elucidation of the ways the sperm whale defies perception and disrupts cognition, there is an unmistakable similarity to theological views of the Absolute. In Pierre Bayle's *Dictionary*, the consideration of Zen philosophy includes considerable time spent grappling with the Buddhist conception of the Absolute, which he calls "the first principle." It should perhaps come as no surprise that his descriptions of the "first principle" reinforce Ishmael's presentation of the unknowable sperm whale. Just as the first principle "is found everywhere . . . [and] exists, say they, from all eternity,"[1] the sperm whale is "immortal in his species, however perishable in his individuality,"[2] and the White Whale himself is "not only ubiquitous, but immortal (for immortality is but ubiquity in time)."[3] The first principle, Bayle writes, is "clear and luminous."[4] Ishmael writes in "The Whiteness of the Whale": "[C]onsider that the mystical cosmetic which produces every one of her hues, the great principle of light, for ever remains white or colorless in itself . . . of all these things the Albino whale was the symbol."[5] As Bayle describes the first principle as "[living] in idleness and a perfect repose,"[6] so too does Ishmael perceive "a gentle joyousness—a mighty mildness of repose in swiftness" the first time he observes the White Whale.[7] When he finally has the opportunity to examine a sperm whale skeleton, he finds it "amid the green, life-restless loom of that Arsacidean wood, the great white, worshipped skeleton lay lounging—a gigantic idler!"[8]

Bayle claims the first principle is "uncapable [*sic*] of increase or diminution . . . it has no figure."[9] And Ishmael has a good deal to say about size and shape as well:

> Would you, you could not compress him.[10]
>
> [S]uch is then the outlandish, eel-like, limbered, varying shape of him, that his precise expression the devil himself could not catch.[11]

103

But it may be fancied, that from the naked skeleton of the stranded whale, accurate hints may be derived touching his true form. Not at all. [12]

For all these reasons, then, any way you may look at it, you must needs conclude that the great Leviathan is that one creature in the world which must remain unpainted to the last. . . . So there is no earthly way of finding out precisely what the whale really looks like. [13]

Bayle seems skeptical that the first principle "is wise but understands nothing" since it also "does not reason," [14] but Ishmael has no such quarrel: "Genius in the Sperm Whale? Has the Sperm Whale ever written a book, spoken a speech? No, his great genius is declared in his doing nothing particular to prove it. It is moreover declared in his pyramidical silence." [15] Ahab, meanwhile, boasts, "I know that of me, which thou knowest not of thyself, oh, thou omnipotent." [16]

Bayle's descriptions of the "first principle" point to the Buddhist teaching of *sunyata*, or emptiness, and are almost certainly taken from what in Japanese is called *Makahannyaharamita Shingyo*—translated as the "Heart of Great Perfect Wisdom Sutra," or "Great Wisdom Beyond Wisdom Sutra"— regarded as the essence of the fundamental Mahayana Buddhist text *Prajnaparamita*. "All dharmas [things] are empty," it reads, "They neither arise nor cease, are neither defiled nor pure, neither increase nor decrease" [17]—this last clause matching Bayle's (rather clumsier) "uncapable of increase or diminution."

The sutra declares that, ultimately, there is "no form" and thus "no eyes, no ears, no nose, no tongue, no body, no mind." [18] It is a teaching repeated by Japanese Zen master Keizan Jokin (1268–1325) in his work *Transmission of Light*: "Monks, you should know that there is Someone who is not only speechless but also mouthless. Not only is He mouthless but He also has no eyes. . . . Even though you say you see things and hear sounds, it is not your eye seeing or your ear hearing; it is this Faceless Fellow doing it." [19] In the chapter "The Prairie," after equating the whale's silence with genius, Ishmael says almost precisely the same thing:

For you see no one point precisely; not one distant feature is revealed; no nose, eyes, ears, or mouth; no face; he has none, proper. . . . Dissect him how I may, then, I but go skin deep; I know him not, and never will. How comprehend his face, when face he has none? I cannot completely make out his back parts; and hint what he will about his face, I say again he has no face. [20]

Deeper than mere superficial features, Bayle's text goes on to address specifically the notion of spiritual practice—that the way we interact with the first principle has a profound effect on our mental well-being. He writes:

> That man may in this world raise himself to the condition and supreme majesty of the first principle, for as much as by the force of meditation he may perfectly know it, and so arrive to the supreme tranquillity which that principle enjoys into itself; that this is all the good that man can acquire, and that till he has obtained it by meditation, and a perfect knowledge, he is tormented with perpetual disquiet. . . . He often passes from one hell to another, and finds rest no where.[21]

This holds true for Ishmael as well, but only partly so. For Ishmael's interest in whaling and worship of the sperm whale is not with the intention that "he may perfectly know it" so much as *know that it cannot be known*. Nevertheless, we can attribute his spiritual development—from his rather inauspicious beginnings to his equanimous bearing thereafter—to this awareness and attention. In composing his story, he begins to "rise and swell with his subject . . . [and] expand to its bulk,"[22] until he can finally "stand among these mighty Leviathan."[23] Captain Ahab, on the other hand, is the one "tormented by perpetual disquiet," whose wooden leg is heard pacing the deck day and night—not only unable to find rest, but indeed being passed through various hellscapes of the mind:

> Often, when forced from his hammock by exhausting and intolerably vivid dreams of the night, which, resuming his own intense thoughts through the day, carried them on amid a clashing of phrensies, and whirled them round and round in his blazing brain, till the very throbbing of his life-spot became insufferable anguish; and when, as was sometimes the case, these spiritual throes in him heaved his being up from its base, and a chasm seemed opening in him, from which forked flames and lightnings shot up, and accursed fiends beckoned him to leap down among them; when this hell in himself yawned beneath him, a wild cry would be heard through the ship; and with glaring eyes Ahab would burst from his state room, as though escaping from a bed that was on fire.[24]

Bayle concludes his section on Japan by lamenting: "One cannot sufficiently admire that so extravagant a notion, and so full of absurd contradictions, should insinuate itself into the mind of so many people so remote from one another, and so different in their humours, education, customs, and genius."[25] But what would appall the rationalist Bayle would surely delight the free-wheeling Melville, who would no doubt see through the apparently "absurd contradictions" on the surface in wondering how "so extravagant a notion" could form the basis to a system of belief. But even more, it is these very contradictions, leading Bayle to reject these doctrines, that lie at the very heart of Melville's philosophy. Bayle's final word on the first principle outlines precisely Ishmael's counsel regarding the sperm whale:

[F]irst he observes that they have but very few doctrines about the nature of the first principles; that they say nothing upon it with any perspicuity, that they cannot resolve questions, and answer the objections proposed to them nor confirm their opinions, and that their only shift is to say, that it does not concern men to enquire into the nature and power of the first principle. [26]

For Ishmael, these are the means through which one comes to "raise himself . . . to the first principle": by *not* having doctrines, *not* resolving questions, *not* saying anything at all with "perspicuity." Ahab's monomaniacal quest can be described as a quest to "confirm his opinion" regarding the White Whale; Ishmael survives precisely because he does not seek to "resolve questions," but rather readily loses himself in "infinite perspectives," knowing that all things "assume different aspects, depending on your point of view."[27] Bayle signs off with a flourish, writing in Latin, "They think they are solving everything with one word, saying that it is not important for people to investigate the force and nature of this primary cause by inquiring and debating. This completely mixes up everything, born (as it is) and arising from ignorance."[28] But again, Ishmael's narrative leaves little ambiguity as to what happens to the man who concerns himself with "investigating the force and nature" of the sperm whale by "inquiring and debating." Ishmael's model is not philosophical deliberation, but immersion in experience. The only way we might be able to join him, he concludes, "is by going a-whaling yourself; but by so doing, you run no small risk of being eternally stove and sunk by him. Wherefore, it seems to me you had best not be too fastidious in your curiosity touching this Leviathan."[29]

Chapter Fifteen

Whiteness

To this point we have mostly concerned ourselves with what Ishmael calls "those more obvious considerations" regarding Moby Dick. While these cetological contemplations might indeed "occasionally awaken in any man's soul some alarm," there is something else, something which causes in Ishmael "vague, nameless horror" concerning the White Whale. In the chapter "The Whiteness of the Whale," Ishmael reveals that it is the whale's "whiteness" which "by its intensity completely overpowered" the whale's other aspects, and thus concerns him "above all things."[1]

This idea of "whiteness"—while here superficially enjoined with the quality of appearing white in color—is, for Ishmael, a psychological experience of the elusiveness and ungraspability of all phenomena, regardless of color. This is what Ishmael is pointing us toward: not the color white, but "the thought of whiteness . . . the innermost idea of this hue."[2] He makes the argument that while this elusiveness is omnipresent in all things, it is more readily apparent in objects that appear white, as we can perceive them without the "earthly hues . . . laid on from without" that otherwise distract the eye.[3] But the color white is also useful to him in that, although it is readily associated with all that is "sweet, and honorable, and sublime"[4]—he cites white elephants, white bulls, white stones, and "sacred White Dogs"[5]—even within these exalted ideals, there still "lurks an elusive something in the innermost idea of this hue."[6] And this elusiveness, the impossibility of getting a clear idea about anything at all, is what "strikes more of panic to the soul."[7] Even further, when this "whiteness" is manifested in "any object terrible in itself," it "heighten[s] the terror to the furthest bounds."[8]

This becomes especially significant in the case of Moby Dick, largely because of the countless intimations and proclamations (from Gabriel's "Shaker God incarnated"[9] to Ishmael's vision of the sperm whale "exalted to

Jove's high seat"[10]) that he represents some semblance of the Ultimate. When coupled with Ishmael's fundamental argument—that Moby Dick is the *ungraspable ungraspable* (i.e., the ungraspable manifestation of the ungraspability of phenomena)—we may arrive at the devastating possibility that the Universal Ultimate must forever remain unknown to us. Perhaps the Thing from which all meaning to earthly existence is derived might itself be without any meaning—that it "cannot amount to much in its totality."[11] As to why this veil is so terrifying, he asks: "Is it that by its indefiniteness it shadows forth the heartless voids and immensities of the universe, and thus stabs us from behind with the thought of annihilation, when beholding the white depths of the milky way?"[12] This is what he finds most frightening, the prospect of a meaningless universe—it is an "atheism from which we shrink." Thus, Ishmael finally describes whiteness as "spiritual whiteness,"[13] as "the very veil of the Christian's deity"[14]—the thing that keeps God (or, to keep in non-theistic terms, the Ultimate)—hidden from us.

What this chapter essentially represents is Ishmael's struggle with the groundlessness he had so passionately embraced in the first chapter. But one gets the impression, particularly toward the end of the chapter, that he is intentionally subjecting himself to this difficulty. That, just as he labors through the sarcastic science of the "Cetology" chapter in order to show the futility of that endeavor, in this chapter, having warned us of the dangers in trying to grasp at the mysterious "invisible spheres" of the universe,[15] he offers himself up as a sacrificial seeker, in order to demonstrate precisely why this is a bad idea.

The horrifying vision he describes is an experience well-documented in Mahayana Buddhist literature, among practitioners who first encounter the doctrine of *sunyata*, or emptiness. Having heard the teaching that all phenomena are empty of inherent existence, one natural reaction would be to shift to "the little lower layer,"[16] as Ahab would say, and postulate that things do in fact have an essence, and that essence is called "emptiness." But emptiness itself is empty of any fixed essence or identity. Emptiness is not an independent thing; it is a word that describes the non-existence of independent things.

This is the focus of C.W. Huntington's book *The Emptiness of Emptiness* (the title of which could very well serve as the title of Ishmael's chapter as well), adapting for a Western audience the philosophical treatises of the Madhyamaka school of Indian Buddhism, particularly the work of Chandrakirti (600–650). Regarding this experience of emptiness Huntington writes: "Again and again [Madhyamaka philosophers] admit that the doctrine of emptiness is frightening—and ought to be frightening for anyone who engages with it at an emotional and volitional level . . . because it lends itself so easily to nihilistic interpretations."[17] It is no surprise, then, that the person who has a vision of "the void" will do anything to protect himself from it; as

Ishmael might say, "He bolts down all events, all creeds, and beliefs, and persuasions, all hard things visible and invisible, never mind how knobby; as an ostrich of potent digestion gobbles down bullets and gun flints."[18] This is why "some whalemen should go even further in their superstitions; declaring Moby Dick not only ubiquitous, but immortal (for immortality is but ubiquity in time),"[19] seeking to attach themselves to something substantial and permanent. This is why God has been turned into a Thing, in "the now egotistical sky."[20]

Despite these nihilistic visions, Huntington argues, the Madhyamaka teachers made no attempt at reassurance or mollification of their students. On the contrary: "Instead they insist on pointing only more resolutely to the groundlessness of all experience, to 'the emptiness of emptiness.'"[21] This is precisely what Ishmael is doing in "The Whiteness of the Whale," contemplating the "vague, nameless horror" the whiteness causes in him[22]—searching deeper and deeper within himself, bravely charging into "the invisible spheres . . . formed in fright,"[23] endeavoring until he has finally "solved the incantation of this whiteness."[24]

Ishmael's visions of the White Whale resemble Shunryu Suzuki Roshi's admonition to "believe . . . in something which has no form and no color—something which exists before all forms and colors appear."[25] R.H. Blyth, wondering what this "something" might be, arrives at a description that might easily be applied to the White Whale: "Then what is the thing if it is devoid of all qualities? It is devoid of the absence of those qualities, and what is meant by this unpalatable conglomeration of negative is that in some mysterious way the thing is alive, it exists with a palpitating stillness."[26] Blyth's phrase "unpalatable conglomeration of negative" could very well be placed within Ishmael's musings on whiteness. For while he may rightly succeed in deconstructing the horror that the whiteness inspires in him, Ishmael correctly recognizes he will never approach the nature of whiteness itself.

On an epistemological level, the whale is white because, although it is the embodiment (and, as we shall see, also the manifestation) of whatever stories our characters have about the universe, none of these various interpretations is inherently existent in the whale itself. Melville uses "white" in much the same way as Shakyamuni Buddha—illustrating this point in the *Samdhinirmocana Sutra* with the example of a crystal—uses the word "clear."

> For example, when a very clear crystal comes in contact with the color blue, it then appears as a previous gem, such as a sapphire or a mahanila. Further, by mistaking it for a precious gem such as a sapphire or a mahanila, sentient beings are deluded. When it comes in contact with the color red, it then appears as a precious gem such as a ruby and, by mistaking it for a precious gem such as a ruby, sentient beings are deluded.[27]

Adapting this to *Moby-Dick*: when the White Whale comes in contact with a whaleman's beliefs about it—Ahab's eternal malice, Stubb's blithe enthusiasm, Flask's dismissive derision—it appears to them in a certain way. By mistaking their belief about the whale to be the actual reality of the whale, the whalemen are deluded.

Hubert Dreyfus takes a similar route, describing whiteness in terms of a prism, in which each whaleman's interpretation of the whale represents a different color, and, adding them all up, the end result is "whiteness." In this reading, the universe is meaningless; people come along and paint it different colors (by, as Ishmael says, wearing "colored and coloring glasses upon their eyes"[28]); but these colors cancel each other out; thus we end up once again with meaninglessness.[29] However, as Melville says, we are not left with simply "meaninglessness" but rather "a dumb blankness, full of meaning."[30] There is no meaning to life outside of the one that we ourselves ascribe to it. So, in this case, while the White Whale is ultimately devoid of intrinsic meaning, conventionally speaking it embodies whatever meaning we ascribe to it. This is why Ishmael considers whiteness "not so much a color as the visible absence of color, and at the same time the concrete of all colors"[31]—for it represents both the conventional reality (the concrete) of each belief and the ultimate reality (the absence) as well.

This is also true about the experience of color. As Ishmael says, "all earthly hues . . . are but subtle deceits, not actually inherent in substances, but only laid on from without."[32] Colors are "deceits" in that what we refer to as "blue," for example, is a dependently co-arisen phenomenon resulting from the interaction of light waves of a certain wavelength and our ocular sense organ, which are then interpreted by our eye consciousness as "blue." Thus, it is not simply that "blue" exists only subjectively, like taste or smell, but that the concept of "blueness" is a product of the *pattern of relationship* between the light particles, the sense organ and the sense consciousness.

Even Ishmael's use of the word "concrete" demonstrates this doctrine of dependent co-origination, since the building material is composed of many disparate components that come together in a certain way to create something to which we can ascribe the word "concrete." Just as concrete is a mixture of materials, and whiteness is the combination of the colors in the spectrum of light, emptiness is described as the dependently co-arisen nature of all phenomena (including itself).

But if these things exist only in the conventional world, is there anything we can say about the ultimate? Near the end of the chapter, Ishmael puts forth his best effort, once again plunging himself into this horrifying nihilistic vision of emptiness, to consider the implications of this "spiritual whiteness": "[A]nd when we proceed further, and consider that the mystical cosmetic which produces every one of her hues, the great principle of light, for ever remains white or colorless in itself, and if operating without medium upon matter, would touch all objects, even tulips and roses, with its own blank tinge."[33] From the ultimate perspective, there are no colors. So "without medium upon matter"—that is, without subject perceiving object—there are no tulips, nor roses. We find a similar teaching in case 26 of the *Book of Serenity*, "Yangshan Points to Snow":

> [T]here is still something beyond white. That is why Yangshan pointed at the snow lion and said, "Is there any that can go beyond this color?" Now white is the basis of all colors, and the color of snow is sheer white—how can there be any going beyond this? I say, since it's called "color" it must relate with the eye—the color that goes beyond white is only the colorless—it does not relate to the eye.[34]

In this place that Ishmael has entered, behind the veil and beyond medium and matter, there is neither black nor white, but rather a "blank"—that is, emptiness. The koan commentary goes on to say, "If you then grasp the point of ultimate blankness, where there isn't even white, this indeed is falling into the formless realm."[35]

We find this color analogy in Blyth's writings as well, specifically regarding ultimate reality:

> It is Pure and Undefiled; things are, just as they are, delivered from all stain of sin or imperfection. It is Unobstructed; all things are free, interpenetrative. That is to say it is age-less, non-moral, law-less. It is like light, containing all colors in it, but itself colorless. It is not a thing but contains all things; not a person but includes all minds; not beautiful or ugly but the essence of both.[36]

This certainly sounds a great deal like the White Whale. But Ishmael's vision of the ultimate is not nearly as harmonious and benign as this. To the contrary, he sees our experience of color (and, thus, our beliefs) as an illusion created by "deified Nature"[37]—that is, "the egotistical sky"[38]—who "paints like the harlot, whose allurements cover nothing but the charnel-house within."[39] If one succumbs to the harlot's advances, as it were, in attaching oneself to her allurements (colors, beliefs), one will find only the "charnel-house within."[40] But Ishmael continues ever deeper, until "pondering all this, the palsied universe lies before us a leper; and like wilful travellers in Lapland, who refuse to wear colored and coloring glasses upon their eyes, so the wretched infidel gazes himself blind at the monumental white shroud that wraps all the prospect around him."[41] Finally the universe begins to crumble before his eyes. When one is fixated on the ultimate ("wilful . . . wretched," ignoring the conventional truth) the universe appears grotesque, paralyzed—for, like all things, it cannot exist from its own side. From a Buddhistic point of view, this expresses "the deep unity between the two truths."[42] A belief in nothing is just as disastrous as an attachment to a specific something. Our effort must not be to explore the mysteries of the universe in hopes of getting some answer to them, or to it, but rather to become intimate with those mysteries so that we no longer find it necessary to seek those answers. Ishmael escapes this fate by immersing himself briefly here and then moving on to the next chapter—"Hark!"—where two whaleman chat beneath "a fair moonlight."[43] Meanwhile Ahab—the "wretched infidel," the "wilful travel-er"—refuses to wear the "colored and coloring glasses" and "gazes himself blind," just as he stares into the icy wind from his place on the deck: "So, with his ivory leg inserted into its accustomed hole, and with one hand firmly grasping a shroud, Ahab for hours and hours would stand gazing dead to windward, while an occasional squall of sleet or snow would all but congeal his very eyelashes together."[44]

But even while Ishmael immerses himself in this nihilistic exercise, we find hints of his spirited buoyancy. He writes, "Though neither knows where lie the nameless things of which the mystic sign gives forth such hints; yet with me, as with the colt, *somewhere those things must exist*" (my italics).[45] He remains fascinated with this "elusive something,"[46] which lies at the root of what he elsewhere calls "the problem of the universe revolving in me."[47] And as Blyth writes: "Above all, the universe is a paradox, and we must laugh with and at it . . . [Things] are bewildering, but that is not so much because we are too stupid to unweave the mingled threads, as that the world is, spiritually speaking, an absolute confusion."[48] In his "profoundest ideal-ized significance,"[49] Moby Dick is the floating apparition of ultimate reality, where no distinctions can be made, and the whale cannot even himself be seen: "I cannot completely make out his back parts; and hint what he will about his face, I say again he has no face."[50] The words of Hongzhi seem particularly apt: "Where emptiness is empty it contains all of existence, where existence exists it joins the single emptiness. Still I ask, what is this?"[51] For one flailing, pivotal chapter, Ishmael subjects himself to "gazing at the monumental white shroud," and, in glimpsing emptiness, reaffirms his devotion to "the fiery hunt," and the cetological exploration of the ungrasp-able ungraspable.[52]

Chapter Sixteen

The Measurements of the Whale Skeleton

One might still wonder whether—despite the sperm whale's impenetrable exterior, and inscrutable physicality—there might still be some permanent, graspable, static entity lying within. What would one find if one could search within (or behind) that "impenetrable veil"?[1] Ishmael explores this question in a series of chapters beginning with "A Bower in the Arsacides."

His first glimpse behind the curtain is the dissection of a young sperm whale cub lifted onto the deck of a ship. But even then, he suggests, what he calls "the contents of that young cub"[2] (i.e., the meat and blood and guts) would only have impeded his search for the mysterious essence. For that task, he needs to strip away all vestiges of the whale's "outer aspect" and view it "stripped of its fathom-deep enfoldings . . . in its ultimatum; that is to say, in his unconditional skeleton,"[3] which he eventually has the opportunity to do, on the island of Tranque in the Arsacides.

The sperm whale skeleton has appropriately been made into "a chapel,"[4] "a grand temple,"[5] befitting Ishmael's theogonic examination. He wanders through and around the archway of bleached bones, trailing twine in his wake (in deference to the sperm whale's disorienting nature)—and finds no basic element, no glittering jewel, no laminated card labeled "sperm whale." He recounts, "I saw no living thing within; naught was there but bones"[6] (sounding perhaps not a little relieved). For it is not merely, as he puts it, "the circumstance, so variously repeated in this book, that the skeleton of the whale is by no means the mould of his invested form,"[7] although we'll get to that in a moment. First, he must deal with two larger, more substantial considerations here, regarding the illusion of independent existence. First, he has argued that the sperm whale cannot be separated from its habitat—that it can only be said to truly exist in concert with the conditions of its environment:

The living whale, in his full majesty and significance, is only to be seen at sea in unfathomable waters; and afloat the vast bulk of him is out of sight, like a launched line-of-battle ship; and out of that element it is a thing eternally impossible for mortal man to hoist him bodily into the air, so as to preserve all his mighty swells and undulations. . . . But it may be fancied, that from the naked skeleton of the stranded whale, accurate hints may be derived touching his true form. Not at all. For it is one of the more curious things about this Leviathan, that his skeleton gives very little idea of his general shape . . . So there is no earthly way of finding out precisely what the whale really looks like.[8]

Ishmael also addresses this point in the chapter "Squid." He laments the paucity of information about the creature believed to "furnish the sperm whale its only food."[9] Specifically, he mentions that little is known of the squid's "nature and form"[10]—the simple reason being that, like the sperm whale, if taken bodily from the water, it will cease to exist in the same way it does unmolested. And since it has no need to come to the surface to breathe, it cannot be observed in its natural habitat.

But Ishmael's most radical conclusion is also the most fundamental. His statement "I saw no living thing within; naught was there but bones"[11] is followed by the *coup de grâce* that the sperm whale, here in its "unconditional skeleton," is "an utter blank!"[12] The sperm whale cannot be separated from its conditions. Separated from its conditions, it no longer exists as a sperm whale; it is "an utter blank."

This expands upon the fruitless search for a "living thing within" or essence beneath the exterior. And it supplants the conclusion that the "blank" might be aligned with the "whiteness" he considers in "The Whiteness of the Whale," or provide a definitive answer to Ahab's concern that there might be "naught beneath." For one finds a "blank" only when one attempts to view an object abstracted from its conditions, and assumes it to have an independent existence. The way things truly exist is in an unfathomably intertwined relationship with the myriad causes and conditions in the universe. To view them in this capacity, Ishmael insists, is to ultimately know them:

How vain and foolish, then, thought I, for timid untravelled man to try to comprehend aright this wondrous whale, by merely poring over his dead attenuated skeleton, stretched in this peaceful wood. No. Only in the heart of quickest perils; only when within the eddyings of his angry flukes; only on the profound unbounded sea, can the fully invested whale be truly and livingly found out.[13]

Only through direct experience do we know the whale, and know ourselves.

The other curious aspect of the Tranque suite is, as I've said, our narrator's preoccupation with the measurements of the whale skeleton. As Ishmael has made quite clear, impressive as the measurements are, they do not come close to conveying the "full majesty and significance" of the living sperm whale "wrapt up in his blubber,"[14] at home in "unfathomable waters."[15] So we can only be surprised when he not only carefully recites these numbers one by one, but reveals he considers this information so precious, he has had the measurements tattooed on his own body!

> The skeletal dimensions I shall now proceed to set down are copied verbatim from my right arm, where I had them tattooed; as in my wild wanderings at that period, there was no other secure way of preserving such valuable statistics. But as I was crowded for space, and wished the other parts of my body to remain a blank page for a poem I was then composing . . .[16]

On the surface, this presents all sorts of problems. How can Ishmael—so wary of the written word, and of definitive statements of belief—decide to engrave something permanent onto his skin? To see how this expresses his attitude of non-grasping, we must look closely at what exactly he is preserving.

Like Queequeg's tattoos—which express nothing in and of themselves but point at a profound unifying truth—these measurements are "a riddle to unfold,"[17] a set of seemingly random numbers that "symbolize something unseen," and unseeable: the great sperm whale.[18] More importantly, we must not forget that, as he has said, these numbers do not come close to conveying the true magnitude of the sperm whale's size. The tattoo serves as reminder—a reminder not of what the measurements are, but of what the measurements *mean*—a reminder that our ideas about things do not come close to what they really are. That removed from their conditions, they are "naught . . . but bones."[19] That our ideas about an object—the descriptive terms and figures we impute upon them—do not encompass that thing's true identity, as it arises and ceases in concert with all the matter and energy in the universe.

Thus, the dimensions are a tangible expression of Way-seeking mind. For although we will never find the "unconditioned ultimatum"—of the sperm whale or of any other object—the only way we realize that profound truth is by constant effort, and ceaselessly searching for it. Ishmael studies the whale until he understands it cannot be understood—a precious realization indeed, and one he literally brands onto his body as a reminder of what is, and what is not.

Chapter Seventeen

Ox-Herding

It is a story of a young man on a quest to discover a sacred animal. This journey—first searching for and finally conquering this animal—awakens in him increasing wisdom and compassion, until finally his journey ends with his liberation.

These words go far toward summarizing *Moby-Dick*, but they are also a description of a famous Zen teaching called the Ten Ox-Herding Pictures (Japanese: *Jugyuzu*). In the twelfth century, a Chinese Zen master named K'uo-an Shih-yuan made a series of illustrations, meant to express the developing stages of realization through Zen practice. The pictures he produced, each accompanied by a four-line verse and short commentary, became popular in Japan in the centuries following their creation, and are widely known today. The images were enthusiastically embraced by a new generation of Western seekers after appearing in Paul Reps's book *Zen Flesh, Zen Bones* in 1957. Before we end our investigation of the sperm whale as an object of meditation, we might take a moment to consider it from this perspective.

The ox, or bull, remains a powerful symbol in Zen Buddhist literature, signifying a person's true nature, or originally enlightened mind, to which the Zen practitioner strives to return. For the whaleman, of course—and especially for Ishmael—the sperm whale is the fruitful symbol of everything worth seeking. Indeed, Ishmael's vision of Noah's Ark at the end of the "Loomings" chapter mentions only pairs of whales; he seems to have no use for any other creature. [1]

The similarities between the Ox-Herding Pictures and *Moby-Dick* are truly striking. For example, regarding the search for the ox, Japanese Zen master Nyogen Senzaki (1876–1958) writes: "Not many people search for the ox. Among those who do, only a fortunate few even discover its traces. In books or in actual life, we may discover such impressions of the ox, but often we confuse these with traces of another sort. Many students wander for years without seeing even traces of wisdom."[2] Ishmael expresses this exact point about pursuing the White Whale, almost verbatim:

> [N]ot all [whalemen] knew of his existence; only a few of them, comparative-
> ly, had knowingly seen him; while the number who as yet had actually and
> knowingly given battle to him, was small indeed. . . . [A]t any rate, there are
> many whalemen . . . who have never hostilely encountered the Sperm Whale,
> but whose sole knowledge of the leviathan is restricted to the ignoble monster
> primitively pursued in the North.[3]

It should be noted that although the White Whale is indeed never caught, that is Ahab's objective, not Ishmael's. Ishmael's goal is to know the whale—to "own the whale"[4]—and I would argue he does indeed succeed. Furthermore, since both stories are primarily journeys of self-discovery (as opposed to literal animal-discovery), we can discern an underlying mutual chronology.

In the first stage, "The Search for the Bull," the ox-herder is at the end of his rope, in an emotional state comparable to Ishmael's in the first chapter:

> In the pasture of this world, I endlessly push aside tall grasses
> Following unnamed rivers, lost upon the interpenetrating paths of distant mountains.
> My strength failing and my vitality exhausted, I cannot find the bull.
> I only hear the locusts chirring through the forest at night.[5]

Although the ox-herder will remain on land for the duration of the story, it is by the riverbank[6] that he first discovers traces of the ox, in the second verse, "Discovering the Footprints": "Understanding the teaching, I see the foot-prints of the bull . . . Not yet having entered the gate, nevertheless I have discerned the path."[7] We can compare this stage to Ishmael's experience on Nantucket, where he finds the "footprints" of the whale—or perhaps not footprints so much as "imprints" (that is, the places where it has left its mark)—all around him (in the chapel and the inn; for better [Queequeg] and for worse [Bulkington]).

The third panel is called "Perceiving the Bull." The ox-herder rhetorically asks, "What artist can draw that massive head, those majestic horns?"[8] Compare this to Ishmael's prolonged attention to "the marvels of [the whale's] outer aspect,"[9] which culminates in three successive chapters in which he derides most attempts to portray the sperm whale in pictorial form. Both the ox-herder and the true whaleman find themselves consumed by thoughts of their respective animal: the ox-herder cries, "Wherever one enters one sees the head of the bull!"[10] and Ishmael describes "catching passing glimpses of the profiles of whales defined along the undulating ridges. But you must be a thorough whaleman, to see these sights."[11]

The fourth stage is "Catching the Bull," which refers to the Zen practitioner's first experiences with *shamatha* meditation practice, and the struggle in calming a mind that for many years has roamed wildly, with impunity. Here the bull (that is, the mind) is difficult to train, and impossible to control: "Infatuation for scenery interferes with his direction . . . he wanders away. His mind is still stubborn and unbridled."[12] In *Moby-Dick*'s "Stubb Kills a Whale," Ishmael is found daydreaming up at the foremast-head. Finding nothing particular to interest him in the surrounding scenery, he is overcome by a more lethargic hindrance:

> The next day was exceedingly still and sultry, and with nothing special to engage them, the Pequod's crew could hardly resist the spell of sleep induced by such a vacant sea. For this part of the Indian Ocean through which we then were voyaging is not what whalemen call a lively ground; that is, it affords fewer glimpses of porpoises, dolphins, flying-fish, and other vivacious denizens of more stirring waters . . . and with my shoulders leaning against the slackened royal shrouds, to and fro I idly swayed in what seemed an enchanted air. No resolution could withstand it; in that dreamy mood losing all consciousness, at last my soul went out of my body.[13]

The ox-herder's verse in this stage—"I seize him with a terrific struggle./His great will and power are inexhaustible"[14]—relates directly to the frenzied hunt that directly follows Ishmael's "dreamy mood," suggesting an unexpected causal connection leading from the wandering mind to the captured whale. Just as close attention to ephemeral thoughts will enable Ishmael to truly observe his mind, the tenacity of the hunt tethers the killed whale to the whaleboat, and for the first time he can finally be seen: "[T]he waning whale relaxed in his wrath. . . . And now abating in his flurry, the whale once more rolled out into view."[15]

"Taming the Bull" (in which the ox "becomes naturally gentle"[16]) carries us through the dissection of Stubb's whale carcass (a "taming" in a different sense entirely), to *Moby-Dick*'s "The Grand Armada," in which Ishmael's whale-boat floats auspiciously into the center of a pod of calving whales. Queequeg pats their foreheads; Starbuck scratches their backs with his lance. But Ishmael looks deeper into the depths, profoundly moved by the creatures' "peaceful concernments."[17] Perhaps only now does our narrator fully realize the equanimity he has achieved through his meditative practices—that "though surrounded by circle upon circle of consternations and affrights . . . I myself still for ever centrally disport in mute calm; and while . . . deep down and deep inland there I still bathe me in eternal mildness of joy."[18]

For the ox-herder, "[t]he struggle is over" already in stage six, Riding the Bull Home: "I observe the clouds above. Onward I go, no matter who may wish to call me back."[19] Reading the second half of the series (panels six through ten) through the lens of *Moby-Dick*, we can see they align with

Ishmael's spiritual development after the events on the Pequod, once his own struggle has ended. In "The Bull Transcended" (stage seven), the ox-herder admits that "We only make the bull a temporary subject" in order to facilitate awakening.[20] In the same way, as I have argued, there is nothing that fundamentally separates the sperm whale from all other dependently co-arisen phenomena, simply that it is particularly well-suited as an object of philosophical inquiry. For Ishmael as well, it serves as a temporary subject— since, as he writes, writers "rise and swell with their subject. . . . To produce a mighty book, you must choose a mighty theme."[21]

The earliest versions of the Ox-Herding Pictures contained either five or eight stages—drawn so that in each succeeding picture, the ox became progressively whiter. The final panel was an empty circle, intended to signify Oneness. But K'uo-an, feeling this ending insufficient, added two further stages after the blankness—"to make it clear," as Philip Kapleau writes, "that the Zen man of the highest spiritual development lives in the mundane world of form and diversity and mingles with the utmost freedom among ordinary men, whom he inspires with his compassion and radiance to walk in the Way of the Buddha."[22] In the modern version, the "empty circle" panel is the eighth of ten stages, titled "Both Bull and Self Transcended":

> Whip, rope, person, and bull—all merge in No-Thing.
> This heaven is so vast no message can stain it.
> How may a snowflake exist in a raging fire?
> Here are the footprints of the patriarchs.[23]

This bears an unmistakable resemblance to Ishmael's meditation on the whiteness of the whale. In Ishmael's construction, all phenomenal objects— "even tulips and roses"[24]—dissolve into the "monumental white shroud"[25] that he uses to describe the indescribable "No-Thing." Beyond this shroud lies a "dumb blankness" where only "nameless things" (that is, no-things within the No-Thing) can reside, for, like a raging fire, it consumes all unique identities and messages. But the "footsteps of the patriarchs" can be found here in the sense that all those who follow the Way must immerse themselves in Nothingness (i.e., whiteness), familiarize themselves with Nothingness, if they are to understand the fundamental equality of all things.

This cyclical immersion and disillusionment appears as well in the penultimate ox-herding panel, "Reaching the Source," which we can compare to Ishmael's union with the whale skeleton in "A Bower In The Arsacides." Both seekers betray a note of disappointment in what they find—namely, in finding that even the source itself is sourceless. The ox-herder laments the chattering mind that leads us from our own original quiescence: "Too many steps have been taken returning to the root and the source./Better to have been blind and deaf from the beginning!"[26] And just as the ox-herder writes,

"Poised in silence, I observe the forms of integration and disintegration,"[27] Ishmael finds "no living thing within; naught was there but bones."[28] Finally he concludes that the source is "an utter blank," and chastises himself for having been so deluded: "How vain and foolish, thought I . . . to try to comprehend aright this wondrous whale, by merely poring over his dead attenuated skeleton, stretched in this peaceful wood."[29]

The final panel of the Ox-Herding Pictures is called "In the World": "Barefooted and naked of breast, I mingle with the people of the world./My clothes are ragged and dust-laden, and I am ever blissful."[30] Zen practice places particular emphasis on what is known as "returning to the market-place"—when a monk has reached the end of his training, he is expected to return to the world and, "with gift-bestowing hands," share his wisdom and compassion with the villagers.

This practice can also be an episodic one—for one may achieve a level of enlightenment while in the peace and solitude of the cloister, but then struggle to maintain that state of mind in the tumult of the world outside the monastery gates. Ishmael shows this is true for the whaleman as well, in the very first paragraph of the book: "Whenever I find myself growing grim about the mouth . . . I account it high time to get to sea soon as I can."[31] But although he moves through fleeting moods and emotions, since he does not allow himself to become attached to any one of them, he is able to "for ever centrally disport in mute calm."[32] While whalemen like Ahab and Bulkington are forever at sea, and the Manhattoes are "tied to counters,"[33] Ishmael is at home everywhere—on far-flung voyages and periodic returns to the marketplace. We find a latter-day Ishmael in Lima's Golden Inn and on an island in the Arsacides. Although he is far from "ragged and dust-laden" in the former, both episodes do recall the figure of Hotei, the "Buddhist god of contentment," whose statue Melville kept on his mantle at Arrowhead. The commentary in the final panel of the Ox-Herding Pictures happily concludes, "I go to the market place with my wine bottle and return home with my staff. I visit the wineshop and the market, and everyone I look upon becomes enlightened."[34] The latter-day Ishmael is serene, even blissful, as he looks upon his readers.

IV

Captain Ahab's Universe

Chapter Eighteen

A Factionalized Consciousness

The conventional view of Captain Ahab is framed by his initial appearance on the deck of the Pequod. Glimpsing the captain for the first time, Ishmael is struck by the "infinity of firmest fortitude, a determinate, unsurrenderable wilfulness, in the fixed and fearless, forward dedication of [his] glance."[1] But Ahab is more accurately characterized by his erratic, impulsive, inconsistent behavior—a condition from which both his fixation on reified identities and his monomaniacal obsession with Moby Dick derive. His descent into madness brings with it a terrifying volatility, as Ishmael describes in the chapter "Moby Dick":

> [A]t intervals during the passage, he was a raving lunatic; and, though un-limbed of a leg, yet such a vital strength yet lurked in his Egyptian chest, and was moreover intensified by his delirium, that his mates were forced to lace him fast, even there, as he sailed, raving in his hammock. In a strait-jacket, he swung to the mad rockings of the gales. And, when running into more suffer-able latitudes, the ship, with mild stun'sails spread, floated across the tranquil tropics, and, to all appearances, the old man's delirium seemed left behind him with the Cape Horn swells, and he came forth from his dark den into the blessed light and air; even then, when he bore that firm, collected front, how-ever pale, and issued his calm orders once again; and his mates thanked God the direful madness was now gone; even then, Ahab, in his hidden self, raved on.[2]

Ahab is shattered into fragments—his "narrow-flowing monomania," his "broad madness," and his "great natural intellect"—the latter two forced into service as "instruments" of the first.[3] This is a grotesque variation on the Buddhist idea of the five aggregates (or *skandhas*), from which each of us derives our own sense of self: form, feeling, perception, volitional forma-tions, and consciousness.[4] While most minds naturally create a neat synthesis

125

of these elements, Ahab is unable to integrate the unraveling threads within him—Ishmael recalls that looking into Ahab's face, it seemed that "two different things were warring."[5] This rupture is expressed most memorably in "The Chart," as Ahab bursts forth from his room onto the deck in the dead of night:

> [A] chasm seemed opening in him. . . . For, at such times, crazy Ahab, the scheming, unappeasedly steadfast hunter of the White Whale; this Ahab that had gone to his hammock, was not the agent that so caused him to burst from it in horror again. The latter was the eternal, living principle or soul in him; and in sleep, being for the time dissociated from the characterizing mind, which at other times employed it for its outer vehicle or agent, it spontaneously sought escape from the scorching contiguity of the frantic thing, of which, for the time, it was no longer an integral. But as the mind does not exist unless leagued with the soul, therefore it must have been that, in Ahab's case, yielding up all his thoughts and fancies to his one supreme purpose; that purpose, by its own sheer inveteracy of will, forced itself against gods and devils into a kind of self-assumed, independent being of its own.[6]

The overarching consequence of this teetering psychological house of cards is an inescapable feeling that something is being hidden from him: "O nature, and O soul of man! how far beyond all utterance are your linked analogies! not the smallest atom stirs or lives in matter, but has its cunning duplicate in mind."[7] If only Ahab could unite the fragments of his consciousness, he would once again be able to grasp the complete picture of his self and the selfhood of all other things. His inability to do so gives rise to a spectral paranoia—for example in his spontaneous challenge to the carpenter, "How dost thou know that some entire, living, thinking thing may not be invisibly and uninterpenetratingly standing precisely where thou now standest; aye, and standing there in thy spite?"[8]

The manifold aspects of Ahab's suffering derive from this inability to locate the things hidden from him—most importantly his sense of self, an omniscient God, and a white whale called Moby Dick. This is predicted in Pierre Bayle's depiction of Buddhist doctrine—that when a man finds himself unable to attain "the supreme majesty of the first principle," he is "tormented with perpetual disquiet," and "passes from one hell to another, and finds rest no where."[9] Indeed, Ishmael writes of the Pequod's tortured captain, "In a strait-jacket, he swung to the mad rockings of the gales."[10]

But it is not only "the first principle" that eludes Captain Ahab, for he is equally unsuccessful in his attempts to define mundane objects. He describes them as "slippery"—telling the carpenter, "I like to feel something in this slippery world that can hold, man"[11]—and Melville returns repeatedly to Ahab's means of keeping things from slipping away from him. In the chapter "The Chart," he sits at a "screwed-down table" in his cabin, studying tides and currents with "reasonable surmises, almost approaching to certainties."[12] When Starbuck descends to meet him, he is "sitting straight in his floor-screwed chair," holding a lantern in his "tightly clenched hand."[13] He has a "pivot-hole" drilled into the very planks of the quarter-deck, to affix himself to the ship and his furious pursuit.[14] In the chapter "The Spirit-Spout," we find Ahab "with his ivory leg inserted into its accustomed hole, and with one hand firmly grasping a shroud . . . for hours and hours [standing] dead to windward, while an occasional squall of sleet or snow would all but congeal his very eyelashes together."[15] Even during a typhoon, he gives advice to "[s]trike nothing, and stir nothing, but lash everything."[16]

Flailing outward from a factionalized consciousness, he attributes his inability to construct a complete picture of phenomena not to their lacking such an identity, but rather to those identities being maliciously hidden from him. He theorizes that "[a]ll visible objects, man, are but as pasteboard masks . . . some unknown but still reasoning thing puts forth the mouldings of its features from behind the unreasoning mask."[17] This thought puts him in direct conflict with the Divine Being he feels is responsible for this cruel obstruction (and, by extension, the supposed agent of His cruelty, Moby Dick), to whom he puts these questions, receiving only silence in response.

The glimpses we receive of the remnants of Ahab's sanity—his "intellect"—reveal a feeble despondency with regard to his present situation, betraying his feeling of being controlled by an external madness: "They think me mad," he cries, "but I'm demoniac, I am madness maddened!"[18] He admits the limits of his knowledge, and despairs that he must rely on tools like the quadrant in searching for "the objects on the unknown, thither side."[19] But most importantly, at times he even seems unable to understand why he is searching for those things—Stubb overhears Ahab mutter, "Here some one thrusts these cards into these old hands of mine; swears that I must play them, and no others."[20] In his final soliloquy, Ahab cries:

> "What is it, what nameless, inscrutable, unearthly thing is it; what cozening, hidden lord and master, and cruel, remorseless emperor commands me; that against all natural loving and longings, I so keep pushing, and crowding, and jamming myself on all the things; recklessly making me ready to do what in my own proper, natural heart, I durst not so much as dare?"[21]

From his limited perspective, trapped between blinders, he knows not whether this "hidden lord and master" is God or the other parts of his fractured self. Appropriately, most of the time—that is, when Ahab is consumed by monomania—he considers there to be very little difference between the two.

In a letter Melville wrote to Hawthorne while writing *Moby-Dick*, we find the emerging spark of Ahab's proclamation of war against the heavens:

[T]he man who, like Russia or the British Empire, declares himself a sovereign
nature (in himself) amid the powers of heaven, hell and earth. He may perish;
but so long as he exists he insists upon treating with all Power upon an equal
basis. If any of those other Powers choose to withhold certain secrets, let them;
that does not impair my sovereignty in myself; that does not make me tribu-
tary. And perhaps, after all, there is *no* secret. We incline to think that the
Problem of the Universe is like the Freemason's mighty secret, so terrible to
children. . . . We incline to think that God cannot explain His own secrets, and
that He would like a little information upon certain points Himself. We mortals
astonish Him as much as He us. [22]

The Captain's questions begin to arise after he loses his leg, when "by this
collision forced to turn toward home, and for long months of days and weeks,
Ahab and anguish lay stretched together in one hammock."[23] He can say
with confidence that he has received an injury from some omnipotent foe.
But is this foe God Himself or merely acting on God's behalf? If the blow
was intended as a punishment, then why the crushing silence that has followed? If it is a test, or some sort of divine quest—"He tasks me; he heaps
me"—what is the efficacy of such an ordeal? Why should he have to take
revenge on a whale? What sort of spiteful God would set him such a task?
Why would He not simply reveal Himself to His subject? What benefit is
there in keeping Himself unknown? These are the "secrets" Melville writes
about to Hawthorne, as he and Ahab become "inclined to think that God
cannot explain His own secrets." When his pleas (and, later, his insults) are
met with nothing but intolerable silence, he begins to wonder if perhaps God
is silent and invisible because He does not exist—that "perhaps, after all,
there is *no* secret," that perhaps there is no God at all. "Sometimes I think
there's naught beyond," Ahab admits. [24]

     This idea, of what we might call an "impotent omnipotent," in turn gives
rise to Ahab's "final monomania,"[25] in which he "insists on treating with all
Power upon an equal basis." In his madness, and in protest against the silence
and apparent disregard of an unknowable God, Ahab "declares himself a
sovereign nature," impervious to any external forces or control, "Immortal on
land and on sea":[26] "But even with a broken bone, old Ahab is untouched. . . .
Nor white whale, nor man, nor fiend, can so much as graze old Ahab in his
own proper and inaccessible being. . . . 'Tis Ahab—his body's part; but
Ahab's soul's a centipede, that moves upon a hundred legs."[27] It is a direct
response to the loss of his leg—a reaction against the universe having rushed
in and violated what Ahab thought were inviolable boundaries, both physical
and metaphysical. While, for example, in "The Castaway," Pip turns a threat
to his personal safety into an experience of the selflessness of all phenomena,
in which his "ringed horizon" expands to include the entire universe, Ahab
emerges from his experience with a self-protective "inveteracy,"[28] drawing
newly defined fixed battle lines between what he believes is under his control

(himself, his ship), and that which he labels "Other." He constructs newly inviolable fortifications for himself and the things he considers "Ahab's," and reaffirms his deluded belief in the existence of independently existing things. Arising from this self-deification is the conviction that he is controlled by nothing but his own will: "What I've dared, I've willed, and what I've willed, I'll do!"[29] But the consequence of this belief is the inescapable feeling of separation that plagues Ahab—permeating the conflicting aspects of his mind, and reinforcing his paranoia that things are being kept hidden from him.

The doomed chase of the White Whale is one with Ahab's furious quest for the answers to these ontological questions, and his violent hatred of the whale the manifestation of his feelings of separation from the God he feels has (first) attacked and (then) abandoned him. But, again, it is Ahab himself who has made himself separate from God—first, through his insistent belief in himself as an independently existing thing, and then by conceiving of such a thing as "God" that exists as a discrete entity outside of himself. Melville tackles this premise directly in another section of the letter to Hawthorne quoted above: "But it is the *Being* of the matter; there lies the knot with which we choke ourselves. As soon as you say *Me*, a *God*, a *Nature*, so soon you jump off from your stool and hang from the beam. Yes, that word is your hangman. Take God out of the dictionary, and you would have Him in the street."[30] Melville takes issue with any religious doctrine that attempts to turn God into a Thing. Bringing God "into the street," he suggests, can be compared to developing an understanding of dependent co-arising—that everything in the universe comes together to create everything in the universe, and that one's actions affect everything and everyone around us. But for Ahab, God is very much a separate Thing—residing, as Ishmael suggests, in "the now egotistical sky."[31] In fact, it may be said that Ahab believes there are but three things in the universe: God, Captain Ahab, and everything else. The thing called "God" includes Moby Dick, the sun, fire, and (sometimes, in saner moments) the Fates; what he considers as "Ahab" includes the Pequod, the engravings on the doubloon, and (other times, in monomaniacal moments) the Fates. He tells his first and second mates, "Ye too are all mankind; and Ahab stands alone among the millions of the peopled earth, nor gods nor men his neighbors!"[32]

But Ahab still notes "an inequality in the deeper analysis" of the cosmic mechanism.[33] While "all earthly felicities"—which we might take to mean "good fortune," or "gratitude for events"—have "a certain unsignifying pettiness" in them, "at bottom, all heart-woes [have] a mystic significance."[34] In other words, Ahab feels suffering to be more "real" than joy—and, going deeper, that the root of the human condition is suffering. Why would this be the case? He continues:

> To trail the genealogies of these high mortal miseries, carries us at last among
> the sourceless primogenitures of the gods; so that, in the face of all the glad,
> hay-making suns, and soft-cymballing, round harvest-moons, we must needs
> give in to this: that the gods themselves are not for ever glad. The ineffaceable,
> sad birth-mark in the brow of man, is but the stamp of sorrow in the signers.[35]

He decides, characteristically, that God is responsible for his suffering. Follow his difficulties to their first cause, he finds the Cause Itself is sad. But
Ahab leaves the thought there for the time being (not surprisingly, since it
happily reinforces his ultimate concern), and with "the unseen, ambiguous
synod in the air, [having] to do or not with earthly Ahab, yet, in this present
matter of his leg, he took plain practical procedures;   he called the carpenter."[36]

    In conversation with the carpenter Ahab continues along this line of
thought, cursing "that mortal inter-indebtedness which will not do away with
ledgers."[37] But it is not "inter-indebtedness" that bothers him; it is "indebted-
ness." He recoils at the idea that any event in the past should have any
consequence on what is happening now, that he could be held accountable
for his (let alone anyone else's) actions in the past: "I would be as free as air;
and I'm down in the whole world's books."[38] This paranoid fixation on
"ledgers," on some Being in the Sky keeping score with Its Celestial Clip-
board, is yet another example of his feeling of separation. Ahab's feeling of
separateness is the fundamental source of all his suffering—something Suzuki Roshi beautifully depicts using the image of a waterfall:

> I went to Yosemite National Park, and I saw some huge waterfalls. The highest
> one there is 1,340 feet high, and from it the water comes down like a curtain
> thrown from the top of the mountain. It does not seem to come down swiftly,
> as you might expect; it seems to come down very slowly because of the
> distance. And the water does not come down as one stream, but is separated
> into many tiny streams. From a distance it looks like a curtain. And I thought it
> must be a very difficult experience for each drop of water to come down from
> the top of such a high mountain. It takes time, you know, a long time, for the
> water finally to reach the bottom of the waterfall. And it seems to me that our
> human life may be like this. We have many difficult experiences in our life.
> But at the same time, I thought, the water was not originally separated, but was
> one whole river. Only when it is separated does it have some difficulty in
> falling. It is as if the water does not have any feeling when it is one whole
> river. Only when separated into many drops can it begin to have or to express
> some feeling.[39]

The ultimate truth—the "one whole river"—is, as Ishmael might say, "far
beyond all visible horizons," where "mild uncontinented seas, interflow with
the blue heavens."[40] It is the place where all things "interpenetrate, and form
one seamless whole."[41] Suzuki Roshi continues:

Before we were born we had no feeling; we were one with the universe. . . .
After we are separated by birth from this oneness, as the water falling from the
waterfall is separated by the wind and rocks, then we have feeling. You have
difficulty because you have feeling. You attach to the feeling you have without
knowing just how this kind of feeling is created. [42]

This passage calls to mind Ahab's self-identification as an orphan, abandoned by an indifferent Universe (even as he himself rejects the "step-mother
world"[43]), left to wander the earth alone: "Where lies the final harbor,
whence we unmoor no more? In what rapt ether sails the world, of which the
weariest will never weary? Where is the foundling's father hidden? Our souls
are like those orphans whose unwedded mothers die in bearing them: the
secret of our paternity lies in their grave, and we must there to learn it."[44]

But, again, Ahab has the mistaken view that God is a "thing" that exists in
the universe—that is, in the same way that he believes Moby Dick exists in
the ocean. This is why, for all his fixation, Ahab never has a very clear
picture of whether he considers Moby Dick to be God's spokesperson or God
Himself. There are the only two possibilities he can conceive—that the whale
is either the principle (aka the first cause, aka God) itself, or is acting under
the agency of that principle—and he never advances beyond that. But the
reason he is unable to delineate between them is because they are both
fallacies, in that they imply independent existence. In reality, things are not
things so much as they are processes, or *patterns of relationship*. Things
emerge from a matrix of conditions, and in turn become part of the matrix of
conditions as other things arise.[45] Nevertheless, requiring a tangible, discernible foe to battle against, he takes Moby Dick as a surrogate:

Ahab . . . at last came to identify with him, not only all his bodily woes, but all
his intellectual and spiritual exasperations. The White Whale swam before him
as the monomaniac incarnation of all those malicious agencies which some
deep men feel eating in them, till they are left living on with half a heart and
half a lung. . . . [D]eliriously transferring its idea to the abhorred White Whale,
he pitted himself, all mutilated, against it. All that most maddens and torments;
all that stirs up the lees of things; all truth with malice in it; all that cracks the
sinews and cakes the brain; all the subtle demonisms of life and thought; all
evil, to crazy Ahab, were visibly personified, and made practically assailable
in Moby Dick. He piled upon the whale's white hump the sum of all the
general rage and hate felt by his whole race from Adam down; and then, as if
his chest had been a mortar, he burst his hot heart's shell upon it. [46]

And just as Ahab's surrogate (the Pequod) and God's surrogate (Moby
Dick) are participating in an intimate dance across the ocean, one can detect a
continuous call-and-response between Ahab and God that permeates the novel. If so, this would suggest that God is indeed responding to Ahab each and
every moment—Ahab has simply made himself blind to the response, as it

has not arrived in precisely the manner that Ahab expects and demands: "If the gods think to speak outright to man," he says, "they will honorably speak outright; not shake their heads, and give an old wives' darkling hint."[47]

Ishmael refers to the ocean as "all-contributed and all-receptive,"[48] a phrase which bears a remarkable similarity to Dogen Zenji's term "Self-Receiving and Self-Employing Awareness." In the "Jijyu Zanmai" section of *Bendowa*, he writes about the benefits of virtuous activity—that all of one's actions extend outward to affect the entire universe, and the universe "resonates back to you and helps you inconceivably."[49] Thus our actions of body, speech and mind can be said to operate much as Newton's Third Law of Motion: the energy we put out into the world, this is precisely what we get back. In Ahab's case, a vicious circle is created: he feels separate from God, and lashes out against Him, trying to push Him further away. This energy reverberates in a number of different ways. In the most immediate sense, it reinforces the feelings of separation in Ahab's own mind, and imprints those habitual tendencies even more deeply. Secondly, just as like poles of a magnet push each other away, this energy causes the universe to push Ahab away as well—manifested, first and foremost, in the White Whale remaining unattainably distant. Finally (and this is the tricky one), since Ahab and God after all are not two different things that influence each other but rather two aspects of the same Stuff that makes up the entire universe, God acts from within Ahab, and Ahab acts from within God. Dogen admits that this truth is difficult to realize ("All this however does not appear within perception"[50]), for our habitually self-centered thinking constantly reinforces our feeling of separation. The following image may be helpful in illustrating this idea: imagine a large oval, with a hundred small circles inside it. The oval is the universe; the circles are all the infinite number of things in the universe. One of those circles is Ahab. And within that circle called "Ahab" are a hundred smaller circles: Ahab's heart, Ahab's will, a fleeting thought in Ahab's mind. Thus while Ahab does indeed have "will"—he is capable of volitional action—it is not what we could call "free will," for it is interpenetrated by all the other circles within the circle called "Ahab." So when Ahab asks, "Is it I, God, or who, that lifts this arm?"[51] the most accurate answer would be "both," or simply "yes."

Additionally, of course, the circle called Ahab is inconceivably interdependent on all the other circles inside the oval called the Universe.[52] Thus Ahab's actions resonate through the *things* around him,[53] and the Universe's responses are manifested through those very same things. Dogen writes: "Grass, trees, and lands which are embraced by this teaching together radiate a great light and endlessly expound the inconceivable profound dharma. Grass, trees, and walls bring forth the teaching for all beings, common people as well as sages, and they in accord extend this dharma for the sake of grass, trees, and walls."[54] As Ahab builds the wall around himself (reinforced by the long hours he spends in his cabin below deck), he is abandoned by things whose bonds he has not before considered. That is, in the White Whale's absence, these reverberations return to him through secondary channels—particularly the enigmatic omens that interject themselves into Ahab's quest. Instead of Dogen's "grass, trees, and walls," one might say, Melville's universe responds, as we are about to see, with bird, fish, and harpoons.

These are the "darkling hints" that Ahab dismisses.[55] When the Pequod meets the Goney, Ahab watches as the "small harmless fish" that had been happily swimming alongside the Pequod suddenly—and "with what seemed like shuddering fins"[56]—forsake the Pequod in favor of the other ship. Ishmael describes the seas as "wearily, lonesomely mild," as if "all space, in repugnance to our vengeful errand, seemed vacating itself of life before our urn-like prow,"[57] at which point he notes in Ahab "more of a deep helpless sadness than the insane old man had ever before evinced."[58] A "red-billed savage sea-hawk" swoops in and inexplicably steals Ahab's hat, flies dead-straight to the horizon and then, just at the edge of sight, drops it into the ocean, as if delivering the hat to Moby Dick.[59]

In a similar way, the nine meetings with other whaleships (or "gams"[60]) scattered through the text are emblematic of the mutually reinforcing character of Ahab's separation. Ishmael explains it is "natural that . . . two whaling vessels descrying each other at the ends of the earth" would relish the opportunity to spend time together, especially since on either ship "not a few of the men are personally known to each other."[61] But given that the act of "gamming" represents the "common pursuit and mutually shared provisions and perils" between all whalemen, we cannot be surprised that Captain Ahab refuses to participate, lest he have to admit such an interwoven bond exists between his own "grand, ungodly, god-like"[62] man and some lowly sailor. So each time the Pequod comes across a passing ship, Ahab asks its captain, "Hast seen the White Whale?"[63] And as befitting selfish Ahab, who "cared not to consort, even for five minutes, with any stranger captain, except he could contribute some of that information he so absorbingly sought,"[64] each time he asks this question, again and again, the universe steps forward with some obstruction that prohibits communication.

For example, when meeting the Goney: "As the strange captain, leaning over the pallid bulwarks, was in the act of putting his trumpet to his mouth, it somehow fell from his hand into the sea; and the wind now rising amain, he in vain strove to make himself heard without it."[65] The Town-Ho has news of Moby Dick, but the story is "the private property of three confederate white seamen of that ship" who "communicated it to Tashtego with Romish injunctions of secrecy,"[66] who in turn the following night "rambled in his sleep" and thus is forced by his shipmates to tell the rest of what he knows. But (as Ishmael is careful to convey) the few who hear the story "kept the secret among themselves so that it never transpired abaft the Pequod's main-mast,"[67] and it never reaches Ahab. The Jeroboam "had a malignant epidemic on board . . . and was fearful of infecting the Pequod's company,"[68] but through the howling wind manages to tell Ahab of Macey, their first-mate, who insisted on chasing Moby Dick and was killed. Finding a letter on board that belongs to the dead first-mate, Ahab tries to pass it off to Macey's former captain, but "as if by magic," it reaches the hand of the mad prophet Gabriel, who throws it back at Ahab's feet, jeering "thou art soon going that way."[69] The Jungfrau (Virgin) admits to being entirely ignorant of any White Whale, and so Ahab disappears without another word, leaving his subordinates to deal with their empty oilcan. With the Rose-bud, not only have they not heard of Moby Dick, they do not even speak English, and Ahab again wordlessly retires to his solitary cabin.

When the Samuel Enderby appears on the horizon, and its captain holds up "a white arm of sperm whale bone,"[70] it seems that Ahab might finally have found a friend. But attempting to step off the boat, Ahab finds himself no longer capable of making this sort of connection—symbolized by his struggle to hoist his mutilated frame onto the other boat, "hopelessly eyeing the uncertain changeful height he could hardly hope to attain."[71] Once he learns Captain Boomer is no longer interested in chasing the whale (having learned his lesson the first time), Ahab cuts him off as well.

And so it goes: the Bachelor is "too damned jolly"[72]; "the dejected Delight" is not jolly enough.[73] All this to emphasize just how Ahab—Ahab who feels he has been so mistreated by God, and abandoned by Him—actively separates himself, and then is somehow still surprised when the world responds in kind. But in meeting the Rachel, Ahab seems finally to realize just how isolated he has become. He listens to Captain Gardiner's devastated wailing, standing "like an anvil, receiving every shock, but without the least quivering of his own."[74] Ahab seems to momentarily wonder why he is not affected by this outpouring of grief in the same way everyone around him seems to be. "I must go," he says, again suggesting he has no say in his decision—the ship will "sail as before," as if nothing has happened.[75]

Chapter Nineteen

Savagery Beyond Savagery

When Captain Ahab first speaks of his secret purpose, and the quest for the White Whale, with the crew gathered round him on the quarter-deck, the three "savage" harpooneers look on "with even more intense interest and surprise than the rest, and at the mention of the wrinkled brow and crooked jaw they had started as if each was separately touched by some specific recollection."[1] In quick succession, Queequeg, Tashtego, and Daggoo each describe a peculiarity of Moby Dick's appearance, assuring Ahab they know the White Whale well. The three mates, on the other hand, though surely they have just as much whaling experience as the three harpooneers, stand rather bewildered, until Starbuck admits he has "heard of Moby Dick," but only as the whale that took Ahab's leg. Later, when Ahab proclaims his power over the heavens by replacing the compromised compass, most of the crew looks on, but only "the pagan harpooneers remained almost wholly unimpressed."[2]

These episodes are emblematic of a theme running through the text—that "savages" are somehow inherently more capable of seeing into Truth than their "civilized" counterparts. Surely it is no coincidence that the harpooneers—hailing from three wildly different regions of the globe but reductively degraded by the term "savage"[3]—are the only men capable of making contact with the sperm whale. They are also solely responsible for feeding the whale blubber into the try-works,[4] and thus rendering the oil that "illuminate[s] the solemn churches" in the white men's hometowns.[5] Captain Peleg indirectly acknowledges their unique abilities, while preventing his partner Bildad from attempting to baptize Queequeg; he avows, "Pious harpooneers never make good voyagers."[6] And while we do not know what changes are wrought in Tashtego upon falling into the great well of the sperm whale's severed head, that Daggoo and Queequeg are the only men who step up to save him suggests that they are the only ones capable of interceding with the "sanctum sanctorum."[7]

Ishmael's transcendent experience with the whale skeleton, which gives him "exact knowledge of the bones of the leviathan,"[8] conspicuously occurs on "one of the Arsacides," a tropical island belonging to his "dear friend Tranquo, king of Tranque" (both names suggesting "tranquillity").[9] But the island priests don't take too kindly to Ishmael's measuring the skeleton, shouting, "Dar'st thou measure this our god! That's for us."[10] Clearly no *civilized* man should be measuring their whale skeleton—but it goes without saying they would not dare measure it themselves.

The fact that the ship—which to Ishmael is a vehicle that brings one close to Truth—is itself named after a Native American tribe, is indicative of this same exaltation of "savageness": "Pequod, you will no doubt remember, was the name of a celebrated tribe of Massachusetts Indians, now extinct as the ancient Medes."[11] Indeed, the tribe's elimination by "civilized" European settlers ties in with Queequeg's having been corrupted by his contact with "Christianity, or rather Christians, [which] had unfitted him for ascending the pure and undefiled throne of thirty pagan kings before him. But by and by, he said, he would return,—as soon as he felt himself baptized again."[12]

The answer may once again lie in the "egotistical sky,"[13] and Melville's exhortation to "take God out of the dictionary."[14] The "savage" has not turned God into a "thing" (as Ishmael argues Christianity has). They are not burdened by philosophy and the scientific method. And thus they can approach the whale, and the locus of spiritual truth, while allowing it to remain shrouded in mystery. Indeed, Ishmael describes "savages" as being both difficult to perceive and endowed with a silent wisdom, just like the whale: "But Savages are strange beings; at times you do not know exactly how to take them. At first they are overawing; their calm self-collectedness of simplicity seems a Socratic wisdom."[15] So while Ahab's furious pursuit of Moby Dick only pushes the whale farther away, the harpooneers are able to easily spear their prey when the opportunity arises.

Queequeg, of course, is the primary example of this "theological savagery," finding no contradiction in hearing a Christian sermon and giving offerings to his Yojo in the same day, allowing both faiths to coexist. After lecturing him on the dangers of religious zealotry, Ishmael admits:

> I do not think that my remarks about religion made much impression upon Queequeg. Because, in the first place, he somehow seemed dull of hearing on that important subject, unless considered from his own point of view . . . and, finally, he no doubt thought he knew a good deal more about the true religion than I did. He looked at me with a sort of condescending concern and compassion, as though he thought it a great pity that such a sensible young man should be so hopelessly lost to evangelical pagan piety.[16]

But Ishmael describes his own path to the true religion largely as aligning himself with this idea of "savagery": "Long exile from Christendom and civilization inevitably restores a man to that condition in which God placed him, i.e., what is called savagery. Your true whale-hunter is as much a savage as an Iroquois. I myself am a savage; owning no allegiance but to the King of the Cannibals; and ready at any moment to rebel against him."[17] It is this final phrase—"ready at any moment to rebel against him"—that actually puts him "beyond savagery," in much the same way that Zen is said to be beyond religion, beyond Buddhism, beyond Zen itself. R.H. Blyth writes: "Zen is the essence of Christianity, of Buddhism, of culture, of all that is good in the daily life of ordinary people. But that does not mean that we are not to smash it flat if we get the slightest opportunity. . . . Zen is the very transcending of Zen."[18] Ishmael's "savagery beyond savagery," beyond conventional models of faith and doubt, is precisely the Zen spirit. And this at least partly explains why he alone survives the sinking of the Pequod.

Chapter Twenty

Faith and the Three Mates

In the chapter "The Chapel," contemplating the memorial plaques laid in honor of whalemen killed on the open ocean, Ishmael addresses the conflicted relationship between faith and doubt. His meditation is inescapably land-based—images of "green grass," "flowers," and "caves" align with the "grief," "desolation," "despair" of the funereal mourners,[1] emphasizing the inescapable nature of their suffering. Without a body to physically lay to rest, the dead whalers' loved ones are denied the closure they desperately seek: "What deadly voids and unbidden infidelities in the lines that seem to gnaw upon all Faith, and refuse resurrections to the beings who have placelessly perished without a grave."[2] Land-based life is once again contrasted against the freedom and "placelessness" of the sea—where even grief cannot abide, for it "permits no records."[3] While the mourners' sorrow is tightly bound to "immovable inscriptions" and "black-bordered marbles,"[4] offering no hope of relief, Ishmael—ever the "Catskill eagle"[5]—plunges into the oceanic depths to share in their suffering and then swoops high again, noting, "Yes, Ishmael, the same fate may be thine. But somehow I grew merry again."[6]

The mourners' ostensible faith falls prey to doubt, as their attachment to the physical form of a body and the cultural form of a coffin "refuse resurrections"[7]—that is, actually prevent the whalers' spirits from ascending to heaven. This narrow idea of faith—faith attached to traditions and conditions—is symptomatic of the general feeling of incongruity, in the way their faith seems to inevitably shade off into doubt. Ishmael asks, "[H]ow is it that we still refuse to be comforted for those who we nevertheless maintain are dwelling in unspeakable bliss."[8] But even within the bleakest gloom, arising from the most ignoble origins, Ishmael once again takes comfort in the possibility (however gruesome) of renewal and rebirth: "But Faith, like a jackal, feeds among the tombs, and even from these dead doubts she gathers her most vital hope."[9] To better understand this seeming paradox, we can look at it through three qualities considered "the three essentials of Zen practice," first expounded by thirteenth-century Chinese Zen master Kao-feng Yüan-Miao, and later popularized by Japanese Zen master Hakuin Eka-ku Zenji: great faith (*daishinkon*), great doubt (*daigidan*), and great determi-nation (*daifunshi*).

In our usual understanding of faith and doubt, we regard them as anto-nyms, inversely proportional to each other: doubts about beliefs lead to a loss of faith; dispelling doubts, faith grows stronger. But the Zen idea of "great faith" does not necessarily entail doctrinal belief, but rather belief in the possibility of overcoming adversity and unwholesome mental states (Japa-nese: *bonno*). As for doubt, the Japanese term for "great doubt," *daigidan*, does not have the connotation of perplexity that the English word "doubt" has, but is rather a state of "probing inquiry, of intense self-questioning."[10] It is the sense that things are not what they seem—which again points toward the possibility of liberation. Great doubt exists both in spite of great faith, and as a direct result of great faith. Zen teacher Victor Sogen Hori writes: "Ordinarily, faith and doubt are related to one another in inverse proportion: where faith is strong, doubt is weak; and vice versa. But in Zen practice, the greater the doubt, the greater the faith. Great Faith and Great Doubt are two aspects of the same mind of awakening (*bodaishin*)."[11]

Ishmael describes his own faith as being *supported by* doubt—in particu-lar the "bitter blanks" and "deadly voids" that send the mourners to despair,[12] but that reinforce his own estimation that they "symbolize something un-seen."[13] He reiterates this view in "The Whiteness of the Whale," writing that while this "visible world seems formed in love" (or faith), "the invisible spheres were formed in fright" (or doubt).

The drive to reconcile these two seemingly disparate sides of ourselves gives rise to Hakuin Zenji's third essential of practice, *great determination*—determination to rid ourselves of our self-centered tendencies, and realize the truth of the interconnectedness of all phenomena. Ishmael's attitude toward the whale—of seeking without grasping, of asking questions without de-manding answers—is a fitting example of great determination. He tackles his metaphysical inquiries with incredible levity, vowing, "I try all things; I achieve what I can."[14] He is well aware that he might not succeed, and feels no anxiety about the possibility: "Can we thus hope to light upon chance clue to conduct us to the hidden cause we seek? Let us try."[15] Ishmael is quite comfortable balancing these aspects of faith and doubt, and, as usual, it is the specter of the sperm whale that gives rise to Ishmael's most eloquent explica-tion of the relationship between the two. Watching a whale swim through tranquil tropical waters, the vapor above its head projecting the image of a rainbow, Ishmael muses on the whale's "incommunicable contemplations," and writes:

And so, through all the thick mists of the dim doubts in my mind, divine intuitions now and then shoot, enkindling my fog with a heavenly ray. And for this I thank God; for all have doubts; many deny; but doubts or denials, few along with them, have intuitions. Doubts of all things earthly, and intuitions of some things heavenly; this combination makes neither believer nor infidel, but makes a man who regards them both with equal eye. [16]

This ability to hold great faith and great doubt equally—"neither to assert in an unqualified way that things exist nor in an unqualified way that things do not exist"[17]—is another way to express the doctrine of the Middle Way.

We might expect Ahab to fulfill his customary role in representing the opposing view, but in this case it is not quite that simple. For Ahab *has no faith*. There are things he believes, things of which he is convinced, but insofar as faith is a belief *not dependent upon proof*, he cannot be said to have faith, and refuses to admit he is even familiar with the term: As he asks the carpenter, "Faith? What's that?"[18] Instead, it is the three mates on the Pequod who represent the contrary models of these three pillars. Rather than "great," we might call them "ordinary": ordinary faith, ordinary doubt, and ordinary determination. These three ideas—respectively employed by Star-buck, Stubb and Flask—are strategies in coping with the mysteries of the universe. Their examples serve as illustrations of the importance of learning to hold all three pillars equally.

Determination is exemplified by Flask, the "pugnacious" third mate, who expresses determination in its most basic sense. Rather than seeking sperm whales as a spiritual activity, he makes his objective nothing less than exter-mination:

[Flask] somehow seemed to think that the great Leviathans had personally and hereditarily affronted him; and therefore it was a sort of point of honor with him, to destroy them whenever encountered. So utterly lost was he to all sense of reverence for the many marvels of their majestic bulk and mysterious ways; and so dead to anything like an apprehension of any possible danger. [19]

His lack of moral bearing and inquisitiveness give rise to an "ignorant, un-conscious fearlessness,"[20] which almost suggests the fixed resolve of Ahab, but without the existential gnawing that drives the captain. No, Flask is driven by a hunger of a different sort, that disallows him the luxury of philosophical inquiry—a gnawing that literally comes from never getting enough to eat: "[E]ver since [Stubb] had arisen to the dignity of an officer, from that moment he had never known what it was to be otherwise than hungry, more or less. For what he ate did not so much relieve his hunger, as keep it immortal in him. Peace and satisfaction, thought Flask, have for ever departed from my stomach."[21] Flask thinks of nothing but attaining goals—

or, more specifically, accruing profit. On the doubloon he sees "nothing here, but a round thing made of gold, and whoever raises a certain whale, this round thing belongs to him."[22] Truly, one cannot expect any more from a man defined by his "pervading mediocrity" than a determination to accumulate wealth.[23]

Unlike great faith and great doubt, which must be held in equal measure, the faith and doubt illustrated by mates Starbuck and Stubb do indeed seem to be, as Ahab suggests, complete opposites: "Ye two are the opposite poles of one thing: Starbuck is Stubb reversed, and Stubb is Starbuck."[24] Starbuck is God-fearing and pious; Ishmael describes Stubb as "unfearing . . . impious."[25] Wrapped in "the invulnerable jollity of indifference and recklessness,"[26] Stubb is "good-humored, easy, and careless."[27] Whereas Starbuck (as we shall see) is haunted by his insights into the great matter of life and death—and works actively to fight them off, lest his faith be shaken—Stubb lives his life wholly indifferent to grand questions: "What he thought of death itself, there is no telling. Whether he ever thought of it at all might be a question."[28] Essentially, Stubb doubts that there be any reason for faith. Both Starbuck's ordinary faith and Stubb's ordinary doubt give rise to a similarly narrow-minded view—the difference being Starbuck has a belief system to fall back on, and Stubb simply refuses to be entangled in such a thing: "Damn me, but all things are queer, come to think of 'em. But that's against my principles. Think not, is my eleventh commandment."[29]

Stubb's lack of existential inquiry—his doubt about faith—fits together with his preoccupation with pleasure. The episode in "Stubb's Supper" in which he eats a whale steak by a whale oil lamp—"[eating] him by his own light, as you might say"—should be a spiritually potent event.[30] But he is completely cut off from the emotions of those around him—decrying the overcooking of the steak, belittling the cook. The cook's sermon to the sharks is surreptitiously directed at Stubb himself, whose voracious appetite for hedonistic pleasures makes him incapable of spiritual advancement: "[He] don't hear one word; no use a-preachin' to such dam g'luttons as you call 'em, till dare bellies is full, and dare bellies is bottomless."[31] So finally, what happens when gaiety is not close at hand? Stubb contends that Ahab "actest right; live in the game, and die in it!"[32] Although he boasts that "I know not all that may be coming, but be it what it will, I'll go to it laughing,"[33] when his end does finally come, it is not with a laugh at all, but with a spiteful grin, and a last wish, "for one red cherry ere we die."[34]

Stubb's epicurean apathy is countered by Starbuck's austere righteousness. There is no shortage of glowing adjectives used to describe Mr. Starbuck. Ishmael calls him "earnest,"[35] "staid, steadfast,"[36] "hardy,"[37] "uncommonly conscientious,"[38] "careful,"[39] "uncommonly prudent,"[40] "respectful and cautious."[41] He is a virtuous man—we hear of his "sobriety,"[42] and "fortitude,"[43] and "deep natural reverence."[44] All of these things stem from his "superstition," which Ishmael describes as "that sort of superstition, which in some organization seems rather to spring, somehow, from intelligence than from ignorance."[45]

Something must be said about this curious thing "ignorance," which can either connote obliviousness, or delusion, or what I refer to above as "willful ignorance," as in purposely "ignoring" something. This ignorance, in my view, is actually at the core of Starbuck's character, and almost indistinguishable from his faith. Zen master Huang Po (d. 850) said, "The foolish reject what they *see*, not what they think; the wise reject what they think, not what they *see*,"[46] scolding those who reject their direct experience when that experience contradicts their beliefs. Huang Po's teacher Baizhang (720-814) said that seeking "nonseeking" is still a form of seeking. This passage from Cleary seems particularly apt in describing Starbuck's thinking: "The ignorant are afraid of insight because they fear that their cherished opinions and beliefs will be threatened, thereby threatening the stability of their worldview and sense of self."[47] Ishmael goes on to say that "brave as [Starbuck] might be, it was that sort of bravery . . . [which] cannot withstand those more terrific, because more spiritual terrors."[48] Starbuck's virtue is based solely in his faith, and cannot exist if that faith is at all shaken. Therefore he spurns all existential inquiry, and even prays for assistance in restraining himself: "Stand by me, *hold* me, *bind* me, O ye blessed influences!" (my italics).[49] Again and again he attempts to isolate himself from the supposed wickedness around him, as in "The Needle": "[W]ith fascinated eyes they awaited whatever magic might follow. But Starbuck looked away."[50] Fittingly (since Starbuck has no interest in seeking Truth), Ahab orders him to stay on board while the rest of the crew does battle with the White Whale: "No, no; stay on board, on board!—lower not when I do; when branded Ahab gives chase to Moby Dick. That hazard shall not be thine. No, no!"[51]

Ishmael even argues that Starbuck's faith is actually a liability for the crew—that they are "morally enfeebled also, by the incompetence of mere unaided virtue or right-mindedness" in Mr. Starbuck.[52] Stubb preaches that "the sea will have its way. Stubb, for one, can't fight it."[53] But in "The Pequod Meets the Virgin," when the carcass of a whale the mates have killed begins to sink, Starbuck so adamantly tries to keep it afloat—"[he] hung on to it to the last; hung on to it so resolutely"[54]—that he almost capsizes the ship. His faith has long been his anchor on the turbulent seas, and he simply cannot understand how his ostensibly omnipotent and infallible truths might be at all shaken by Ahab's will. So he tries to block out the world of the Pequod, and reground himself: "Tell me not of thy teeth-tiered sharks, and thy kidnapping cannibal ways. Let faith oust fact; let fancy oust memory; I look deep down and do believe."[55]

The difference between Starbuck's faith and Ahab's certitude is given sharp contrast in the late chapter "The Deck Toward the End of the First Night Watch." It is the height of the typhoon, and Starbuck approaches the Captain to tell him the "main-top-sail yard" is coming loose in the wind, and must be taken down. Ahab scoffs at this suggestion, and commands that everything instead be lashed tighter. So we see that, when faced with a situation that might waver his "fond faith," Starbuck backs off. But Ahab is so blindly sure of his purpose that he cannot imagine anything shaking it from its course, and so clings ever more tightly.

As it happens, Ahab comes to recognize this difference as well. Early in the voyage, he worries about Starbuck's potential for rebellion. But soon he recognizes that Starbuck's disposition makes him incapable of taking such a stand: "He waxes brave, but nevertheless obeys; most careful bravery that! . . . Thou art but too good a fellow, Starbuck."[56] In this instance he even grants Starbuck's request, being so little worried of a power struggle. It is a gambit that again proves wise in the chapter "The Musket," when Starbuck finally has a chance to kill Ahab—thus saving himself and everyone on board—but (either admirably or pathetically, depending on the reader's perspective) cannot bring himself to do it. Starbuck admits, "I can't withstand thee, then, old man,"[57] and though he wrestles "with an angel"[58]—that is, weighing the response called for by the situation against that which his faith commands—he places the musket back in its rack, and ascends back to the deck.

This "angel-wrestling" sets the two apart even further, for when Starbuck beseeches God for guidance—"Great God, where art thou? Shall I? Shall I?"[59]—he receives naught but silence in return, yet nevertheless acts as he imagines God would prefer. This pointed silence is of course precisely what Ahab finds so intolerable about existence, and he shows empathy during the chase when Starbuck publicly implores the heavens, "Great God! but for one single instant show thyself."[60] While Ahab has long ago moved from such supplication to bellicose threats and taunts, Starbuck remains pious to the watery end—"Is this the end of all my bursting prayers? all my life-long fidelities? Oh, Ahab, Ahab, lo, thy work."[61] He never begrudges God for His silence, but meekly lays the blame at his own feet, for having allowed himself to be caught up in Ahab's vengeful errand.

Chapter Twenty-One

The Doubloon

Melville's clearest statement on the range of experience and belief among the Pequod's crew is the short chapter "The Doubloon." Just as each sailor's ideas about God and the universe are expressed in his thoughts on the White Whale, so too are these ideas expressed in each man's unique interpretation of the gold coin nailed to the main-mast. As Ahab says, standing before the doubloon, "this round gold is but the image of the rounder globe, which, like a magician's glass, to each and every man in turn but mirrors back his own mysterious self."[1] Direct perception might give each whaleman roughly the same information ("there is a gold coin")—and for most of us, that perception is ineluctably followed by discursive cognition ("the coin is x," "the meaning of the coin is y," etc.). So just as each sailor's temperament and beliefs dictate his ideas about the whale, so too do they affect his cognition of the doubloon. All perception is filtered through the patterns and tendencies of our minds, and then we project back onto the world our ideas of things based on what is happening in our minds. Bodhidharma said, "Everything good and bad comes from your own mind. To find something beyond the mind is impossible."[2] Ishmael concurs: "It all depends on what mood you are in; if in the Dantean, the devils will occur to you; if in that of Isaiah, the archangels."[3] As if to illustrate this subjectivity as strikingly as possible, most of this scene with the doubloon is not even narrated directly by Ishmael. It is the second mate Stubb, rather, who stands reporting as the whalemen approach the doubloon one by one (in hierarchical order)—and whose monologue (we can only assume) is overheard somewhere by Ishmael, and in turn relayed to us.

The only people whose considerations of the doubloon come to us directly—that is, without the additional filter—are the second mate's two superiors on the ship. With monomaniacal Ahab, this makes perfect sense—certainly as formidable a self as his cannot be analyzed by the simple second mate. As we might expect, the captain is unable to see anything in the coin that does not refer directly to himself. He declares the coin to be "egotistical,"[4] and sees only himself reflected back: "The firm tower, that is Ahab; the volcano, that is Ahab; the courageous, the undaunted, and victorious fowl, that, too, is Ahab; all are Ahab."[5] The grandiose adjectives he uses—"firm, courageous, undaunted, victorious"[6]—reinforce this sense of self-aggrandizing hauteur, especially considering the coin's status as the talisman of his supposedly heroic chase.

We then watch Starbuck approach the coin and state matter-of-factly, "I have never marked the coin inspectingly"[7]—typifying his lack of interest in the mysteries of the universe, his lack of Way-seeking mind. Now examining the coin for the first time, he faithfully considers it from a Christian perspective. The mountains are "mighty, heaven-abiding peaks," while the valley is "faint" and "earthly."[8] He praises the "sun of Righteousness" that "shines a beacon and a hope," and proposes that "God girds us" only if we lift our eyes to heaven, in which case "the bright sun meets our glance half way."[9] But at that moment, something unexpected overtakes him, as he cries, "Yet, oh, the great sun is no fixture; and if, at midnight, we would fain snatch some sweet solace from him, we gaze for him in vain!"[10] A moment ago, the sun (which he has all but equated with God) could shine "over all our gloom," but now having seen the "dark valley" on the coin, he views the Pequod as cloaked in darkness (i.e., "at midnight").[11] Being that he is now bound up in Ahab's quest, however Starbuck may beseech for the Almighty's guidance, He will not hear the whaleman's cry. Starbuck's final thought matches his first: "This coin speaks wisely, mildly, truly, but still sadly to me. I will quit it, lest Truth shake me falsely."[12] He has glimpsed Truth, and has no doubt of the veracity of his thoughts. But though they may be wise, mild and true, they make him sad—and thus he will shake them off, lest they shake his beliefs. He chooses blind faith over seeing Truth.

Stubb demonstrates his own surprisingly astute awareness of the subjectivity of meaning in his journalistic endeavor. When Stubb looks at the coin himself, he conspicuously avoids claims of finding any one definitive meaning to the coin, but announces simply, "I'll try my hand at raising a meaning."[13] And his interpretation is indeed idiosyncratically Stubb-ian—a vision of the Zodiac in which the sun shines "jollily" despite its "toil and trouble."[14] But he shows little interest even in his own interpretation ("I'd not look at it [the doubloon] very long ere spending it"[15]), and he does not exert himself deciphering his shipmates' thoughts.[16] Instead, we find him deciphering the men themselves, reading into them even as they stand reading the coin: "There's another rendering now; but still one text. All sorts of men in one kind of world, you see."[17]

But it is Pip (fittingly the last to arrive) who makes explicit what Ahab and Stubb have each alluded to regarding the subjectivity of interpretation, as he repeats over and over: "I look, you look, he looks; we look, ye look, they look."[18] Pip, as we will soon see, has lost his sense of self, and is no longer able to make any interpretation himself; he can only make what we may call a "meta-interpretation" of the doubloon. Thus, "watching all these interpreters," he seems unable to perceive the doubloon as a static object, but only as it exists in relation to the ship ("Here's the ship's navel") and in the way it affects his shipmates ("they are all on fire to unscrew it").[19] As Pip's own "navel" has been thoroughly unscrewed, his cognition of the "pattern of relationship" between things is self-referential as well—he describes himself as a crow standing at the top of a pine tree, surveying the scene below, searching hopefully (rather counter-intuitively) for the scare-crow.

Notably absent from the scene is Ishmael, who speaks of the doubloon only in retrospect. Perhaps having waited to cultivate the wisdom necessary to understand such things, his description of the coin is almost entirely removed from individual interpretation, as befitting someone who has risen above the fickle subjectivity of cognition. Thomas Cleary writes, "When we realize that the way we are experiencing things is mixed up with our own interpretations of things and our reactions to our own interpretations, we learn to refrain from taking our own representations for ineluctable realities, and thus reduce our susceptibility to compulsion and obsession."[20] As Seng-Ts'an says, "Do not search for the truth; only cease to cherish opinions."[21] Ishmael recognizes that all things "assume different aspects, depending on your point of view,"[22] and thus makes only simple declarative statements about the doubloon, describing it in terms of perception (what it looks like) and conception (it is, in a word, "gold"). While his shipmates make judgments based on the "colored and coloring glasses" that control their perceptions,[23] Ishmael alone can view the doubloon (and everything else around him) with clarity and receptivity.

Chapter Twenty-Two

Pip, Who Jumped from the Whale-Boat

Ishmael's brave consideration of "whiteness" comes after years of psychological and emotional preparation. Thus he is able to thoroughly immerse himself in a mental space that would simply overwhelm the unprepared and uninitiated. We see the potentially devastating effects of a spontaneous insight into ultimate reality in Pip's experience in "The Castaway."

As we have seen, Ishmael joins the Pequod not only willingly, but desperately, seeing it as a vessel for and emblem of existential liberation. But Pip is described as being "entrapped" on the ship, and arrived there not willingly, but "somehow unaccountably"—it is clear he misses life on shore, "and all its peaceable securities."[1] He wants his feet on the ground; he wants to be comfortable. It isn't that he's unintelligent—Ishmael ensures us Pip is "at bottom very bright, with [a] pleasant, genial, jolly brightness," and even calls him "brilliant"[2]—he simply has no connection to the existential questions being asked elsewhere on the Pequod. He is quite uninterested in troubling himself with the Great Matter, as evidenced by his status as one of the "ship-keepers,"[3] the few men who stay onboard when the boat crews are off chasing after whales.

But it comes to pass that Pip ends up in a whale-boat as a replacement for another sailor, and thus embarks on an unintentional pursuit after truth. We can consider the whale-boat as Ishmael's surrogate for the soul, the heart, the "sense of self," which carries the men in their adventures on the ocean—most importantly toward the object of our spiritual quest. For example, in "The Gilder," Ishmael describes the contentment of sitting in the whale-boat, abiding in this sense of self: "These are the times of dreamy quietude, when beholding the tranquil beauty and brilliancy of the ocean's skin. . . . These are the times, when in his whale-boat the rover softly feels a certain filial, confident, land-like feeling toward the sea; that he regards it as so much flowery earth."[4] Ahab's attachment to Self is epitomized by his habit of spending long hours standing defiantly in his personal whale-boat, "high-hoisted" off the side of the ship.[5] And in "The Pequod Meets the Rachel," his usual call "Hast seen the White Whale?" is met with the thrilling news, "Aye, yesterday. Have ye seen a whale-boat adrift?"[6] The metaphysical analogue here could translate as something like, "Have you been seeking Meaning?" "Yes, have you seen a lost soul?"

Dogen Zenji uses a similar analogy to address our usual belief in a fixed unchanging self, emphasizing the difference between looking inwardly and outwardly: "When you ride in a boat and watch the shore, you might assume that the shore is moving. But when you keep your eyes closely on the boat, you can see that the boat moves."[7] Turning our attention to the boat, we see that it is rolling with the waves, and not at all a fixed entity. The shore is moving as well, for "nothing at all has unchanging self." But it is not moving the way we think it is, since we can see it only from the vantage of the boat. Our goal is not to rid ourselves of the boat, but to pay close attention to the way that boat, sea, and shore are all constantly changing (and are also inextricably interdependent) in hopes that eventually we will no longer be controlled by the capricious waves. Ishmael offers a similar teaching in describing that "the whale line,"[8] which on one end is attached to the harpoon, is, on the other end, never tied to the whale boat, "for were the lower end of the line in any attached to the boat, and were the whale then to run the line out . . . the doomed boat would infallibly be dragged down after him into the profundity of the sea."[9] If one chases after Meaning (the whale) while still clinging (tied) to fixed views of an independent self (the boat), one may be dragged down to a place from which one cannot return.[10]

So Pip joins a whale-boat. But during his second lowering for a whale, in a tense moment of "involuntary consternation,"[11] he leaps out of the boat and into the sea. In much the same way that the hypothetical dreamy sailor in "The Mast-Head" slips his grasp and his "identity comes back in horror,"[12] Pip feels a threat to his personal safety and cannot help jumping. As the crew is forced to stop and save him, a whale is lost, and despite Stubb's stern warning to "Stick to the boat, Pip, or by the Lord, I won't pick you up if you jump,"[13] the next time he finds himself in harm's way, Pip jumps again:

> But we are all in the hands of the Gods; and Pip jumped again. . . . In three minutes, a whole mile of shoreless ocean was between Pip and Stubb. . . . Now, in calm weather, to swim in the open ocean is as easy to the practised swimmer as to ride in a spring-carriage ashore. But the awful lonesomeness is intolerable. The intense concentration of self in the middle of such a heartless immensity, my God! who can tell it?[14]

Not only are there miles of ocean surrounding Pip horizontally; there are miles of ocean beneath his feet as well. So the "awful loneliness" is self-explanatory—and it brings about an "intense concentration" of his sense of self, in the literal sense of having a body, being a body, floating alone in the infinite ocean. For a moment, the boundary between Self and Other is palpable, visceral. We can imagine his limbs paddling frantically, struggling to keep afloat, perhaps considering his options of rescue or escape.

But then something shifts. From this "intense concentration of self," there is a sudden switch, as Ishmael tells us that "Pip's ringed horizon began to expand around him miserably."[15] It is similar to the switch that Dogen Zenji expresses in *Genjo Koan*: "To study the self is to forget the self. To forget the self is to be actualized by myriad things."[16] Looking for one's self, one finds nothing but the "myriad things" in the universe. We might imagine that Pip, for the first time in his life, looks closely at himself, asking, "Who am I?" or "What is this self that I feel so intensely?" or "Is the self the same as the body, lost out here in the ocean? If so, then where is my mind?"

What Pip sees is the subjectivity of perception, and the fallacy of the instinctual impression that each of us is at the center of the universe. For Pip, floating in the middle of the ocean, the "intense concentration of self" momentarily puts the center squarely in his own mind. But then, "Out from the centre of the sea, poor Pip turned his crisp, curling, black head to the sun, another lonely castaway, though the loftiest and the brightest."[17] The idea that the sun could exist on the fringe—as "another lonely castaway," lost and alone itself—is another way that Ishmael denies us the comfort of a convenient "center" to our experience and also pulls us ineluctably toward the margins.[18] Instead of its mythologically ascribed role as the ubiquitous source of light and intelligibility in religious symbolism, as well as the literal (and eponymous) center of the solar system[19]—the sun now exists only in relation to Pip, burning somewhere in the distance, "out from the centre of the sea."[20] If the sun is just "another lonely castaway," ostensibly having a similar experience to Pip's, then from its heliocentric perspective the center would be with it, some ninety-three million miles away. So the center lies both everywhere and nowhere, for ultimately there cannot even be fixed distinctions drawn between Pip and the sun—they, along with the ocean and the ship and the "multitudinous, God-omnipresent, coral insects," are all dependently co-arisen.[21] Indeed, the sun is only called "the loftiest and brightest" in relation to Pip's being less lofty, and less bright.[22] Even Ishmael's curious reference to the "coral insects"[23] might reflect this relationship—that just as coral reefs are composed of millions upon millions of mutually co-dependent organisms that together form what we call "coral," innumerable phenomena are every moment "multitudinously" creating what we refer to as "the universe." Thus the "little negro lad, five feet high"[24] and the flaming ball of gas, almost a million miles high, while obviously not the same, cannot truly be said to be different.

On the surface, this interaction between Pip and the sun appears comparable to mythological archetypes wherein an unprepared mortal gains insight into the world of the divine: Zeus's lover Semele (taking Hera's devious advice) demanded to see the Olympian god in his full glory, and when he reluctantly obliged, she "sizzled, shrank, and was vaporized."[25] In Exodus, Moses makes a similar request of God, and God refuses, knowing the prophet would not survive the sight.[26] Pip's experience in "The Castaway," however, illustrates precisely the opposite point of view. For the two Classical examples are emphasizing difference: the human seeks a close relationship with the god (or God), and the Deity makes clear the fundamental separation between them. In Pip's case, the insight is one of sameness—that human, deity, and the relationship between them, are all One, and all indispensible parts of the universe. While this might sound encouraging at first—that we are one with God and God is one with us—it can actually be a terrifying prospect. For although we might easily grasp the idea of everything around us being a part of God (and thus lacking inherent existence), eventually we will have to dismantle the idea of our self as independently existent as well. Again, it is not that individual things don't exist; it is that they do not exist independently of everything else. But the idea that the self is a delusion, and what we refer to as the self is a mere amalgamation of sense perceptions, is, to say the least, unsettling.

And this is how Pip loses his mind: "By the merest chance the ship itself at last rescued him; but from that hour the little negro went about the deck an idiot; such, at least, they said he was."[27] It is also precisely why Pip's "mad" post-castaway ravings are almost entirely concerned with his search for Pip—"Pip, that jumped from a whale-boat," and left behind his idea of self.[28] Thus he is no longer able to understand the connection between the name "Pip" and the person "Pip": "Pip? whom call ye Pip? Pip jumped from the whale-boat. Pip's missing. . . . Pip! Pip! Pip! Reward for Pip!"[29]

But Pip is no idiot, as Ishmael well knows. The experience of insight is literally outside the realm of language—and, as mid-twentieth-century Buddhist scholar John Blofeld remarks, "those who have actually achieved this tremendous experience, whether as Christians, Buddhists or members of other faiths, are agreed as to the impossibility of communicating it in words."[30] Shakyamuni Buddha himself is said to have initially decided against attempting to share his teaching with others, assuming that no one would be able to understand it. And remember, these are the experiences of people who have spent their lives preparing for such a moment! We cannot expect Pip to fare very well when thrust unwillingly into this arena.

Buddhist texts make frequent mention of the dangers of seeing the ultimate truth without being firmly grounded in the conventional truth. Cleary writes, "When individuals are still at a stage where they need externally imposed structures of belief and practice . . . insight can be a shattering experience, beyond the capacity of an immature or unbalanced mind to bear with equanimity."[31] So, again, "Pip's ringed horizon [begins] to expand around him miserably,"[32] until finally he can no longer distinguish between Self and Other. Dogen concludes, "When actualized by myriad things, your body and mind as well as the bodies and minds of others drop away."[33] But for Pip this happens "miserably," as he is unprepared for the loss of his belief in a separate Self. It is curious that Melville says, "The sea had jeeringly kept his finite body up, but drowned the infinite of his soul,"[34] for that seems precisely the opposite of what happens—it is his sense of the *finite* that is drowned, and the *infinite* kept afloat.

Pip is then "carried down to wondrous depths [where] the miser-merman, Wisdom, revealed his hoarded heaps."[35] Surprising, then, that the idea that Pip is turned into an idiot has persisted among scholars, since Melville explicitly states that his guide in this adventure is none other than Wisdom itself. In this strange alliterative phrase, is Wisdom revealing the heaps that he himself has hoarded? Or is he revealing to Pip the truth of his own hoarded heaps? If we take this latter view, Melville appears again to be pointing to Pip's elusive self. The Buddha taught that what we consider our separate self is actually "a combination of ever-changing physical and mental forces or energies."[36] As mentioned earlier, these are divided into the five *skandhas*: form, feeling, perception, volitional formations, and consciousness.[37] And while the Sanskrit word *skandhas* (*khandha* in Pali) is usually translated as "aggregates," a more literal definition is "heaps" or "piles." The word "hoarded" usually connotes something saved for future use, but here can suggest something to which one is attached, or clinging. In fact, the Buddha specifically defined *dukkha*, or suffering, as "*Upadana* [clinging] *panca* [five] *skandha* [aggregates] *dukkha* [suffering]."[38] So when Melville says "Wisdom revealed his hoarded heaps," he is pointing to something like the revelation described above—that what we usually think of as the self is revealed to be nothing more than a delusion based upon clinging to these five heaps:

> We seem to believe that there is some self lurking behind the awareness of the body and mental objects. But if you turn and look for this "somebody" behind your awareness, you do not find a self independent from awareness. . . . This is not to say that there is no self, it's just that there is no independent self. The self exists only in dependence upon mind and its objects. When you clearly observe the dependent co-arising of self, mind, and objects, the belief in a self independent of mind and objects drops away.[39]

This idea of "boundaries" recalls once again the ancient text *Hsin Hsin Ming*, which states, "Emptiness here, Emptiness there, but the infinite universe stands always before your eyes. Infinitely large and infinitely small, no difference, for definitions have vanished and no boundaries are seen."[40]

Ken Wilber deals with this subject at length in his book *No Boundary*. He describes the usual human experience as drawing a mental boundary around ourselves: everything on the inside of that boundary is the "self"; everything outside the boundary is "not-self."[41] The boundary is malleable, and exists on several levels, as in our connections with objects and people—for example "my coffee," "my job," "my husband"—and we often feel threatened when our relationship to those things is compromised (as we have seen with Ahab and the loss of his leg). But what is important for our purposes here is Wilber's argument that the boundary can be eliminated altogether:

> The most radical re-mapping or shifting of the boundary line occurs in experiences of the supreme identity, for here the person expands his self-identity boundary to include the entire universe. We might even say that he loses the boundary line altogether, for when he is identified with the "one harmonious whole" there is no longer any outside or inside, and so nowhere to draw the line.[42]

Wilber also argues that the ultimate aim of Zen Buddhism—one might say this is true of all religions—is "to heal the split between the total organism and the environment to reveal an identity, a supreme identity, with the entire universe."[43] Ishmael's remark that the "pointless centres" of "great hearts . . . contain the entire circumferences of inferior souls" suggests a similar idea of the permeability of boundaries.[44]

So Melville equates "man's insanity" with "heaven's sense," and "wandering from all mortal reason, man comes at last to that celestial thought."[45] For Pip, poor Pip, the trouble comes only when he attempts to return to the conventional world, after having been united with the ultimate. "Lines are drawn in the mind. There are no lines in nature," Batchelor writes.[46] What happens when one loses one's line-drawing capacity? Pip feels "uncompromised, indifferent"[47]—for he cannot take care of a self he no longer feels exists.

Chapter Twenty-Three

Ahab's Awakening

Ishmael's telepathic insights into Captain Ahab's mind make clear that the captain is not at all the static, unchanging entity he is often assumed to be. Belying his infamous obstinacy and self-proclaimed invulnerability, his tortured soliloquizing reveals he is indeed searching within his mind, even as he searches the empty seas. Ahab maintains a powerful self-awareness throughout—not only of the nature of his condition, but on its self-destructive impact as well:

> Nor, at the time, had it failed to enter his monomaniac mind, that all the anguish of that then present suffering was but the direct issue of a former woe; and he too plainly seemed to see, that as the most poisonous reptile of the marsh perpetuates his kind as inevitably as the sweetest songster of the grove; so, equally with every felicity, all miserable events do naturally beget their like.[1]

Reading this passage, we might at first assume simply that by "former woe" he means the loss of his leg. But "woe" does not specifically refer to a misfortune itself, but rather the mental suffering that follows the misfortune—that is to say, "woe" does not arise from an injury itself, but from the self-pitying story one tells oneself about having been injured. And Ahab makes continual reference—vacillating between celebration and lamentation—to his wretched philosophy. When he tells the carpenter, "I like to feel something in this slippery world that can hold, man," we might take it to be his credo.[2] "That lively cry upon this deadly calm might almost convert a better man,"[3] he says, but of course he himself is unconvertible: "Would now St. Paul would come along that way, and to my breezelessness bring his breeze!"[4]

When Ahab does receive moments of "breeziness," he immediately dismisses them. Watching from the deck as a sperm whale slowly dies, he does experience some calming joy, and is momentarily soothed, "but only soothed to deeper gloom."[5] One cannot help but wonder what would happen if Ahab succeeded in killing the White Whale? Are we to believe he would retire contentedly in Nantucket with his wife and son? Or would he simply find another surrogate through whom to continue waging war on the heavens? This is a man who claims for himself the exclusive right to suffer: "In no Paradise myself," he tells the blacksmith, "I am impatient of all misery in others."[6] The answer is clear: this is no passing fancy; there is no walking away. Having dedicated himself to the pursuit of Moby Dick, Ahab will continue it at all costs, and against all reason. The English Captain asks him whether he does not agree that the whale is best left alone: "He is. But he will still be hunted, for all that. What is best let alone, that accursed thing is not always what least allures. He's all magnet!"[7] He is unyielding to the last, even in his final order to Tashtego, to nail a new flag to the mast of his ship as it sinks to the bottom of the ocean.

In this way, Ahab exemplifies the consequence of the Buddha's warning against clinging to a fixed view, or having rigid assurance in and insistence on one's beliefs.[8] But when we examine the nature of the Captain's beliefs, we find them not very clearly defined. In fact, Ahab does not have a consistently held philosophy, but oscillates wildly between conflicting proclamations—while never diminishing, of course, his conviction in their veracity. It is indeed distressing to watch fractured Ahab ricochet between a fierce belief in his absolute independence and a wailing despair of his enslavement to some "cozening, hidden lord and master,"[9] insisting that while his heart is fundamentally good, an evil spirit forces him to do what in his "own proper, natural heart, [he] durst not so much as dare."[10]

Determined to get a definitive answer as to God's ontological status—the two possibilities, in his mind, being that he is either a knowable Thing or utterly non-existent—as the book progresses, Ahab begins *taunting* God, hoping He will respond in some concrete way. He calls himself "demoniac,"[11] smuggles a crew of "dusty phantoms" on board with him,[12] and baptizes a harpoon in the name of the devil[13]—all of which fail to elicit an immediate response from the heavens. Eventually, in the sequence of chapters surrounding the typhoon, Ahab's focus shifts to the tools of his trade—the objects aiding his pursuit of the White Whale—finding intolerable his reliance on them for information. Perhaps by removing the buffer between himself and God, he surmises, he will be brought closer to the White Whale.

These interactions convey both the interdependent relationship he has with the universe, and his volatile recognition of—and revolt against—that relationship. The first casualty is the quadrant, which Ahab crushes beneath his "live and dead feet."[14] While its "colored glasses"[15] have long allowed Ahab to gaze directly at the sun, he now comes to resent this filter—both for refusing him direct contact with the sun, and, by its very existence, leading his eyes to seek that contact:

> "Curse thee, thou vain toy; and cursed be all the things that cast man's eyes aloft to that heaven, whose live vividness but scorches him, as these old eyes are even now scorched with light, O sun! Level by nature to this earth's horizon are the glances of man's eyes; not shot from the crown of his head, as if God had meant him to gaze on his firmament. Curse thee, thou quadrant!"[16]

In smashing the quadrant, Ahab admits his powerlessness—first, that he is so separate from God that he cannot find Him, and second, that the universe has cruelly made him into such a person that he cannot stop looking for Him. He now pledges his allegiance to the other (ostensibly more honorable) tools at his disposal: "the level ship's compass, and the level dead-reckoning, by log and by line; these shall conduct me, and show me my place at sea."[17]

But even as Ahab denies himself the use of the quadrant and places his faith elsewhere, the typhoon arrives (in energetic response to his destructive mood) to deny him these things as well. When the compass needles are turned, Ahab momentarily considers the symbolism of such a thing, and as his arm falls to his side, "for a moment he almost seemed to stagger."[18] He regrets his impulsive rebuke of the quadrant, eulogizing its crushed pieces still lying on the deck: "Thou poor, proud heaven-gazer and sun's pilot! yesterday I wrecked thee, and to-day the compasses would feign have wrecked me."[19] But seconds later he launches into action, his creation of a new compass needle allowing him to extend his consideration of "self" into a tool that he hopes will bring him to Moby Dick.

This does not work quite as simply with the log and line, which, as Ahab "remembered how his quadrant was no more, and recalled his frantic oath about the level log and line,"[20] he attempts to deploy. But it is weathered and rotten, and when tossed into the sea, it snaps the line and sinks. This leads to an offhand admission that—even now, in his monomania—Ahab may no longer consider himself self-powered. Meeting a sailor from the Isle of Man, he muses, "Here's a man from Man; a man born in once independent Man, and now unmanned of Man; which is sucked in—by what? Up with the reel! The dead, blind wall butts all inquiring heads at last."[21] This cryptic remark suggests that his belief in his "inexorable self" has begun to be corroded by the "dead, blind wall" of Moby Dick. Collecting himself, the monomaniacal Ahab both acknowledges his relationship with the universe but refuses to renounce the power of his obstinate will: "I crush the quadrant, the thunder turns the needles, and now the mad sea parts the log-line. But Ahab can mend all."[22]

As the book nears its conclusion, Ahab becomes increasingly aware of his inescapable interdependence with the people and things surrounding him, and with the universe itself. During the typhoon in "The Candles," as the corpusants burn in the main-mast, Ahab asks to be brought closer to the flames, so that he can "feel this pulse, and let mine beat against it; blood against fire!"[23] His furious challenge to the heavens—daring the "clear spirit" to "come as more supernal power"[24]—is met by "sudden, repeated flashes of lightning."[25] When Ahab responds by repeating himself more loudly, lightning sets fire to the tip of his diabolically christened harpoon, sufficient proof for Starbuck that "God, God is against thee, old man; forbear! 'tis an ill voyage!"[26] When the crew attempts to retreat from Ahab—as with "the hurricane that sweeps the plain, men fly the neighborhood of some lone, gigantic elm"[27]—the Captain reminds them, "All your oaths to hunt the White Whale are as binding as mine; and heart, soul, and body, lungs and life, old Ahab is bound."[28]

Ahab is confronted again by the "all-contributed and all-receptive" universe the following morning, when it is discovered the compasses have been "exactly inverted" by the magnetic energy of the previous evening's storm.[29] He has no doubt that the turned compasses are a direct response to his smashing of the quadrant the previous day, but his response remains the same, as he reaffirms his power to supersede this relationship: "So, so. But Ahab is lord over the level loadstone, yet."[30] This is mirrored, in a way, by Ahab's proximity to his men on deck: as the chapter opens, Ishmael tells us, "Ahab stood apart."[31] Once he has fashioned his new compass, he urges them forward—"Look ye, for yourselves"[32]—but though "one after another they peered in,"[33] just as quickly "one after another they slunk away."[34] He remains unaware of the heavy implications of the needles turning (the universe trying to lead him away from the White Whale) as the Pequod once again turns east and "thrust[s] her undaunted bows into the opposing wind, for the supposed fair one had only been juggling her."[35]

Captain Ahab truly undergoes a profound change in the final chapters of the novel. We see traces of regret begin to undermine his recalcitrant rhetoric. Saying goodbye to the Rachel, he almost whispers, "Good bye, good bye. God bless ye, man, and may I forgive myself"[36]—suggesting that, though he no longer feels deserving of His divine grace, he may still wish it on others. As Ahab's self-imposed isolation begins to crumble, he has deeply illuminating interactions with the outside world—progressing quickly from objects (compass, quadrant) to people (Starbuck, Pip) and finally the White Whale himself. It is through these experiences—most important among them his relationship with Pip and his consideration of the "coffin life-buoy"—that Ahab, for the first time, begins to question his motives, and the efficacy of his actions. It is only then that, in direct response to his taking this introspective step backward, Moby Dick rushes forward to meet him. As Zen master Linji said, "If you seek him, he retreats farther and farther away; If you don't seek him, then he's right there before your eyes, his wondrous voice resounding in your ears."[37]

This process climaxes in the chapter "The Symphony," with an episode which also serves as the most explicit portrayal of Ahab's Narcissistic tendencies (in the most literal sense of the term). Leaning over the side of the Pequod, a despondent Ahab stares at his reflection below, which "sank and sank to his gaze, the more and the more he strove to pierce the profundity,"[38] and drops a single tear into the sea. Like Narcissus, in his final hours, Ahab's mind is occupied by thoughts of impermanence, and the fickle, ephemeral nature of existence:

> "Forty—forty—forty years ago! . . . Here, brush this old hair aside; it blinds me, that I seem to weep. Locks so grey did never grow but from out some ashes! But do I look very old, so very, very old, Starbuck? I feel deadly faint . . . bitter, bitter mockery of grey hairs, have I lived enough joy to wear ye; and seem and feel thus intolerably old?"[39]

This soliloquy is Ahab at his most human, and signals a fundamental change in Old Thunder's heart. Looking up from his own reflection, he addresses Starbuck: "Close! stand close to me, Starbuck; let me look into a human eye; it is better than to gaze into sea or sky, better than to gaze upon God."[40] As the sea, sky and God will only reflect back "his own inexorable self,"[41] here Ahab—perhaps seeking to avoid Narcissus's fate—finally seeks solace in something outside Self, something Other.

The curious image of "the step-mother world" introduced in "The Symphony" is also indicative of this feeling of isolation. Ahab, the petulant stepson, shuns Mother Earth, and thus is shunned by her. Howling at the infinite, he cries, "My sweet mother, I know not. What hast thou done with her?"[42] But a few chapters later he admits it is he who has abandoned her. And, crucially, the moment he drops his posturing, she does immediately "stroke and caress him: the step-mother world, so long cruel—forbidding—now threw affectionate arms round his stubborn neck, and did seem to joyously sob over him, as if over one, that however wilful and erring, she could yet find it in her heart to save and to bless."[43] Having long seen the universe as vindictive, malicious, he now feels its gentle, nurturing grace. In this immediate response to and reflection of his own actions, he cannot help seeing that his intention—the volitional energy he puts out into the universe—is precisely what he gets in return. And thus, "From beneath his slouched hat Ahab dropped a tear into the sea; nor did all the Pacific contain such wealth as that one wee drop."[44]

The episode with the coffin life-buoy is the defining example of Ahab's reification of phenomena, and the catalyst for his great realization. Here a man falls from the mast-head into the sea, and the Pequod's life-buoy is thrown to him. But so long has it been hanging in the scorching sun that it no longer floats, and sinks to the bottom along with the fallen sailor, "as if to yield him his pillow, though in sooth but a hard one."[45] So, first, we are essentially presented with a koan: Is a life-buoy still a life-buoy if it is no longer buoyant? Can a life-buoy become a pillow for a man on the bottom of the sea?

A replacement is then needed for the lost life-buoy, and when the men have difficulty finding "a cask of sufficient lightness,"[46] Queequeg suggests they use his coffin (the one he didn't use after he decided not to die). The coffin is dutifully prepared—its lid nailed, its seams caulked—and will soon be called a life-buoy. But at what defining moment does this change occur? At what point does the coffin cease to be a coffin and take on its new existence as a life-buoy? For that matter, what exactly defined its previous existence as a coffin? It cannot be necessarily tied to functionality, for this object never held a corpse, and since his recovery Queequeg has been using it, "with a wild whimsiness,"[47] as a sea-chest. The only possible answer is that its existence as a thing, its *thingness*, depends entirely on the labels applied to it from without.

Ahab agrees that things are not as they seem—that, as he says early on in the book, "all visible objects . . . are but as pasteboard masks."[48] This is indeed true—that, for example, what we see as a banana is not simply a banana, but all the myriad causes and conditions that have come together to allow that banana to exist. And even then, the banana cannot be said to truly exist as a "thing" until someone comes along to give it the label "banana." Until that moment, it is just a banana-shaped portion of the universe. Another example: say I walk into a friend's kitchen. The kitchen is full of utensils and appliances, but right now as I stand there it is just "the kitchen." It is only after I point at individual things and say "toaster," kettle," "can opener" that those things exist in the way we normally speak of "existence"—that is, for example, as an apparently independently existing thing called "kettle." In the Buddhist view, the only place that supposedly independent thing exists is as an idea in my own mind.

Returning to Ahab, the Captain is convinced that "some unknown but still reasoning thing puts forth the mouldings of its features from behind the unreasoning mask."[49] The idea that the "mouldings" exist somewhere behind the mask is no different from saying the mask has an essence, or intrinsic existence. It is reifying the mask, making it into a thing. What we find when we look behind the mask are myriad causes and conditions (that is, everything else in the universe). Still, the mask is conventionally real—or, as R.H. Blyth says, "The mask *is* the face."[50] The mask's "true" face, one might say, is its lack of a face. Bodhidharma says, "If we practice thus, whatever the object is, then it will take off its mask and reveal its true face, saying, I am you; you are me."[51] The last in the series of *things* that betray Ahab—after the quadrant, the needle, the log and line—the incident with the life-buoy challenges Ahab's belief in "mouldings," forcing him to ask what it is that makes a life-buoy a life-buoy.

Ahab arrives on deck as the carpenter prepares the coffin for its new life, and their brief dialogue is a telling one. "What's here?" Ahab asks—as if to say, what is this thing that I cannot easily define? "Life-buoy, sir," the carpenter says. Ahab's response? "Thank ye, man. *Thy coffin* lies handy to the vault" (my italics).[52] He completely ignores the ambiguity in the carpenter's response. As he is unable to internalize something that is not "either/or" but rather "both," he insists that the thing remains what he believes it to be.

He takes similar issue with the carpenter as well: "Art not thou the leg-maker? . . . Art thou not also the undertaker?"[53] Ahab clearly considers it blasphemy that a man might exist in different capacities, and placates himself by denouncing the carpenter as "unprincipled" and assigning him the label of "jack-of-all-trades"[54]—this for exhibiting the same qualities that had earned him Ishmael's praise.

But this interaction provokes an unexpectedly profound insight within Ahab. As he is walking away from the carpenter, he hears the continuous banging of the carpenter's mallet, and has a bewildering change of heart:

> "There's a sight! There's a sound! The greyheaded woodpecker tapping the hollow tree! Blind and deaf might well be envied now. . . . Oh! how immaterial are all materials! What things real are there, but imponderable thoughts? Here now's the very dreaded symbol of grim death, by a mere hap, made the expressive sign of the help and hope of most endangered life. A life-buoy of a coffin! Does it go further?"[55]

The sound of the mallet against the (former) coffin and (soon-to-be) life-buoy brings to his mind the image of a woodpecker tapping a hollow tree. Given what we know about Ahab's insistence on self-control, we can assume he would not appreciate his mind's involuntary reactions to outside stimulus. Thus, the "blind and deaf" should be envied, for they are not prone to manip-ulation by such wayward insolent mallets. This banging gives Ahab a flash-ing realization of the interdependence of all phenomena—echoing a famous Zen story of a monk who was sweeping the monastery courtyard and, when a pebble hit a piece of bamboo, he heard the sound and was greatly enlight-ened. There can be no separation between the mallet, the sound reaching Ahab's ear, and the thought of the woodpecker, since for the "blind and deaf," none of them would exist. And the banging of the mallet cannot have an essence, for the sound, immediately abstracted from connection to the mallet, gives rise to Ahab's thoughts of a woodpecker. So, finally, as usual, Ahab is left with only the belief in himself: "Does it go further?" he wonders aloud—asking, rather frightfully, is my own identity as much of an illusion as the coffin life-buoy's? But he dismisses this without another thought, and likewise dismisses the offensively ambiguous object at fault: "Let me not see that thing here when I return again."[56]

The other major episode in the Captain's epiphany is his bond with Pip. Ahab has previously met Starbuck's offer, "Shall we not understand each other better than hitherto, Captain Ahab?" by pulling a loaded musket on him.[57] But later on in his journey he is able to connect with Pip, expressly because the boy is without an individual identity, and thus cannot reflect Ahab's sense of self: "And who art thou, boy? I see not my reflection in the vacant pupils of thy eyes."[58] Not only does Ahab feel unthreatened by this empty shell, but also it momentarily relieves him of his Narcissistic obsession with his separate self, allowing him to feel connected to someone else: "Thou touchest my inmost centre, boy; thou art tied to me by cords woven of my heart-strings."[59]

Separately, the two represent opposite sides of the extreme views of existence, as Pip nihilistically denies there is anything called "Pip," and Ahab is obsessed with the fundamental existence of this thing called "Ahab." By joining hands they are merged, and their positions intermingle. Ahab says, "Now, then Pip, we'll talk this over; I do suck most wondrous philosophies from thee!"[60] and specifically notes that caring for this boy is further wearing away his feeling of separation: "There is that in thee, poor lad, which I feel too curing to my malady."[61] Pip, in turn, moves from feeling he is nothing, to feeling that he is a part of Ahab—indeed, as he says, the missing piece: "No, no, no! ye have not a whole body, sir; do ye but use poor me for your own lost leg . . . so I remain a part of ye."[62] This relationship also gives Ahab an opportunity to once again shake his fist at the "immortal souls" cruel enough to inflict such a fate on this boy.[63] But instead of aligning himself with their power, as he might have before, he now despairs that they are simultaneously "omniscient" and "oblivious" to man's suffering—while this boy, having shed his sense of self, is somehow "full of the sweet things of love and gratitude."[64] Ahab sounds a note of envy.

As they walk hand in hand, an old sailor calls them daft: "one daft with strength, the other daft with weakness."[65] As R.H. Blyth writes, "Some minds have a tendency to over-emphasize difference, some to make everything of a meaningless sameness. Both are wrong, the latter perhaps more than the former."[66] So Pip, nudged back from the edge of nihilism, comes quite close to the idea of the Ultimate Truth. Ahab, for his part, does begin to move from the idea of a separate self to the idea of a dependently co-arisen

self. Unfortunately, he knows he is too far gone to abandon his quest now—
and though he acknowledges the remedy, he wants not to be cured: "for this
hunt, my malady becomes my most desired health."[67] Pip is finally left alone
once again—as he says, without even himself to keep him company: "I'm
alone. Now were even poor Pip here I could endure it, but he's missing. Pip!
Pip! Ding, dong, ding! Who's seen Pip?"[68]

Ahab's affection for Pip leads directly toward his heart being flooded in
"The Symphony"—for Starbuck, and Starbuck's family, and Ahab's own
family. He speaks about this feeling of separation, which has caused him so
much misery, with candor and sensitivity: "When I think of this life I have
led; the desolation of solitude it has been; the masoned, walled-town of a
Captain's exclusiveness . . . oh, weariness! heaviness! Guinea-coast slavery
of solitary command!—when I think of all this; only half-suspected, not so
keenly known to me before."[69] He is a changed man, Captain Ahab. Having
opened himself up to the world outside his mind, he meets a succession of
reflections—in the ocean, in Starbuck, in Fedallah—but he is no longer trying to grasp them, as was Narcissus. He is shaken to the core, but nevertheless, he knows he cannot leave his quest unfinished; he still wants answers.
So, leaning over the rail, he makes what seems like an informed, conscious
decision to continue his quest. The world is no longer his enemy; he now
looks out upon a "smiling sky," and "unsounded sea," and "a mild, mild
wind."[70] For somewhere, finally, the White Whale awaits.

Chapter Twenty-Four

Pacific

In the book's final pages, Moby Dick, having been chased by the Pequod across the Pacific, finally turns around and confronts his aggressor. Doing battle with the whaleboats, he kills Ahab and Fedallah, just as the prophecies have foretold. Ramming and sinking the ship, he ensures the death of everyone onboard, save one: Ishmael alone is spared.

In considering these events, and the philosophical implications behind them, we are returned to two questions Ishmael poses earlier in the narrative regarding the White Whale: whether he is intelligent and whether he is malicious. Regarding the former, Ishmael is unequivocal, answering resoundingly in the affirmative. The sperm whale, he tells us, is "knowing"[1]; in its forehead one sees the "mark of genius."[2] It is a "ponderous profound being . . . thinking great thoughts."[3] Regarding the sperm whale's capacity for malice, however, Ishmael is nowhere near as definitive, leaving himself a conditional escape hatch each time he addresses it:

> The Sperm Whale is *in some cases* sufficiently powerful, knowing, and judiciously malicious, as with direct aforethought to stave in, utterly destroy, and sink a large ship . . . I might proceed with several more examples, one way or another known to me, of the great power and malice *at times* of the Sperm Whale. . . . Again, *it is very often observed* that . . . he then acts, *not so often* with blind rage, as with wilful, deliberate designs of destruction to his pursuers. (all my italics)[4]

In his description of Ahab's first encounter with the White Whale, Ishmael first describes Moby Dick as having "reaped away Ahab's leg, as a mower a blade of grass in the field"—suggesting not only that it was an accident, but that the whale is no more aware of its actions than a reaper.[5] If the whale represents the order of the universe, this suggests indifference at best, chaos at worst. But then in the very next sentence, Ishmael states that the whale "could not have smote him with more seeming malice."[6] The word "seeming" emphasizes that if the whale is indeed malicious, it is solely because Ahab believes it to be so—just as Captain Boomer, in his own battle with the whale, makes unconvincing note of "the boiling rage he seemed to be in."[7] It is this ambiguity that incenses Ahab: "I see in him outrageous strength, with an inscrutable malice sinewing it. That inscrutable thing is chiefly what I hate."[8] It is not the malice that troubles Ahab; it is that he does not know whether the malice resides in the whale himself, or in Ahab's perception of the whale.

Where this supposed malice truly resides, it seems, is within the pattern of relationship between the two of them. That Ishmael describes the "salt-sea Mastodon" as being "clothed with such portentousness of unconscious power"[9] suggests that this is an attribute applied from without—as if the whale is wearing a costume, performing a role—and not at all inherent in the being itself. Our narrator is alone in his awareness that, just as the image in the water is a reflection of whatever is before it, the whale is not only the *symbol* of whatever meaning is attached to it, it is the *manifestation* of that thing for each of them. Since Ahab believes the whale to be malicious and vengeful, it *is* malicious and vengeful—when it finally attacks at novel's end, it does so "with that malicious intelligence *ascribed to him*" (my italics).[10] As he bears down to smite the ship, "retribution, swift vengeance, eternal malice were in his whole aspect."[11] This does not necessarily mean the whale is malicious, or vengeful, but rather this is what is manifesting through the whale, in response to Ahab's quest.

Despite the ways in which Ahab has changed over the course of the voyage, he remains fixated on his final battle with the supposed source of his suffering. The fatal encounter, in many ways, is not the unambiguous verdict we would like (though by now we should have stopped expecting). The manner of Ahab's death acutely illustrates the dependently co-arisen nature of his suffering. The rope recalls the death of Fedallah on the second day of the chase, and Stubb's comment that he had been "caught among the tangles of your line—I thought I saw him dragging under."[12] Ahab responds incredulously, "*My* line? *My* line?"[13] in disbelief that he could somehow be responsible—that actions have unwelcome consequences, trailing after us like lines behind harpoons. His death is the perfect manifestation of this truth, as well as his egoistic quest—as he hurls his harpoon, the rope trailing behind it gets caught around his neck and pulls him along after it, and into the sea. Thus, crucially, Ahab is not killed by Moby Dick, but rather (almost literally) by his own hatred and malice, as the unintended consequence of his throwing the spear—again pointing to the "simultaneousness of volition and action" of the whale line.[14]

If we take Ahab's death as retributive, and thus neatly tied up (and pulled under), must we assume the same of the rest of the Pequod's crew? Or can we argue that, as nothing occurs in a vacuum, those around Ahab are simply in the wrong place at the wrong time? Just as Elijah shrugs and says, "Any how . . . some sailors or other must go with [Ahab], I suppose; as well these as any other man, God pity 'em!"[15] some sailors must necessarily end up going down with the ship. What is it that connects and condemns both Starbuck's active disengagement and Flask's careless bellicosity?

One possible answer comes from a most unexpected arrival during the ship's destruction—the valedictory nailing of the sea-hawk to the mast-head. The bird is a most noble creature: it is "the bird of heaven, with archangelic shrieks, and . . . imperial beak."[16] That this noble bird (who of course has had nothing to do with the drama of the White Whale) can be "folded in the flag of Ahab" and "dragged . . . to hell" is testament to the gravitational pull of Ahab's volition. But more than that, the manner of its death—being "nailed down"—symbolizes the philosophical quality that unites (and dooms) each member of the crew. The extreme example is Ahab, whose possessions are nailed to the ship,[17] just as an "infinity of firmest fortitude, a determinate unsurrenderable wilfulness" is nailed to his countenance.[18] It is the other connotation of "nailing something down"—that of being finalized, or decided upon—that applies to every member of the crew. Just as the bird is being nailed down as a fixed ontological entity—"Yes, the bird is a bird"— so too is each man on the Pequod confident of his unique identity: as a Christian, as a cook, as a cannibal. And so too are all the objects on the ship readily identifiable as discrete entities: the doubloon is a doubloon, the smashed quadrant is a smashed quadrant.

There are only two places where our convenient labels fall short—the coffin life-buoy, and our elusive narrator. Not at all coincidentally, these are the two things that survive the Pequod's destruction.

In the book's final scene—as the swirling whirlpool consumes the Pequod and her crew—rather than being pulled toward the center as well, Ishmael is instead "floating on the margin of the ensuing scene, and in full sight of it."[19] The vortex suggests the force of Captain Ahab's will, which drags the crew along with him on his vengeful errand, and eventually sucks them down after him into the black depths. While Ishmael is not immune to Ahab's gravitational pull, he remains a *marginal* figure—spinning in orbit around Ahab, revolving around the events on the Pequod, maintaining his distance without ever being pulled in (or thrown off) himself.

In a literal sense, Ishmael survives by clinging to the coffin life-buoy. "[L]iberated by reason . . . and, owing to its great buoyancy,"[20] it cannot be dragged down by the Pequod, and thus shoots out from the sea and floats

happily over to Ishmael's side. But in a metaphorical sense as well, it is his
association with the coffin life-buoy that allows Ishmael alone to survive the
drowned wreckage of Ahab's fatal pursuit. The coffin life-buoy has been
"liberated by reason" for it has been liberated from its identity. As we have
seen, close scrutiny shows that it can be called either a coffin or a life-buoy
or a sea chest or a box of wood and nails—its identity depends exclusively on
the label applied to it. Thus, no longer weighed down by the illusion of a
static individual essence, it is "buoyant." Pressing the point, this nameless
object is covered in Queequeg's hieroglyphics, which—although we are told
they contain the mysteries of the universe within their indecipherable
script—cannot possibly express those secrets, for the symbols mean nothing
in themselves. It is through our interpretation that meaning is applied, and
only then can it be said to exist.

Ishmael is no longer weighed down by any attachment to identity, having
(skillfully, gradually) shed such clingings during the course of his journey. In
"Loomings," he describes his impending loss of status in transitioning from a
schoolmaster's position of authority to a lowly sailor's acquiescence, con-
fessing to relying upon "a strong decoction of Seneca and the Stoics" to deal
with the existential whiplash. "But even this wears off in time," he smirks.[21]
By the time he sets off for New Bedford he is carrying his carpet-bag ("that
is, the Ego," as Melville wrote to Hawthorne), suggesting an immediate
disassociation with his identity, a token collection of attributes he is willing
to trade or shed any moment. While in New Bedford, he muses on the precise
nature of this "self":

> Methinks we have hugely mistaken this matter of Life and Death. Methinks
> that what they call my shadow here on earth is my true substance. Methinks
> that in looking at things spiritual, we are too much like oysters observing the
> sun through the water, and thinking that thick water the thinnest of air. Me-
> thinks my body is but the lees of my better being. In fact take my body who
> will, take it I say, it is not me.[22]

From there he doubts that there be "any as yet undiscovered prime thing in
me"[23] beyond his senses, speaks of a man who "loses his identity,"[24] makes
references to both the "hidden self"[25] and the "invisible self,"[26] and laments
"the intense concentration of self."[27]

When he meets Queequeg, he is intrigued by the possibility of adopting
new exotic entrapments—but trying on the harpooneer's strange "South
American poncho," he immediately throws it off: "I put it on, to try it, and it
weighed me down like a hamper . . . I tore myself out of it in such a hurry
that I gave myself a kink in the neck."[28] Later he assures us that carrying
Locke's and Kant's "thunderheads" makes one "sorely strained" and "in very
poor plight"; it is only by throwing them overboard that one can "float light
and right."[29] It is this process of disposal—of identity, of ideology—that

Ishmael follows through the book and that ultimately allows him to survive the wreckage.

After brushing death in "The Hyena," he takes a further step away from his attachment to self, happily writing up his last will and testament, feeling "all the easier; a stone was rolled away from my heart," and declaring, "I survived myself."[30] With his "death and burial locked up in [his] chest," he looks around "tranquilly and contentedly . . . cool and collected."[31] But the pivotal moment for Ishmael appears in "Stubb Kills a Whale":

> It was my turn to stand at the foremast-head; and with my shoulders leaning against the slackened royal shrouds, to and fro I idly swayed in what seemed an enchanted air. No resolution could withstand it; in that dreamy mood losing all consciousness, at last my soul went out of my body; though my body still continued to sway as a pendulum will, long after the power which first moved it is withdrawn.[32]

He writes "*at last* my soul went out of my body" (my italics), implying the attainment of a goal, or the conclusion of a long struggle—finally he has achieved the state of selflessness. He is ultimately "buoyed up by that coffin," having used the same process applied to the coffin life-buoy to deconstruct and dismantle his sense of self.

The final image in *Moby-Dick*, of Ishmael calmly floating amidst the wreckage of the Pequod, recalls a story Melville tells in the journal of his trip to Europe in 1849. During the voyage there, a man jumped overboard from the ship. Melville wrote of the man: "His conduct was unaccountable; he could have saved himself, had he been so minded. I was struck by the expression of his face in the water. It was merry. It afterwards turned out, that he was crazy, & had jumped overboard."[33] We can imagine Melville's mind set to wondering what within a man could lead him to drown himself merrily in the North Atlantic. As Ishmael floats alone in Pacific (and pacific) waters, not only is he merry, but the universe seems quiescent as well: "[F]or almost one whole day and night, I floated on a soft and dirge-like main. The unharming sharks, they glided by as if with padlocks on their mouths; the savage sea-hawks sailed with sheathed beaks."[34] While Ishmael attributes his survival to having been "ordained" by the Fates, it is no idle coincidence that such a singular consciousness would alone be spared. As depicted in the chapter "The Mat-Maker," the sword of chance exists in concert with the actions of the shuttle, and vice versa. Zen master Hongzhi suggests something similar: "Only do not let yourself interfere with things, and certainly nothing will interfere with you. First, do not establish your own identity, then beings will not impose their own conditions."[35] Ishmael, through his unique nonattachment to self, has been removed from the laws to which the rest of the crew are subject. Just as the universe responds to Ahab's actions with thunder and lightning, and then drowns him with a white whale, it embraces

Ishmael with soft rolling seas and gentle sea creatures. As it "jeeringly kept [Pip's] finite body up, but drowned the infinite of his soul,"[36] it keeps Ishmael afloat, for he alone understands there is no difference between the two. And when it sends him a ship to carry him to shore, he is no longer an outcast—he is an orphan, free from attachment and obligation.

Conclusion

Herman Melville is buried in Woodlawn Cemetery, in the Bronx, New York. On his headstone, above his name and the dates of his life, there is a scroll chiseled out of the marble. There is no epitaph; the scroll is blank. But tucked behind the blank scroll, a quill is poised—suggesting the time was not yet right to offer any conclusions for his life.

Ishmael's conclusions about conclusions evolve during the course of his narrative. In New Bedford, he considers the possibility that an investigative approach might lead to some concrete understanding of phenomena—"I took it up, and held it close to the light, and felt it, and smelt it, and tried every way possible to arrive at some satisfactory conclusion concerning it"[1]—but once at sea, he steps away from certainty, and urges us toward a sort of meta-conclusion: "Still, we can hypothesize, even if we cannot prove and establish."[2] Ishmael presents us with his thoughts and experiences in hopes that each reader will come to his or her own conclusion (in much the same way that Melville has Captain Ahab nail a doubloon to the mast in order that each sailor may publicly ponder its meaning). As mentioned earlier, Ishmael writes in "The Affidavit," "I care not to perform this part of my task methodically; but shall be content to produce the desired impression by separate citations of items, practically or reliably known to me as a whaleman; and from these citations, I take it,—the conclusion aimed at will naturally follow of itself."[3] On the rare occasion he offers his own theory on a subject—"My hypothesis is this: that the spout is nothing but mist"[4]—it is a theory dispelling the grandiose conclusions of his brethren in favor of an explanation that is at once uncomplicated (it is simply water vapor) and ungraspable (it is simply water vapor).

So that accounts for Ishmael, but where does that leave the rest of us? Having argued that Ishmael's refusal to adhere to any tidy conclusions is what ends up saving his life—that such static certainties and conclusions are like weights, binding one to a fixed view of reality, dragging one down beneath the crashing waves—surely I cannot now profess to have arrived at any conclusions of my own. If we return once more to Dongshan's comment "My idea is to have no particular idea," we can place alongside it a possible maxim of Ishmael's own: "My conclusion is to have no particular conclusion." When Ishmael is tattooed, it is with the dimensions of the sperm whale skeleton—abstract numbers like answers to a question that will never be found. The tattoo is a reminder to continue asking questions, to keep searching for the whale—not *although* he will never be found, but *because* he will never be found. It is an inconclusive conclusion, leading us out once again to further uncertain seas.

Of course, I cannot claim to live up to Ishmael's ideal, nor to Dongshan's. I have my own view of the text, that reaches both backward to the accounts of Buddhism to which Melville had access, and forward to the Zen Buddhist literature which would have been unknown to him, but to which his book is so surprisingly linked. So I read Ishmael's reverent description of "the mystical treatise" carved onto the coffin life-buoy,[5] and draw a line to John Francis Davis's account of Chinese monks worshipping scriptures they cannot understand. I read about the "trances of torment" that accompany Ahab's "unachieved revengeful desire" to find the White Whale,[6] and connect it to Pierre Bayle's warning that the one who seeks after the first principle will suffer "perpetual disquiet."[7] And I read Ishmael's manifold descriptions of the White Whale, and am reminded of a teaching from Huang Po: "[It] is without beginning, is unborn and indestructible. It is not green nor yellow, and has neither form nor appearance. . . . It transcends all limits, measures, names, traces and comparisons. It is that which you see before you—begin to reason about it and you at once fall into error."[8]

Melville's spiritual restlessness continued in the work that followed *Moby-Dick*. Glimmers of his indefatigably curious mind shine through the deep, twisted gloom of 1852's *Pierre* (along with continued references to interdependence, causation, and, yes, "Hindostan"[9]). The ascetic scrivener in 1855's "Bartleby" is frequently compared to a Buddhist mendicant. *The Confidence-Man* is almost solely concerned with the question of whether there is an abiding self within our changeable exteriors. Even in *Battle-Pieces*, his collection of Civil War poetry, "The Conflict of Convictions" makes reference to "the Middle Way."[10]

By the time he wrote *Clarel*, however, the metaphysical possibilities of the open ocean had been subsumed by a vast spiritual (and literal) desert, Ishmael's search for illumination replaced by a sighing wish for annihilation. Whatever Melville's insights into Buddhist thought may have been, they seem to have been either forgotten—or, more likely, eclipsed by the coalescing American Buddhist orthodoxy. Perhaps, as with the ungraspable sperm whale, seeking to define a religious tradition only occludes us from engaging with it in any meaningful way. Melville seems to have allowed his Ahabian tendencies to overcome his Ishmaelean ones, and was sunk by them.

In arguing for this reading's historical basis, as well as its fidelity to the text, I am not seeking to convert the reader to my view, but to offer a persuasive argument for its legitimacy. For in the end, maybe Melville does have Ishmael survive as an endorsement of his peaceable philosophy. Maybe the fatalist in him would have preferred him to die with the rest of the crew, if not for the necessity of having a narrator to relate his story. Maybe both, or maybe neither. We can discuss the validity of these conclusions without adopting or rejecting them ourselves, just as Ishmael "cherish[es] the greatest respect" toward the conclusions others make about life and the universe, "never mind how comical."[11] Ultimately, it is not the conclusion itself that is problematic, but the way one clings to it that creates its burdensome weight. The text itself remains "blank"—like the whale, like the doubloon, and like the scroll above Herman Melville's grave.

Acknowledgments

This document only exists through the contributions of innumerable others, known and unknown. Fitting, then, that between this project's inception and its completion I've moved nearly across the world: from Wellington, New Zealand; to New Haven, Connecticut; and finally to Berkeley, California. In addition to the restaurant cooks whose laksa, pizza, and tacos (respectively) kept me nourished these past five years, I'd like to briefly offer thanks to a few people in particular.

First and foremost to Vincent O'Sullivan, whose guidance and support has been one of the great blessings of my life. I am also deeply indebted to Peter Whiteford, who was an endless source of both sage counsel and expert assistance.

Many of my dharma brothers and sisters provided kind criticism and advice. Reverend Bryan Clark devoted significant time reading the first completed draft, and offered invaluable commentary. He also introduced me to Professor Hubert Dreyfus, whose lectures helped shape some of my earliest thoughts on this topic. Heartfelt thanks to Reverend Korin Charlie Pokorny, Reverend David Rutschman, Devon Miller, Amy Parker (whose devotion to *Moby-Dick* convinced me to read it in the first place), and Lauren Bouyea. I also corresponded with dozens of scholars—both Buddhist scholars and Melville scholars—who were very charitable with their time, and gracious in responding to my queries. (Countless librarians assisted in this effort as well.) I send sincere thanks also to everyone at Victoria University of Wellington, San Francisco Zen Center, and Lehigh University Press.

I won't be able to express my gratitude for the encouragement and support I've received from my family and friends, so I won't try. Thank you for everything; I love you all. Special thanks to my parents: to my father for being my first editor when I was eleven years old; and to my mother for providing the beautiful cover illustration—which, true to form, she conceived and executed in a matter of minutes. To my wife Erin, who, throughout the writing process, untangled every knot in my thinking, without fail, in that effortless way of hers, every step of the way. To our daughter Ada, who must wonder why our house is filled with whales. And to our sweet dog Mako.

Deepest gratitude to my teachers Tenshin Reb Anderson Roshi and Daigan Lueck Sensei. Also to great teachers Shunryu Suzuki Roshi, Eihei Dogen Zenji, Shakyamuni Buddha, and all buddhas and ancestors.

Finally, to Herman Melville, thank you for writing this strange book about a whale. It breaks my heart to think you died without knowing what your work would one day mean to the world. Maybe somewhere, now, you do.

May whatever merit I have accumulated in writing this text be dedicated to the benefit of all beings. May they be happy and free from suffering.

Notes

INTRODUCTION

1. Since there are literally dozens of editions of *Moby-Dick*, and hopes of encouraging the reader to follow along in his or her own copy while reading, all passages from *Moby-Dick* will be cited by chapter and paragraph, rather than page number (e.g., 16.4, 42.15, etc.). These citations will be preceded by the abbreviation *M-D*. In this case, the quote is from *M-D* 41.19.

2. Seng-Ts'an, *Hsin-Hsin Ming: Verses on the Faith-Mind*, trans. Richard Clarke (Buffalo: White Pine Press, 2001), 22.

3. *M-D* 55.14.

4. William B. Dillingham, *Melville & His Circle: The Last Years* (Athens: The University of Georgia Press, 1996), 32–34.

5. *Clarel* 1.V.203–208.

6. H. Bruce Franklin, *The Wake of the Gods: Melville's Mythology* (Stanford: Stanford University, 1963), 192

7. qtd. in David Chadwick, *Crooked Cucumber: The Life and Zen Teaching of Shunryu Suzuki* (New York: Broadway Books, 1999), 202.

8. Nathaniel Hawthorne, *The Portable Hawthorne*, ed. Malcolm Cowley (New York: Viking Press, 1969), 650.

9. Qtd. in Thomas Cleary, *Zen Antics: Classics of Buddhism and Zen, Volume Four* (Boston: Shambhala, 2001), 316.

10. *M-D* 55.14.

11. Ibid. 104.2.

12. Dongshan Liangjie, "Song of the Precious Mirror Samadhi," in *Cultivating the Empty Field: The Silent Illumination of Zen Master Hongzhi*, trans. Taigen Daniel Leighton with Yi Wu, 76–78.

13. *M-D* 1.1.

14. Masao Abe, *Zen and Western Thought* (Honolulu: University of Hawaii Press, 1985), 7.

15. R.H. Blyth, *Zen and Zen Classics, Volume 1* (Tokyo: Hokuseido Press), 54.

16. Abe, *Western Thought*, 7.

17. Edward F. Edinger, "The Meaning of the Whale," in *Critical Essays on Herman Melville's* Moby-Dick, ed. Brian Higgins and Hershel Parker (New York: Macmillan, 1992), 470-475.

18. Newton Arvin, *Herman Melville* (London: Methven and Co., 1950), 188.

19. *M-D* 36.38.

20. Thomas Cleary, ed. and trans., *Book of Serenity: One Hundred Zen Dialogues* (Hudson: Lindisfarne Press, 1990), xii.
21. Thanks to Reverend Bryan Clark for helping articulate this idea.
22. *M-D* 113.23.
23. Ibid. 46.1.
24. Ibid. 42.26.
25. Ibid.
26. Ibid.
27. Eihei Dogen, *Genjo Koan*, in *Enlightenment Unfolds: The Essential Teachings of Zen Master Dogen*, ed. Kazuaki Tanahashi (Boston: Shambhala, 1999), 37.
28. Andrew Ferguson, *Zen's Chinese Heritage: The Masters and Their Teachings* (Somerville: Shambhala, 2011), 79–81.
29. Sekito Kisen, *Sandokai*, trans. Soto-shu Liturgy Conference, in Shunryu Suzuki, *Branching Streams Flow in the Darkness: Zen Talks on the Sandokai*, ed. Mel Weitsman and Michael Wenger, (University of California Press: Berkeley, 1999), 21.
30. There is, I suppose, the possibility that Melville had some contact with Zen during his years as a sailor—for example, trading tales with sailors recently returned from China. But to suggest anything more than a fleeting encounter strains credulity.
31. *M-D* 45.2.
32. I also hope this will set the present volume apart from Van Meter Ames's *Zen and American Thought* (Greenwood Press, 1962). Couched in the lofty language of D.T. Suzuki, Ames's book places the "Zen spirit" at the foundation of the nation's intellectual history: lauding the "Zen-freshness" of Jonathan Edwards, finding in Thomas Jefferson "the Zen-pleasure in homely chores," and declaring Emerson an "American Bodhisattva" (203, 30, 58, 78).
33. *M-D* 75.3.
34. Robert Sharf, "The Rhetoric of Experience and the Study of Religion." *Journal of Consciousness Studies*, 7, No. 11–12, 2000, 267–87.
35. Sharf, "Rhetoric," 273.
36. Robert Sharf, "The Zen of Japanese Nationalism." *Curators of the Buddha: The Study of Buddhism Under Colonialism*, ed. Donald S. Lopez. Chicago: University of Chicago Press, 1995, 107–160.
37. Those interested in reading more about the Beat Generation's relationship with Buddhism and Zen may enjoy *The Emergence of Buddhist American Literature*, an essay collection edited by John-Whalen Bridge and Gary Storhoff (SUNY Press, 2009).
38. Alan Watts, "Beat Zen, Square Zen, and Zen." *Chicago Review*, Vol. 12, No. 2, (Summer 1958), 3–11. http://www.jstor.org/stable/i25293446, 8.
39. Ibid. 10.
40. There are many good books on this topic. One particularly valuable one is Rick Fields's *How the Swans Came to the Lake* (Shambhala, 1992).
41. *M-D* 99.2.
42. Ibid. 32.9.

1. THE PROLOGUE TO BUDDHIST STUDIES

1. *M-D* 1.12.
2. Thomas A Tweed, *The American Encounter with Buddhism, 1844–1912* (Chapel Hill: University of North Carolina Press, 1992), xxx.
3. Brian Houghton Hodgson, *Essays on the Languages, Literature, and Religion of Nepal and Tibet* (London: Trubner & Co., 1874), 32.
4. Donald S. Lopez Jr. "The Ambivalent Exigete: Hodgson's Contribution to the Study of Buddhism," in *The Origins of Himalayan Studies: Brian Houghton Hodgson in Nepal and Darjeeling 1820–1858*, ed. David M. Waterhouse (New York: Routledge, 2004), 63.
5. Stephen Batchelor, *The Awakening of the West* (Berkeley: Parallax Press, 1994), 238.

6. Lopez, "Ambivalent Exigete," 56.

7. Tweed xxxi; Andy Nagashima, in his unpublished essay "Who Translated the Preaching of Buddha," quotes the following letter, from Charles Lane to Isaac Hecker, dated 29 December 1843: "While you have been reading some of the Budhist [as spelled in the letter] Books, I find Miss Peabody has been doing the same in French, and translating them for the Dial if Mr. Emerson approves."

2. A UNIVERSAL ABSORBER

1. Lewis Mumford, *Herman Melville* (London: Jonathan Cape, Ltd., 1929), 5.
2. *M-D* 55.3.
3. Ibid.
4. *M-D* 106.4.
5. William Braswell, *Melville's Religious Thought* (New York: Octagon Books), 118.
6. John M.J. Gretchko, *Melvillean Loomings: Essays on Moby-Dick* (Cleveland, Falk & Bright Publishers, Inc.), 42.
7. Herman Melville, *White-Jacket or The World in a Man-of-War* (Evanston and Chicago: Northwestern University Press and The Newberry Library), 4.
8. Millicent Bell, "Pierre Bayle and *Moby-Dick*," *PMLA*, Vol. 66, No. 5 (September 1951), 626–648. 24 August 2010. Web. http://www.jstor.org/stable/459528, 626.
9. Howard P. Vincent, *The Trying-Out of* Moby-Dick (Carbondale: Southern Illinois University Press, 1967), 277.
10. William Potter, *Melville's* Clarel *and the Intersympathy of Creeds* (Kent: Kent State University Press, 2004), 172.
11. *M-D* 32.7.
12. Ibid. 77.3.
13. Ibid. 82.8.
14. James Freeman Clarke, *Ten Great Religions* (Boston: Houghton-Mifflin Company, 1871), 4.
15. In an interesting twist, it was at this precise moment of *Moby-Dick*'s conception that the first wave of Buddhist immigrants began to arrive in America, as over twenty thousand Chinese arrived in the years immediately following the discovery of gold in Northern California in 1848.
16. James Freeman Clarke writes:

> A paper in his [Jones's] own handwriting tells us that he knew critically eight English, Latin, French, Italian, Greek, Arabic, Persian, and Sanskrit; less perfectly eight others,—Spanish, Portuguese, German, Runic, Hebrew, Bengali, Hindi, Turkish; and was moderately familiar with twelve more,—Tibetan, Pali, Phalavi, Deri, Russian, Syriac, Ethiopic, Coptic, Welsh, Swedish, Dutch, and Chinese. (J.F. Clarke, *Ten Great*, 79.)

17. *M-D* 79.6.
18. This finds Melville more in line with the sentiment of Neo-Confucian scholar Fang I-chih (1611–1671), who had come into contact with Jesuits in China, and observed that the "Westerners were clever at examining and fathoming things, but incapable of penetrating the innermost workings of the universe" (qtd. in Batchelor, *Awakening*, 176).
19. Herman Melville, *Mardi: And a Voyage Thither* (Evanston and Chicago: Northwestern University Press and The Newberry Library, 1970), 228.
20. Potter, *Clarel*, 174.
21. Tweed, *American*, xxx
22. William J. Wolf, *Thoreau: Mystic, Prophet, Ecologist* (Philadelphia: United Church Press, 1974), 18.

23. Wolf, *Thoreau*, 16.
24. Ralph Waldo Emerson, *Works* (London: George Rutledge and Sons, 1883), 621.
25. Henry David Thoreau, *A Week on the Concord and Merrimack Rivers* (Princeton: Princeton University Press, 1980), 67.
26. Herman Melville, *Correspondence*, ed. Lynn Horth (Evanston and Chicago: Northwestern University Press and The Newberry Library, 1993), 196.
27. Qtd. in Tweed, *American*, 27; Tweed's book (particularly the first two chapters) is also an excellent source of information on the Victorian era's response to Buddhism.
28. J.J. Clarke, *Oriental Enlightenment: The Encounter Between Asian and Western Thought* (London: Routledge, 1997), 88.
29. Dillingham, *Circle*, 41–42.
30. Herman Melville, "Buddha," in *Collected Poems of Herman Melville*, ed. Howard P. Vincent (Chicago: Packard and Company, 1947), 232.
31. Eleanor M. Tilton, *Melville's "Rammon": A Text and Commentary*. Offprint from Harvard Library Bulletin, Volume XIII, Number 1, Winter 1959, 84.
32. Carol Rollyson and Lisa Paddock, *Herman Melville, A to Z: The Essential Reference to His Life and Work* (New York: Checkmark Books, 2001), 22.
33. Melville, *Collected Poems*, 411.
34. Ibid.
35. Braswell, *Religious Thought*, 4–5.
36. Hawthorne, Portable, 650–651.
37. See, for example, James H. Austin's *Zen and the Brain* (Cambridge: MIT Press, 1999), 678.
38. Meanwhile, recent works including R.K. Gupta's *The Great Encounter: A Study of Indo-American Literary and Cultural Relations* (1986), I. Joseph Ladislaus's *The Quest for Spirituality in Herman Melville and Swami Vivekananda* (2001), have placed Melville more deeply in a Hindu framework; D.J. Ferrantello argues for the importance of trade with China on Melville's worldview in her *Moby-Dick and Peace: Melville's "Gospel of the Century" Revisited: The Influence of the China Trade, Orientalism and Universalism on Melville's Romanticism* (2000).
39. Franklin, *Wake*, 192.
40. Dillingham, *Circle*, 34.
41. V.200–210.
42. Frederick Denison Maurice, *The Religions of the World and their Relations to Christianity* (Boston: Gould and Lincoln), 66.
43. Dillingham, *Circle*, 39–40.
44. J.W.N. Sullivan, "Melville's Lonely Journey" in *Moby-Dick as Doubloon*, eds. Hershel Parker and Harrison Hayford (New York: Norton, 1970. 1923), 165.
45. Herman Melville, *Omoo: A Narrative of Adventures in the South Seas* (Evanston and Chicago: Northwestern University Press and The Newberry Library, 1968), 195.
46. Melville, *Mardi*, 604.
47. Melville, *White-Jacket*, 285.
48. *M-D* 106.4.
49. J.F. Clarke, *Ten Great*, 448.
50. Ibid. 171.
51. Ibid. 139.
52. Dillingham, *Circle*, 37.
53. Clarke, *Ten Great*, v.
54. Qtd. in Parker, *Melville 2*, 230–231.
55. Patricia Turner and Charles Russell Coulter, eds., *Dictionary of Ancient Deities* (New York: Oxford University Press, 2000), 224.
56. Hershel Parker, *Herman Melville, A Biography*. 2 vols. (Baltimore: Johns Hopkins University Press, 1996–2002), 647.
57. *M-D* 1.4.
58. Cf. Ibid. 4.6, 10.4, 12.4.
59. Ibid. 16.55.

60. Ibid. 45.2.
61. Ibid. 45.19.
62. Ibid. 74.8.

3. BAYLE'S *DICTIONARY*

1. Herman Melville. "To Evert A. Duyckinck." 5 April 1849. *The Writings of Herman Melville, Volume 14: Correspondence,* ed. Lynn Horth Evanston. Chicago: Northwestern University Press and The Newberry Library, 1993, 126–129.
2. Franklin, *Wake,* 2.
3. Parker, *Herman Melville,* 623.
4. Bell, "Pierre Bayle," 628.
5. *M-D* 75.10.
6. Pierre Bayle, *The Dictionary Historical and Critical of Mr. Peter Bayle, Second Edition.* 5 vols. (London: Printed for D. Widwinter, et al., 1738), 202.
7. Ibid.
8. "[A] primary proposition, considered self-evident, upon which further reasoning or belief is based" (*Oxford English Dictionary*).
9. Bayle, *Dictionary,* 202.
10. Ibid.
11. *M-D* 36.39.
12. Bayle, *Dictionary,* 202.
13. Ibid.
14. *M-D* 33.6.
15. Bayle, *Dictionary,* 202.
16. Cleary, *Serenity,* xiv.
17. Bayle, *Dictionary,* 549.
18. Gudo Wafu Nishijima and Chodo Cross, trans., *Master Dogen's Shobogenzo.* 4 vols. (London: Windbell Publications, 1994–1999), 49.
19. *M-D* 35.10.
20. Masao Abe, *A Study of Dogen: His Religion and Philosophy* (Albany: State University of New York Press, 1992), 42.
21. Qtd. in Abe, *A Study,* 42.
22. *M-D* 35.10.
23. *M-D* 35.11.
24. Abe, *A Study of Dogen,* 42.
25. Bayle, *Dictionary,* 549.
26. Mumon, *The Gateless Gate: The Classic Book of Zen Koans,* trans. Koun Yamada (Boston, Wisdom Publications, 2004), 138.
27. *M-D* 35.8.
28. Ibid. 35.8, 35.10.
29. Andrew Ferguson, *Zen's Chinese Heritage* (Somerville: Wisdom Publications, 2000), 68.
30. Cf. *M-D* 52.1, 61.6, 86.12.
31. Ibid. 61.4–6.

4. POSSIBILITIES AND PROBABILITIES

1. Herman Melville, *Redburn: His First Voyage* (Evanston and Chicago: Northwestern University Press and The Newberry Library, 1969), vii; Parker explains the inconsistent timeline by speculating that Melville conceived of this dedication before even writing the book.

2. Herman Melville, *Journal of a Visit to London and the Continent, 1849–1850*, ed. Eleanor Melville Metcalf (Cambridge, MA: Harvard University Press, 1948), 44.

3. *M-D* 55.3.

4. Ibid. 56.8.

5. Ibid. 54.32.

6. Ibid. 77.5.

7. Ibid. 64.1.

8. John Francis Davis, *The Chinese: A General Description of China and Its Inhabitants* (New York: Harper Brothers, 1836), 135–136.

9. Another conspicuous item in Davis's text is a reference to the "Grand Lama of Thibet" (Davis, *General Description*, 216), who, as mentioned above, is mentioned in four of Melville's first six books. Melville may have first encountered the term there, or in E.E. Salisbury's lectures before the American Oriental Society, or somewhere else entirely, as it seems to have already become a reasonably well-known term by that time. The lectures are particularly tantalizing, for although they were originally given in 1844, they appeared collected in the *Journal of the American Oriental Society* in 1849—once again, just as Melville was beginning *Moby-Dick*. Salisbury heralds the great advances in Buddhist scholarship that had occurred over the past few years, most notably through the partnership of Brian Hodgson and Eugene Burnouf. These new materials allow him to refer explicitly to the *Prajnaparamita* ("Perfection of Wisdom") literature, quoting its doctrine of ultimate truth far more directly than Bayle was able: "Form itself is illusion, and illusion itself is form," he writes, following Burnouf's translation of the Sanskrit *sunyata* (now generally rendered "emptiness") as "illusion" (Salisbury, "Memoir," 289).

10. Davis, *General Description*, 214.

11. Ibid.

12. Ibid. 220. (This statement is repeated by E.E. Salisbury, who observes that since Buddhism's "distinctive peculiarities are philosophical, and not derived from any particular mythological conceptions, it could take to itself any mythology.")

13. Ibid. 214.

14. Ibid.

15. Ibid. 219.

16. Ibid. 223.

17. Ibid. 220.

18. *M-D* 110.19.

19. Ibid.

20. Davis, *General Description*, 224.

21. *M-D* 10.5.

22. Potter, *Clarel*, xix, 74, 162.

23. "Robert Boyle," *The Living Age*, No. 264, 9 June 1849, 26.

24. In all, *The Living Age* published seven articles on Melville before the publication of *Moby-Dick*: "Herman Melville's Residence in the Marquesas," *The Living Age*, No. 100, 18 April 1846, 26–37; "Herman Melville's *Omoo*," *The Living Age*, No. 159, 29 May 1847, 41–42; "Pacific Rovings," *The Living Age*, No. 167, 24 July 1847, 1–8; "Herman Melville's *Redburn*," *The Living Age*, No. 293, 29 December 1849, 3–7; "Mr. Melville and South Sea Missions," *The Living Age*, No. 339, 16 November 1850, 37–42; "Melville's New Book *Mardi*," *The Living Age*, No. 258, 28 April 1849, 39–41; "*White-Jacket*, or The World in a Man-of-War," *The Living Age*, No. 311, 4 May 1850, 37–40.

25. Here is the note in full, appended to an article about the lectures of Robert Boyle:

> We cannot deny ourselves the pleasure, and its author the justice, of adverting to one of the most recent works which has appeared . . . "The Religions of the World," by the Rev. F. Maurice. This treatise is perhaps less known in the circles of nonconformity than it deserves to be. The few minds in England that are attentive to the development of our higher theological literature, know Mr. Maurice to be one of the most accomplished writers of the age, in all topics that respect the theory of religious belief, and the relations of Christianity to philosophical systems. The

work to which we have referred more than sustains his high reputation. A less speculative mind might perhaps object to it, too great a fondness for the discovery of system and order in the *disjecta membra* of non-Christian creeds and superstitions . . . but every candid person will be pleased with the spirit of deep and liberal sympathy, in combination with extensive learning, with which he has divined not less than investigated the pecularities of the religions which prevail *in partibus infidelium*. . . . We willingly pay this tribute to an able scholar, a genial thinker, a liberal divine, who has not been soiled by the philosophy and vain deceit in which he has been much conversant ("Robert Boyle," *The Living Age*, No. 264, 9 June 1849, 26).

26. Frederick Denison Maurice, *The Religions of the World and their Relations to Christianity* (Boston: Gould and Lincoln, 1854), 74.
   27. "Letter to Nathaniel Hawthorne," 16 April 1851. Horth, *Correspondence,*186.
   28. Maurice, *Religions,* 75.
   29. *M-D* 42.2, 42.11.
   30. Ibid. 42.2.
   31. Ibid. 42.17.
   32. Maurice, *Religions,* 93, 76.
   33. Ibid. 77.
   34. *M-D* 127.21.
   35. Maurice, *Religions,* 76.
   36. Ibid. 78–79.
   37. Ibid. 80.
   38. Ibid. 199.
   39. *M-D* 36.39.
   40. Maurice, *Religions,* 89.
   41. *M-D* 132.17.
   42. Maurice, *Religions,* 92.
   43. *M-D* 132.17.
   44. Maurice, *Religions,* 76.
   45. Ibid. 92–93.
   46. Ibid. 83.
   47. *M-D* 132.19.

5. *MARDI* AND OTHER MYSTERIES

   1. Sullivan, "Lonely Journey," 165.
   2. "Letter to Richard Bentley," 26 June 1850. Horth, *Correspondence,* 163.
   3. "Letter to Nathaniel Hawthorne," 1 June 1851. Horth, *Correspondence,* 193.
   4. Parker, *Melville I,* 574.
   5. Melville, *Mardi,* 13, 603.
   6. Ibid. 13.
   7. Ibid. 14, 3.
   8. Ibid. 383.
   9. Ibid. 296.
   10. Ibid. 12.
   11. Ibid. 428.
   12. Ibid. 352.
   13. Parker, *Melville I,* 623.
   14. Ibid. 693.
   15. "Letter to Sophia Hawthorne," 8 January 1852. Horth, *Correspondence,* 219.
   16. Melville, *Mardi,* 389.

6. GROUNDLESSNESS

1. *M-D* 1.1.

2. Gerry Shishin Wick, *Book of Equanimity: Illuminating Classic Zen Koans* (Somerville: Wisdom Publications, 2005), 114.

3. Eihei Dogen, *Yuibutso Yobutsu—Buddhas Alone, Together With Buddhas*. In Nishijima and Cross, *Book 4*, 213.

4. Nikkyo Niwano, *A Guide to the Threefold Lotus Sutra* (Tokyo: Kosei Publishing Co., 1981), 24.

5. *The Holy Bible: New Revised Standard Version*, Genesis 16.12.

6. Genesis 21.17.

7. Shunryu Suzuki, *Zen Mind, Beginner's Mind* (New York: Weatherhill, 1970), 38, 40.

8. Eihei Dogen, *Guidelines for Studying the Way (Gakudo Yojin-shu)*, in *Moon in a Dewdrop: Writings of Zen Master Dogen*, ed. Kazuaki Tanahashi (New York: North Point Press, 1985), 31.

9. *M-D* 1.1.

10. Ibid.

11. Ibid.10.4.

12. Ibid.1.1.

13. Ibid.

14. Cleary, *Insight*, 126.

15. Seng-Ts'an, *Hsin Hsin Ming*, 22.

16. Eihei Dogen, *Fukanzazengi*, in *The Heart of Dogen's Shobogenzo*, trans. Norman Waddell and Masao Abe (Albany: SUNY Press, 2002), 3.

17. *M-D* 1.1.

18. Ibid. 2.1.

19. "Letter to Nathaniel Hawthorne," 16 April 1851. Horth, *Correspondence*, 186.

20. *M-D* 8.4.

21. Ibid.35.4.

22. Bodhidharma, *The Zen Teaching of Bodhidharma*, trans. Red Pine (New York: North Point Press, 1989), 3.

23. *M-D* 1.9.

24. Ibid.1.12.

25. Ibid. 1.7.

26. Ibid. 1.6.

27. Ibid. 13.6.

28. Ibid. 1.5.

29. Ibid. 14.5, 26.3, 86.12, 132.2.

30. Ibid. 35.12.

31. Suzuki, *Zen Mind*, 34–35.

32. *M-D* 1.3.

33. Ibid. 13.6.

34. Ibid. 13.6.

35. Thomas Cleary, *Zen and the Art of Insight* (Boston: Shambhala, 1999), 20.

36. "To embrace landlessness . . . is to trade certainty for doubt and thus to find ourselves, like Ishmael, compelled not only to wander but to wonder." Carolyn Porter, "Call Me Ishmael, or How to Make Double-Talk Speak," in *Bloom's Modern Critical Interpretations: Herman Melville's* Moby-Dick: *Updated Edition*. (New York: Bloom's Literary Criticism, 2007), 134.

37. *M-D* 1.8.

38. Ibid. 60.9.

39. Reb Anderson, *Being Upright: Zen Meditation and the Bodhisattva Precepts*. (Berkeley: Rodmell Press, 2001), 12.

40. *M-D* 14.5.

41. Ibid. 115.14.

42. Ibid. 23.2.

43. Ibid. 23.4.
44. Ibid. 1.3.
45. Ibid. 23.3.
46. Ibid. 23.2–23.4.
47. Ibid. 3.22.
48. Hubert Dreyfus and Sean Kelly, *All Things Shining: Reading the Western Classics to Find Meaning in a Secular Age* (New York: Free Press, 2011), 50–52.
49. *M-D* 23.2, 23.4.
50. Ibid. 58.11.
51. Ibid. 23.2-3.
52. Ibid. 23.4.

7. NARCISSUS AND DONGSHAN

1. *M-D* 1.6.
2. Ibid.
3. Ibid. 42.12–13.
4. Ibid. 79.1.
5. Ibid. 52.8.
6. Ibid. 1.6.
7. Ovid III. 485–487.
8. Ferguson, *Heritage*, 184.
9. *M-D* 1.6.
10. Ibid. 109.16.
11. Ibid. 108.12.
12. Dogen, *Fukanzazengi*, 3.
13. Steve Hagen, *Buddhism Is Not What You Think* (San Francisco: Harper, 2003), 13–14.
14. Dogen, *Genjo Koan*, 36.
15. *M-D* 109.9.
16. The word "leak," in an interesting coincidence, happens to be the most common translation of the Sanskrit word *asvara* (Pali: *asava*), used to refer to the "attachments to sense objects and therefore to passions" (Taigen Daniel Leighton, *Cultivating the Empty Field: The Silent Illumination of Zen Master Hongzhi,* trans. Leighton with Yi Wu [San Francisco: North Point Press, 1991], 77).
17. *M-D* 1.4.
18. Ibid. 1.3.
19. Ibid. 52.8.
20. Ibid. 76.4.

8. SEARCHING FOR ISHMAEL

1. Porter, "Ishmael," 139.
2. John Bryant, "*Moby-Dick* as Revolution," in *Bloom's Modern*, 199–224.
3. Andrew Delbanco, *Melville: His World and Work* (New York: Vintage Books, 2005), 145.
4. As Chinese Zen master Hongzhi (1091–1157) said, "The essential function . . . is to know without touching things and to illuminate without encountering objects. Knowing without touching things, this knowledge is innately subtle" (Leighton, *Cultivating*, 39).
5. *M-D* 41.1.
6. Ibid. 104.11.
7. Bryant, "Revolution," 202.

8. *M-D* 76.2, 125.14.
9. Ibid. 114.4.
10. R.P. Blackmur, "The Real Center of Interest" (1938), in Parker and Hayford, *Doubloon*, 179.
11. Genesis 21:8–21:25.
12. *M-D* 12.4.
13. Ibid. 10.5.
14. Ibid. 12.6.
15. Ibid. epilogue.
16. Alfred Kazin, "Introduction to Moby-Dick," in *Bloom's Modern*, 10–19.
17. Porter, "Ishmael," 149.
18. *M-D* 4.5.
19. Ibid. 3.34, 3.40.
20. Ibid. 3.44.
21. Ibid. 3.74.
22. Ibid. 11.2.
23. Ibid. 4.3.
24. Ibid. 4.4.
25. Ibid. 4.3.
26. Ibid. 4.1.
27. Ibid. 4.3, 4.4.
28. Ibid. 10.7.
29. Ibid. 10.4.
30. Ibid. 4.4.
31. Ibid.
32. Ibid.
33. Ibid. 5.1.
34. Ibid. 17.14.
35. Ibid. 17.15; Melville's scene fits Englebert Kaempfer's 1727 description (in his bestseller *History of Japan*) of the meditation practice of the Japanese *bonzes*, both in posture—"sitting upon their knees and ancles"—and in imperturbability: "Sasen is a profound meditation of divine misteries and holy things, which so entirely takes up a man's mind, that his body lies, as it were, destitute of all sense and life, unmov'd by any external object whatsoever" (Englebert Kaempfer, *The History of Japan* [Richmond: Curzon Press, 1993], 10, 150).
36. Melville would have read Buddha referred to as a "sage" both in Thomas Maurice's *History of Hindostan* and in "The Preaching of Buddha" in *The Dial*.
37. In effect saving him twice—first, of course, literally saving the man's life, but also, as Ishmael contends, teaching everyone a lesson about the "mutual, joint-stock world" (*M-D* 13.15).
38. *M-D* 78.8–14.
39. Ibid. 110.2.
40. Ibid. 110.17.
41. Karen Armstrong, *Buddha* (New York: Penguin, 2001), 174.
42. *M-D* 110.17; Stories abound about enlightened masters choosing the manner of their demise. One notable story is that of Zen master Dongshan:

> Then the master had his head shaved, bathed and put on robes. He struck the bell and announced his departure to the assembly. Sitting solemnly, he began to pass away. Immediately the large assembly began to wail and lament. This continued for some time without stopping. The master suddenly opened his eyes and addressed the assembly, saying, "For those who have left home, a mind unattached to things is the true practice. People struggle to live and make much of death. But what's the use of lamenting?" Then he ordered a temple official to make arrangements for a "delusion banquet." However, the assembly's feeling of bereavement did not go away, so preparations for the banquet were extended over seven days. The master joined with the assembly in completing the preparations, saying, You monks have

made a great commotion over nothing. When you see me pass away this time, don't make a noisy fuss." Accordingly, he retired to his room, sat correctly, and passed away in the third month of the tenth year of the Hsien-t'ung era (qtd. in William F. Powell, *The Record of Tung-shan* [University of Hawaii Press, Honolulu, 1989], 68.)

43. *M-D* 10.4.
44. Ibid. 7.3.
45. Ibid. 66.4.
46. Ibid. 17.14.
47. Ibid. 17.29.
48. Ibid. 10.5.
49. Ibid. 10.9.

9. WHALING LIFE, MONASTIC LIFE

1. *Mahasaccaka Sutta*, in *The Middle-Length Discourses of the Buddha: A Translation of the Majjhima Nikaya*, trans. Bhikku Nanamoli and Bikkhu Bodhi (Somerville: Wisdom Publications, 1995), 36:12.
2. Qtd. in Dogen, *Ceaseless Practice*, in Tanahashi, *Enlightenment*, 120.
3. D.T. Suzuki, *The Training of the Zen Buddhist Monk* (New York: University Books, 1965), 53.
4. In fact, the Chinese phrase *qinggui*, meaning "monastic regulations," is an abbreviation of *qingjinghaizhongqinggui*, meaning "the regulations of the pure oceanlike community."
5. Herman Melville, "Hawthorne and His Mosses," in *The Literary World* (1847–1853) 17–24 August 1850, American Periodicals Series Online, ProQuest. Web, 21 October 2010.
6. "Works in Press." *The Literary World* (1847–1853) 20 Nov. 1847.
7. qtd. In William M. Bodiford, *Soto Zen in Medieval Japan* (Honolulu: University of Hawaii Press, 1993), 58.
8. *M-D* 98.7.
9. Ibid. 98.5.
10. One brief example, connecting the rituals of the whaleship to those in the monastery: In Dogen's *Fushukuhanpo*, "The Dharma for Taking Food," he outlines the forms of *oryoki*, the ritualized eating-style in Zen monasteries. Dogen writes, "sitting places for meals depends on the number of years since ordination or the time spent in that monastery" (85), and in "The Cabin-Table" we watch the three mates go down to dinner, descending to the cabin strictly by rank. Starbuck accepts his meal "as though receiving alms; and cut it tenderly . . . and chewed it noiselessly . . . not without circumspection" (34.5). Dogen writes, "The manner for receiving food is to accept it respectfully. Buddha said, 'Receive food with reverence.' We should study this" (Eihei Dogen, *Fushukuhanpo*, in *Pure Standards for the Zen Community: A Translation of Eihei Shingi*, trans. Taigen Daniel Leighton and Shohaku Okamura [Albany: SUNY Press, 1996], 91).
11. Leighton, *Training*, 3.
12. *M-D* 1.1.
13. Ibid. 112.5, 112.7.
14. Ibid. 112.4.
15. Ibid. 112.7.
16. Ibid.
17. Ibid. 112.1.
18. Ibid. 112.8.
19. Ibid. 112.7.
20. *Literary World*, 381.
21. *M-D* 112.1.

22. Ibid.
23. Ibid.
24. Ibid. 113.4.
25. Ibid.
26. Ibid. 112.1.
27. Hongzhi, *Cultivating*, 21.
28. *M-D* 107.2.
29. Ibid. 107.4.
30. Ibid. 107.2.
31. Ibid. 107.5.
32. *Literary World*, 381.
33. *M-D* 107.5.
34. Ibid. 107.6.
35. Ibid.
36. Suzuki, *Training*, 60.
37. *M-D* 112.1.
38. Ibid. 127.10.
39. Eihei Dogen, *Tenzokyokun*, in *Dogen's Pure Standards for the Zen Community: A Translation of Eihei Shingi*, trans. Taigen Daniel Leighton and Shohaku Okamura (Albany: SUNY Press, 1996), 44.
40. *M-D* 107.5–6.
41. D.T. Suzuki, *Essays in Zen Buddhism, First Series* (Auckland: Rider and Co., 1970), 317.
42. *M-D* 108.10.
43. Salisbury, *Memoir*, 96.
44. *M-D* 16.29–33, 16.38–39.
45. Eihei Dogen, *Shukke Tokudo*, in Nishijima and Cross, *Shobogenzo IV*, 177–178.
46. *M-D* 94.6.
47. Ibid. 1.6.
48. Ibid. 94.5.

10. ISHMAEL'S MEDITATION

1. *M-D* 10.5.
2. Ibid. 20.7.
3. Dogen, *Fukanzazengi*, 4.
4. Seng-Ts'an, *Hsin Hsin Ming*, 23.
5. *M-D* 16.82.
6. Ibid. 94.4.
7. Ibid. 87.20.
8. Ibid. 133.17–19.
9. Dogen, *Genjo-Koan*, 38.
10. *M-D* 41.24.
11. Ibid. 41.1.
12. Ibid. 96.8.
13. Seng-Ts'an, *Hsin Hsin Ming*, 24.
14. *M-D* 96.10.
15. Ibid. 96.11.
16. Ibid. 96.12.
17. Ibid. 61.4.
18. Ibid. 51.8.
19. Ibid. 111.3.
20. Ibid. 42.1.
21. Ibid. 1.22.

22. Qtd. in Cleary, *Insight*, 8.
23. *M-D* 10.4, 2.9.
24. Seng-Ts'an, *Hsin Hsin Ming*, 23.
25. *M-D* 11.3.
26. Ibid. 7.7.
27. Maurice, *Religions*, 68.
28. Hongzhi, *Cultivating*, 23.
29. *M-D* 41.21.
30. Ibid. 18.12.
31. Ibid. 16.3.
32. Ibid. 17.1–2.
33. Ibid. 10.9.
34. Ibid. 107.5.
35. Ibid. 85.11.
36. Ibid. 85.12.
37. Ibid. 49.1.
38. Ibid. 18.12.
39. Ibid. 3.53.
40. Ibid. 68.1.
41. Ibid. 3.2.
42. Ibid.
43. Ibid. 61.1.
44. Eihei Dogen, *Sansuikyo* (*Sutra of Mountains and Water*), in Nishijima and Cross, *Shobogenzo I*, 241.
45. *M-D* 76.4.
46. Cleary, *Insight*, 21.
47. *M-D* 68.7.
48. "In ancient times a monk asked a venerable patriarch, 'When a hundred thousand myriad circumstances converge all at once, what should I do?' The venerable patriarch said, 'Do not try to manage them'" (Eihei Dogen, *Yuibutso*, in Nishijima and Cross, *Shobogenzo I*, 216–217).
49. *M-D* 87.27.
50. Cleary, *Insight*, 126.
51. *M-D* 68.6.
52. Ibid. 68.7.
53. Ibid. 60.9.
54. Seng-Ts'an, *Hsin Hsin Ming*, 22.
55. *M-D* 96.2.
56. Ibid. 35.8
57. Ibid. 64.7
58. Ibid. 106.3.
59. Dogen, *Genjo Koan*, 36.
60. *M-D* 3.1.
61. Ibid. 85.1–2.
62. Ibid. 2.2.
63. Ibid. 85.3.
64. This passage is also notable in mentioning, as Philip Hoare does in *Leviathan*, that the sperm whale remains constantly mindful of its breath. Its respiration, unlike our own, is not involuntary; it must make a conscious decision to breathe, with every inhale and exhale (Philip Hoare, *Leviathan, or The Whale* [London: Fourth Estate], 2008, 28.) As Huike might say, "It is always clearly aware" (Cook, *Transmitting the Light*, 156).
65. *M-D* 85.7.
66. Ibid. 98.7.
67. Ibid. 82.1.
68. Ibid. 72.3.
69. Ibid. 17.29.
70. Ibid. 48.47.

71. Ibid. 110.2.
72. Ibid. 16.79.
73. Ibid. 22.16.
74. Ibid. 87.12.
75. Ibid. 132.1.
76. Ibid. 114.4.
77. Ibid. 130.2.
78. Ibid. 119.30.
79. Ibid. 64.23.
80. Ibid. 106.3.
81. Ibid. 127.21.
82. Ibid. 85.8.
83. Ibid. 93.1.
84. Ibid. 93.13.
85. Ibid. 108.1.
86. Ibid. 11.2.

11. IMPERMANENCE AND INTERDEPENDENCE

1. *M-D* 18.12–13.
2. Ibid. 49.8.
3. Ibid. 49.1.
4. Ibid. 49.8.
5. Bodhidharma, *Zen Teaching*, 41.
6. *M-D* 49.9.
7. "Letter to Nathaniel Hawthorne," 17 November 1851. Horth, *Correspondence*, 212.
8. *M-D* 11.2.
9. Ibid. 11.3.
10. Dogen, *Fukanzazengi*, 3.
11. *M-D* 24.22.
12. Ibid. 25.2.
13. Ibid. 47.1.
14. Ibid. 47.2.
15. Ibid. 1.12.
16. Ibid. 47.2
17. This phrase coined by Tenshin Reb Anderson.
18. *M-D* 72.3.
19. Ibid. 72.4.
20. Ibid. 72.7.
21. Ibid.
22. Ibid.
23. Ibid. 72.4.
24. Reb Anderson, *Warm Smiles from Cold Mountains: Dharma Talks on Zen Meditation* (Berkeley: Rodmell Press, 2005), 133.

12. PHILOSOPHY, KOANS, AND SILENCE

1. *M-D* 1.1.
2. Ibid. 73.40.
3. Ibid. 35.9.
4. Ibid.

5. Ibid.
6. Ibid. 1.5.
7. Ibid. 60.10.
8. Ibid. 10.4.
9. Dogen, *Genjo Koan*, 35.
10. *M-D* 1.5.
11. Qtd. in Blyth, *Zen*, 48.
12. *M-D* 16.31–32.
13. Ibid. 3.45.
14. Ibid. 16.15, 16.27.
15. Ibid. 49.6.
16. Ibid. 5.7, 17.3–22.
17. Ibid. 85.6.
18. Ibid. 79.5; The Buddha is said to have maintained a similar "noble silence"—as Stephen Batchelor writes, "When asked what he was doing, the Buddha replied that he taught 'anguish and the ending of anguish.' When asked about metaphysics (the origin and end of the universe, the identity or difference of body and mind, his existence or nonexistence after death), he remained silent" (Stephen Batchelor, *Buddhism Without Beliefs* [London: Bloomsbury, 1997], 15.)
19. Seng-Ts'an, *Hsin Hsin Ming*, 22.
20. *M-D* 4.3.
21. Ibid. 87.14.
22. Ibid. 85.6.
23. Ibid. 93.13.
24. Ibid. 13.6.
25. Ibid. 110.4.
26. Ibid. 32.6–32.16.
27. Ibid. 99.9.
28. Ibid. 57.9.
29. Ibid. 55.14.
30. Hongzhi, *Cultivating*, 12–16.
31. *Gabyo*, Nishijima and Cross, *Shobogenzo II*, 343.
32. *M-D* 42.2.
33. Ibid. 104.2.
34. Ibid. 104.3.
35. Ibid. 104.3.
36. Ibid. 55.14.
37. Ibid. 32.9.
38. Ibid. 32.43.
39. Ibid. 55.14.
40. Ibid. 32.43.
41. Ibid. 32.9.
42. Ibid. 110.19.
43. Ibid. 110.19.
44. Ibid. 99.13.
45. Ibid. 110.19.
46. Ibid. 10.2.
47. Ibid. 6.1.
48. Ibid. 17.2.
49. Ibid. 10.3.
50. Ibid. 68.5.
51. Ibid.
52. Ibid.
53. Ibid. 68.1.
54. Ibid. 102.8.
55. Ibid. 104.11.

56. Ibid. 70.7.
57. Ibid. 70.5–6.
58. Ibid. 36.39.
59. Ibid. 44.1.
60. Ibid. 44.2.

13. SARCASTIC SCIENCE

1. Bernie Glassman, *Infinite Circle: Teachings in Zen* (Boston: Shambhala, 2002), x.
2. *M-D* 36.39.
3. Ibid. 79.4.
4. Ibid.
5. Ibid.76.4.
6. Ibid.76.2.
7. Ibid. 36.39.
8. Ibid.
9. Ibid. 36.39.
10. Ibid. 76.4.
11. Ibid. 80.3.
12. Ibid. 76.4.
13. Ibid. 86.14.
14. Ibid. 133.24.
15. Ibid. 36.38.
16. Ibid. 100.36.
17. Ibid. 42.26.
18. Ibid. 42.24.
19. Ibid. 68.3.
20. Ibid. 32.20.
21. Ibid. 59.11.
22. Ibid. 59.11.
23. Ibid. 55.12.
24. Ibid. 86.12.
25. Ibid. 79.2, 79.4; Philip Hoare, in his extended encomium to whales and whaling *Leviathan*, writes of his experience viewing sperm whales for the first time in person: "They were giant jigsaw puzzles: no matter how hard I looked, I could not grasp the entirety of the creatures, the sense of their structure, the components from which they were made. It was as if they were shifting in and out of focus" (Hoare, *Leviathan*, 212).
26. *M-D* 70.2.
27. Ibid. 76.2.
28. Ibid.
29. Ibid. 79.6.
30. Ibid. 80.3.
31. Ibid. 80.2–3.
32. Ibid. 100.35.
33. Ibid. 86.14.
34. Ibid. 79.6.
35. Ibid. 86.14.
36. Ibid. 68.2.
37. Ibid. 68.3.
38. Ibid. 42.12.
39. Ibid. Extracts.
40. Ibid. 32.5.
41. Ibid. 32.2.
42. Ibid. 32.9.

43. Ibid. 32.42.
44. Ibid. 32.34.
45. Ibid. 32.27.
46. Ibid. 32.10.
47. Ibid. 32.11.
48. Ibid.
49. Ibid. 32.14.
50. Ibid. 32.13.
51. Ibid. 32.21.
52. Ibid. 32.44.
53. Ibid.
54. Ibid.
55. Ibid. 68.6.
56. Ibid. 32.22.
57. Ibid. 79.6.
58. Ibid. 32.24.

14. THE FIRST PRINCIPLE OF ALL THINGS

1. Bayle, *Dictionary*, 549.
2. *M-D* 105.15.
3. Ibid. 41.13.
4. Bayle, *Dictionary*, 549.
5. *M-D* 42.26.
6. Bayle, *Dictionary*, 549.
7. *M-D* 133.17.
8. Ibid. 102.9.
9. Bayle, *Dictionary*, 549.
10. *M-D* 104.1.
11. Ibid. 55.12.
12. Ibid. 55.13.
13. Ibid. 55.14.
14. Bayle, Dictionary, 549.
15. *M-D* 79.5.
16. Ibid. 119.31.
17. "Heart of Great Perfect Wisdom Sutra," in Shohaku Okamura, *Realizing Genjokoan: The Key to Dogen's Shobogenzo* (Somerville: Wisdom, 2010), 205–206.
18. Ibid. 205.
19. Keizan Jokin, *The Record of Transmitting the Light: Zen Master Keizan's Denkoroku*, trans. Francis Dojun Cook (Somerville: Wisdom Publications, 2003), 210.
20. *M-D* 79.4.
21. Bayle, *Dictionary*, 549.
22. *M-D* 104.3.
23. Ibid. 104.7.
24. Ibid. 44.11.
25. Bayle, *Dictionary*, 549.
26. Ibid. 549.
27. *M-D* 69.2, 75.3.
28. Bayle, *Dictionary*, 549.
29. *M-D* 55.14.

15. WHITENESS

1. *M-D* 42.2.
2. Ibid. 42.3–4.
3. Ibid. 42.26.
4. Ibid. 42.3.
5. Ibid.
6. Ibid.
7. Ibid.
8. Ibid. 42.4.
9. Ibid. 71.17.
10. Ibid. 79.5.
11. Ibid. 25.2.
12. Ibid. 42.26.
13. Ibid. 42.6.
14. Ibid. 42.25.
15. Ibid. 42.24.
16. Ibid. 36.39.
17. C.W. Huntington Jr., *The Emptiness of Emptiness: An Introduction to Early Indian Madhyamaka* (Honolulu: University of Hawaii Press, 1989), 26.
18. *M-D* 49.1.
19. Ibid. 49.13.
20. Ibid. 79.5.
21. Huntington, *Emptiness*, 26.
22. *M-D* 42.2.
23. Ibid. 42.24.
24. Ibid. 42.25.
25. Suzuki, *Zen Mind*, 116.
26. Blyth, *Zen*, 77.
27. John Powers, trans., *Wisdom of Buddha: The Samdhinirmocana Mahayana Sutra* (Berkeley: Dharma Publishing, 1995), 85.
28. *M-D* 42.26.
29. Dreyfus and Kelly, *All Things Shining*, 169–173.
30. *M-D* 42.26.
31. Ibid.
32. Ibid.
33. Ibid.
34. Cleary, *Book of Serenity*, 120.
35. Ibid. 126.
36. Blyth, *Zen*, 75.
37. *M-D* 42.26.
38. Ibid. 79.5.
39. Ibid. 42.26.
40. Ibid.
41. Ibid.
42. Jay L. Garfield, *The Fundamental Wisdom of the Middle Way: Nagarjuna's Mulamadhyamakakarika* (New York: Oxford University Press, 1995), 90.
43. *M-D* 43.2.
44. Ibid. 51.10.
45. Ibid. 42.24.
46. Ibid. 42.3.
47. Ibid. 35.8.
48. Blyth, *Zen*, 16.
49. *M-D* 42.11.
50. Ibid. 86.14.

51. Hongzhi, *Cultivating*, 26.
52. *M-D* 42.26.

16. THE MEASUREMENTS OF THE
WHALE SKELETON

1. *M-D* 32.5.
2. Ibid. 102.3.
3. Ibid. 102.1–6.
4. Ibid. 102.10.
5. Ibid. 102.6.
6. Ibid. 102.10.
7. Ibid. 103.8.
8. Ibid. 55.12–14; Dogen Zenji makes a similar point, regarding the inseparable nature between an object and the brocade of conditions surrounding it:

> A fish swims in the ocean, and no matter how far it swims there is no end to the water. A bird flies in the sky, and no matter how far it flies there is no end to the air. However, the fish and the bird have never left their elements . . . If the bird leaves the air it will die at once. If the fish leaves the water it will die at once (Dogen, *Genjo Koan*, 37–38).

9. *M-D* 59.11.
10. Ibid.
11. Ibid. 102.10.
12. Ibid. 103.8.
13. Ibid. 103.9.
14. Ibid. 68.6.
15. Ibid. 60.13.
16. Ibid. 102.14.
17. Ibid. 110.19.
18. Ibid. 8.4.
19. Ibid. 102.10.

17. OX-HERDING

1. "By reason of these things, then, the whaling voyage was welcome; the great flood-gates of the wonder-world swung open, and in the wild conceits that swayed me to my purpose, two and two there floated into my inmost soul, endless processions of the whale, and, mid most of them all, one grand hooded phantom, like a snow hill in the air" (*M-D* 1.15).
2. Nyogen Sensaki, *Like a Dream, Like a Fantasy: The Zen Teachings and Translations of Nyogen Senzaki*, ed. Eido Shimano (Boston: Wisdom Publications, 2005), 120.
3. *M-D* 41.2, 41.6.
4. Ibid. 76.4.
5. Paul Reps, *Zen Flesh, Zen Bones*, compiled by Paul Reps and Nyogen Senzaki (Boston: Tuttle Publishing, 1998), 168.
6. As Ishmael instructs, "Take almost any path you please, and ten to one it carries you down in a dale, and leaves you there by a pool in the stream . . . [it] will infallibly lead you to water" (*M-D* 1.5).
7. Reps, *Zen Flesh*, 168.

8. Ibid. 172.
9. *M-D* 102.1.
10. Reps, *Zen Flesh*, 173.
11. *M-D* 57.9.
12. Reps, *Zen Flesh*, 174.
13. *M-D* 61.3–4.
14. Reps, *Zen Flesh*, 174.
15. *M-D* 61.19.
16. Reps, *Zen Flesh*, 175.
17. *M-D* 87.27.
18. Ibid.
19. Reps, *Zen Flesh*, 178.
20. Ibid. 180.
21. *M-D* 104.3.
22. Kapleau, *Pillars*, 313.
23. Reps, *Zen Flesh*, 182.
24. *M-D* 42.26.
25. Ibid.
26. Reps, *Zen Flesh*, 184.
27. Ibid.
28. *M-D* 102.10.
29. Ibid. 103.9.
30. Reps, *Zen Flesh*, 186.
31. *M-D* 1.1.
32. Ibid. 87.27.
33. Ibid. 1.3.
34. Reps, *Zen Flesh*, 186.

18. A FACTIONALIZED CONSCIOUSNESS

1. *M-D* 28.5.
2. Ibid. 41.20.
3. Ibid.
4. *Samyutta Nikaya* 22.56.
5. *M-D* 51.3.
6. Ibid. 44.11.
7. Ibid. 70.11.
8. Ibid. 108.26.
9. Bayle, *Dictionary*, 549.
10. *M-D* 41.20.
11. Ibid. 108.6.
12. Ibid. 44.4.
13. Ibid. 51.10.
14. Ibid. 28.5.
15. Ibid. 51.10.
16. Ibid. 120.6.
17. Ibid. 36.39.
18. Ibid. 37.4.
19. Ibid. 118.2.
20. Ibid. 118.8.
21. Ibid. 132.17.
22. "Letter to Nathaniel Hawthorne," 16 April 1851. Horth, *Correspondence*, 186.
23. *M-D* 41.20.
24. Ibid. 36.39.

25. Ibid. 41.20.
26. Ibid. 117.14.
27. *M-D* 134.29, 134.43.
28. Ibid. 44.11.
29. Ibid. 37.4.
30. "Letter to Nathaniel Hawthorne," 16 April 1851. Horth, *Correspondence*, 186.
31. Ibid. 79.5.
32. Ibid. 133.44.
33. Ibid. 106.3.
34. Ibid.
35. Ibid. 106.3.
36. Ibid. 106.5.
37. Ibid. 108.32.
38. Ibid.
39. Suzuki, *Zen Mind*, 93.
40. *M-D* 110.5.
41. Ibid. 114.4.
42. Suzuki, *Zen Mind*, 93–94.
43. *M-D* 132.7.
44. Ibid. 114.6.
45. Batchelor, *Beliefs*, 76.
46. *M-D* 41.19.
47. Ibid. 133.44.
48. Ibid. 112.7.
49. Dogen, *Bendowa*, in Tanahashi, *Dewdrop*, 146.
50. Ibid.
51. Ibid. 132.17.
52. In Ahab's view—that is, the idea of the "egotistical sky"—God-as-thing would also be one of these circles, within the larger circle the Universe. But since this idea requires postulating a higher "GOD," I am using God and Universe as synonyms.
53. Ishmael admits being infected by Ahab's fury himself: "[M]y shouts had gone up with the rest; my oath had been welded with theirs; and stronger I shouted, and more did I hammer and clinch my oath. . . . A wild mystical, sympathetical feeling was in me; Ahab's quenchless feud seemed mine" (*M-D* 41.1).
54. Dogen, *Bendowa*, 146.
55. *M-D* 133.44.
56. Ibid. 52.5.
57. Ibid. 51.6.
58. Ibid. 52.6.
59. Ibid. 130.11, 130.15.
60. Ibid. 53.8.
61. Ibid. 53.2.
62. Ibid. 16.79.
63. Cf. *M-D* 100.1, 115.9, 128.3, 131.3.
64. Ibid. 53.1.
65. Ibid. 52.4.
66. Ibid. 54.2.
67. Ibid.
68. Ibid. 71.4.
69. Ibid. 71.27–28.
70. Ibid. 100.4.
71. Ibid. 100.6.
72. Ibid. 115.11.
73. Ibid. 131.11.
74. Ibid. 128.14.
75. Ibid. 128.16.

19. SAVAGERY BEYOND SAVAGERY

1. *M-D* 36.24.
2. Ibid. 124.13.
3. "[T]hese three savages" (*M-D* 34.8).
4. Ibid. 96.7.
5. Ibid. 81.36.
6. Ibid. 18.23.
7. Ibid. 78.15.
8. Ibid. 102.4.
9. Ibid.
10. Ibid. 102.11.
11. Ibid. 16.3.
12. Ibid. 12.6.
13. Ibid. 79.5.
14. "Letter to Nathaniel Hawthorne," 16 April 1851. Horth, *Correspondence,* 186.
15. *M-D* 10.4.
16. Ibid. 17.29.
17. Ibid. 57.3.
18. Blyth, *Zen*, 7, 13.

20. FAITH AND THE THREE MATES

1. *M-D* 7.4; thanks to Amy Parker for her help with this idea.
2. Ibid.
3. Ibid. 13.5.
4. Ibid. 7.4.
5. Ibid. 96.12.
6. Ibid. 7.7.
7. Ibid. 7.4.
8. Ibid. 7.5.
9. Ibid. 7.6.
10. Philip Kapleau, *The Three Pillars of Zen* (Garden City: Anchor Books, 1980), 64.
11. Victor Sogen Hori, "The Nature of the Rinzai (Linji) Koan Practice," in *Sitting with Koans*, John Daido Loori, ed. (Boston: Wisdom Publications, 2006), 118–119.
12. *M-D* 7.4.
13. Ibid. 8.4.
14. Ibid. 79.1.
15. Ibid. 42.12–13.
16. Ibid. 85.12.
17. Garfield, *Fundamental Wisdom*, 223.
18. *M-D* 127.15.
19. Ibid. 27.4.
20. Ibid.
21. Ibid. 34.6.
22. Ibid. 99.10.
23. Ibid. 41.24.
24. Ibid. 133.44.
25. Ibid. 27.2.
26. Ibid. 41.24.
27. Ibid. 27.1.
28. Ibid.

29. Ibid. 29.10.
30. Ibid. 65.1.
31. Ibid. 64.25.
32. Ibid. 118.8.
33. Ibid. 39.1.
34. Ibid. 135.53.
35. Ibid. 26.1.
36. Ibid.
37. Ibid.
38. Ibid.
39. Ibid. 26.2.
40. Ibid. 49.3.
41. Ibid. 109.12.
42. Ibid. 26.1.
43. Ibid.
44. Ibid.
45. Ibid.
46. Qtd. in Hagen, *Not What You Think*, 22.
47. Cleary, *Insight*, 24.
48. *M-D* 26.4.
49. Ibid. 38.2.
50. Ibid. 124.18.
51. Ibid. 132.12.
52. Ibid. 41.24.
53. Ibid. 119.4.
54. Ibid. 81.42.
55. Ibid. 114.8.
56. Ibid. 109.17–18.
57. Ibid. 123.8.
58. Ibid. 123.12.
59. Ibid. 123.9.
60. Ibid. 134.42.
61. Ibid. 135.52.

21. THE DOUBLOON

1. *M-D* 99.7.
2. Bodhidharma, *Zen Teachings*, 77.
3. *M-D* 86.12.
4. Ibid. 79.5.
5. Ibid. 99.7.
6. Ibid.
7. Ibid. 99.8.
8. Ibid.
9. Ibid.
10. Ibid.
11. Ibid.
12. Ibid.
13. Ibid. 99.9.
14. Ibid.
15. Ibid.
16. For example: wondering aloud if Old King-Post (aka Flask) is "wise or foolish" (and concluding that he's both: "if it be really wise it has a foolish look to it; yet, if it be really foolish, then has it a sort of wiscish look to it"); reckoning Queequeg's tattoos bear a resem-

blance to the zodiac; assuming Fedallah has some secret understanding of the doubloon, making "a sign to the sign" (*M-D* 99.11, 99.13).

17. Ibid. 99.13.
18. Ibid. 99.14.
19. Ibid. 99.13, 99.22.
20. Cleary, *Insight*, 89.
21. Seng-Ts'an, *Hsin Hsin Ming*, 23.
22. *M-D* 75.3.
23. Ibid. 42.26.

22. PIP, WHO JUMPED FROM THE WHALE-BOAT

1. *M-D* 93.3.
2. Ibid. 93.3.
3. Ibid. 93.2.
4. Ibid. 114.2–3.
5. Ibid. 100.2, 118.1.
6. Ibid. 128.3–4.
7. Dogen, *Genjo Koan*, 36.
8. *M-D* 60.4.
9. Ibid. 60.6.
10. In the fascicle "Zenki," Dogen Zenji extends this connection between boat and Self even further:

> Life can be likened to a time when a person is sailing in a boat. On this boat, I am operating the sail, I have taken the rudder, I am pushing the pole; at the same time, the boat is carrying me, and there is no "I" beyond the boat. Through my sailing of the boat, this boat is being caused to be a boat—let us consider, and learn in practice, just this moment of the present. At this very moment, there is nothing other than the world of the boat: the sky, the water, the shore have all become the moment of the boat, which is utterly different from moments not on the boat. So life is what I am making it, and I am what life is making me. While I am sailing in the boat, my body and mind and circumstances and self are all essential parts of the boat; and the whole earth and the whole of space are all essential parts of the boat. What has been described like this is that life is the self, and the self is life (Eihei Dogen, *Zenki*, in Nishijima and Cross, *Shobogenzo II*, 244).

11. *M-D* 93.6.
12. Ibid. 35.13.
13. Ibid. 93.9.
14. Ibid. 93.11.
15. Ibid. 93.13.
16. Dogen, *Genjo Koan*, 36.
17. *M-D* 93.10.
18. Ibid.
19. Hubert Dreyfus, "Ishmael and the Sacred," University of California, Berkeley, 11 November 1997. Lecture.
20. *M-D* 93.10.
21. Ibid. 93.13.
22. Ibid. 93.10.
23. Ibid. 93.13.
24. Ibid. 129.8.

25. Melville would have read this story in Ovid's *Metamorphoses* (III.308–309), a few pages before reading about Narcissus.
26. Exodus 33:20.
27. *M-D* 93.13.
28. Ibid. 110.15.
29. Ibid. 125.20, 125.25.
30. John Blofeld, *The Zen Teaching of Huang Po: On the Transmission of Mind* (London: Rider & Company, 1958), 17.
31. Cleary, *Insight*, ix–x.
32. *M-D* 93.13.
33. Dogen, *Genjo Koan*, 36.
34. *M-D* 93.13.
35. Ibid.
36. Walpola Rahula, *What the Buddha Taught* (New York: Grove Press, 1974), 20.
37. *Samyutta Nikaya*, 22.56.
38. Anderson, *Warm Smiles*, 33.
39. Anderson, *Upright*, 162.
40. Seng-Ts'an, *Hsin Hsin Ming*, 26.
41. Ken Wilber, *No Boundary* (Boston: Shambhala, 1979), 4.
42. Wilber, *Boundary*, 5.
43. Ibid. 12.
44. *M-D* 133.33.
45. Ibid. 93.13.
46. Batchelor, *Beliefs*, 76.
47. *M-D* 93.13.

23. AHAB'S AWAKENING

1. *M-D* 106.3.
2. Ibid. 108.6.
3. Ibid. 70.9.
4. Ibid. 70.11.
5. Ibid. 116.3.
6. Ibid. 113.4.
7. Ibid. 100.37.
8. See, for example, *Majjhima Nikaya* 38.
9. *M-D* 132.17.
10. Ibid.
11. Ibid. 37.4.
12. Ibid. 47.14.
13. Ibid. 113.26.
14. Ibid. 118.4.
15. Ibid. 42.26.
16. Ibid. 118.3.
17. Ibid.
18. Ibid. 124.8.
19. Ibid. 124.15.
20. Ibid. 125.1.
21. Ibid. 125.14.
22. Ibid. 125.18.
23. Ibid. 119.28.
24. Ibid. 119.30.
25. Ibid. 119.31.
26. Ibid. 119.34.

27. Ibid. 119.36.
28. Ibid. 119.35.
29. Ibid. 124.12.
30. Ibid. 124.15.
31. Ibid. 124.2.
32. Ibid. 124.19.
33. Ibid. 124.20.
34. Ibid.
35. Ibid. 124.11.
36. Ibid. 128.16.
37. Abe, *Western Thought*, 7.
38. *M-D* 132.7.
39. Ibid. 132.12.
40. Ibid.
41. Ibid. 9.21.
42. Ibid. 119.31.
43. Ibid. 132.17.
44. Ibid. 132.7.
45. Ibid. 126.6.
46. Ibid. 126.8.
47. Ibid. 110.19.
48. Ibid. 36.39.
49. Ibid.
50. Blyth, *Zen*, 83.
51. Qtd. in Anderson, *Upright*, 108.
52. *M-D* 127.2–3.
53. Ibid. 127.5, 127.7.
54. Ibid. 127.9.
55. Ibid. 127.21.
56. Ibid.
57. Ibid. 109.14.
58. Ibid. 125.24.
59. Ibid. 125.26.
60. Ibid. 127.21.
61. Ibid. 129.1.
62. Ibid. 129.2.
63. Ibid. 125.24.
64. Ibid. 125.28.
65. Ibid. 125.29.
66. Blyth, *Zen*, 90.
67. *M-D* 129.1.
68. Ibid. 129.8.
69. Ibid. 132.12.
70. Ibid. 132.16–7.

24. PACIFIC

1. *M-D* 64.5.
2. Ibid. 79.4.
3. Ibid. 85.11.
4. Ibid. 45.10, 45.19.
5. Ibid. 41.19.
6. Ibid.
7. Ibid. 100.19.

8. Ibid. 36.39.
9. Ibid. 14.4.
10. Ibid. 133.24.
11. Ibid. 135.55.
12. Ibid. 133.44.
13. Ibid. 134.45.
14. Ibid. 60.9.
15. Ibid. 19.27.
16. Ibid. 135.61.
17. Surely, all members of the crew have attached personal objects to the ship, as this is common practice on sea vessels, but all such descriptions in *Moby-Dick* refer exclusively to Ahab.
18. *M-D* 28.5.
19. Ibid. epilogue.3.
20. Ibid. epilogue.3.
21. Ibid. 1.8.
22. Ibid. 7.7.
23. Ibid. 24.22.
24. Ibid. 35.10.
25. Ibid. 41.20.
26. Ibid. 47.1.
27. Ibid. 93.11.
28. Ibid. 3.52.
29. Ibid. 73.40.
30. Ibid. 49.8.
31. Ibid.
32. Ibid. 61.3–4.
33. Melville, *Journal*, 6–7.
34. *M-D* epilogue.3.
35. Hongzhi, *Cultivating*, 27.
36. *M-D* 93.13.

CONCLUSION

1. *M-D* 3.52.
2. Ibid. 85.11.
3. Ibid. 45.2.
4. Ibid. 85.11.
5. Ibid. 110.19.
6. Ibid. 44.10.
7. Bayle, *Dictionary*, 549.
8. Huang Po, *Zen Teaching*, 29–30.
9. Melville, *Pierre*, 24.
10. Herman Melville, *Published Poems: The Writings of Herman Melville, Volume 11*, Hershel Parker, ed. (Evanston and Chicago: Northwestern University Press and The Newberry Library, 2009), 11.
11. *M-D* 17.1.

Bibliography

Abe, Masao. *A Study of Dogen: His Religion and Philosophy*. Albany: State University of New York Press, 1992.

——. *Zen and Western Thought*. Honolulu: University of Hawaii Press, 1985.

Alger, William Rounseville. *The Solitudes of Nature and of Man*. Boston: Roberts Brothers, 1867.

Ames, Van Meter. Zen and American Thought. Westport: Greenwood Press, 1962.

Anderson, Tenshin Reb. *Being Upright: Zen Meditation and the Bodhisattva Precepts*. Berkeley: Rodmell Press, 2001.

——. *Warm Smiles from Cold Mountains: Dharma Talks on Zen Meditation*. Berkeley: Rodmell Press, 2005.

Armstrong, Karen. *Buddha*. New York: Penguin, 2001.

Arnold, Sir Edwin. *The Light of Asia*. Wheaton, IL: Theosophical Publishing House, 1969.

Arvin, Newton. *Herman Melville*. London: Methven and Co., 1950.

Austin, James H. *Zen and the Brain*. Cambridge: MIT Press, 1999.

Baizhang Huaihai. *The Baizhang Zen Monastic Regulations*. Translated by Shohei Ichimura. Berkeley: Numata Center for Translation and Research, 2006.

Batchelor, Stephen. *The Awakening of the West*. Berkeley: Parallax Press, 1994.

——. *Buddhism Without Beliefs*. London: Bloomsbury, 1997.

Bayle, Pierre. *The Dictionary Historical and Critical of Mr. Peter Bayle, Second Edition*. 5 vols. London: Printed for D. Widwinter, et al., 1738.

Bell, Millicent. "Pierre Bayle and Moby Dick." *PMLA*, Vol. 66, No. 5 (September 1951), 626–648. 24 August 2010. Web. http://www.jstor.org/stable/459528.

Blackmur, R.P. "The Real Center of Interest." Parker and Hayford, 1938, 179–180.

Bloom, Harold. "Introduction." *Bloom's Modern Critical Interpretations. Herman Melville's Moby-Dick: Updated Edition*. New York: Bloom's Literary Criticism, 2007.

Blyth, R.H. *Zen and Zen Classics, Volume 1*. Tokyo: Hokuseido Press, 1960.

Bodhi, Bikkhu, trans. *The Connected Discourses of the Buddha: A translation of the Samyutta Niakaya*. Boston: Wisdom Publications, 2000.

Bodhidharma. *The Zen Teaching of Bodhidharma*. Translated by Red Pine. New York: North Point Press, 1989.

Bodiford, William M. *Soto Zen in Medieval Japan*. Honolulu: University of Hawaii Press, 1993.

Braswell, William. *Melville's Religious Thought*. New York: Octagon Books, 1973.

Bryant, John. "*Moby-Dick* as Revolution." Bloom, 199–224.

Burnouf, Eugene. *Introduction to the History of Indian Buddhism*. Translated by Katia Buffetrille and Donald S. Lopez Jr. Chicago: University of Chicago Press, 2010.

Chadwick, David. *Crooked Cucumber: The Life and Zen Teaching of Shunryu Suzuki*. New York: Broadway Books, 1999.

Clarke, J.J. *Oriental Enlightenment: The Encounter Between Asian and Western Thought*. London: Routledge, 1997.

Clarke, James Freeman. *Ten Great Religions*. Boston: Houghton-Mifflin Company, 1871.

Cleary, Thomas, ed. and trans. *Book of Serenity: One Hundred Zen Dialogues*. Hudson: Lindisfarne Press, 1990. xi–xlii.

———. *Zen and the Art of Insight*. Boston: Shambhala, 1999 .

———. *Zen Antics: Classics of Buddhism and Zen, Volume Four*. Boston: Shambhala, 2001.

Davis, John Francis. *The Chinese: A General Description of China and its Inhabitants*. New York: Harper Brothers, 1836.

Delbanco, Andrew. *Melville: His World and Work*. New York: Vintage Books, 2005.

The Dial: A Magazine for Literature, Philosophy, and Religion. 4 vols. Boston: James Munroe and Co., 1841–1849.

Dillingham, William B. *Melville & His Circle: The Last Years*. Athens: University of Georgia Press, 1996.

Dogen, Eihei. *Dogen's Pure Standards for the Zen Community: A Translation of Eihei Shingi*. Translated by Taigen Daniel Leighton and Shohaku Okamura. Albany: SUNY Press, 1996, 33–62.

———. *Enlightenment Unfolds: The Essential Teachings of Zen Master Dogen*. Edited by Kazuaki Tanahashi. Boston: Shambhala, 1999.

———. *Moon in a Dewdrop: Writings of Zen Master Dogen*. Edited by Kazuaki Tanahashi. New York: North Point Press, 1985.

———. *The Heart of Dogen's Shobogenzo*. Translated by Norman Waddell and Masao Abe. Albany: SUNY Press, 2002.

———. *Master Dogen's Shobogenzo*. 4 vols. Translated by Gudo Wafu Nishijima and Chodo Cross. London: Windbell Publications, 1994 –1999.

Domoulin, Heinrich. *Zen Buddhism: A History*. Bloomington: World Wisdom, 2005.

Dongan, Alan. "Spinoza's Theology." *Cambridge Companion to Spinoza*. Edited by Don Garrett. Cambridge: Cambridge University Press, 1996, 343–382.

Dongshan. "Secret of the Mind Elixir." *Classics of Buddhism and Zen, Volume One*. Edited by Thomas Cleary, 315–316.

Dreyfus, Hubert and Sean D. Kelly. *All Things Shining: Reading the Western Classics to Find Meaning in a Secular Age*. New York: Free Press, 2011.

Dumoulin, Heinrich. "The Song Period: A Time of Maturation." Loori, 17–40.

Edinger, Edward F. "The Meaning of the Whale." Higgins and Parker, 470–475.

Eitel, Ernest J. *Hand-Book of Chinese Buddhism, being a Sanskrit-Chinese Dictionary with Vocabularies of Buddhist Terms in Pali, Singhalese, Siamese, Burmese, Tibetan, Mongolian and Japanese*. Hong Kong: Lane, Crawford, & Co, 1888.

Emerson, Ralph Waldo. *Works*. London: George Rutledge and Sons, 1883.

"Extracts from New Books: Rev. of *De Hell's Travels*." *The Literary World* (1847–1853) 17 July 1847: American Periodicals Series Online, ProQuest. Web, 21 October 2010.

Ferguson, Andrew. *Zen's Chinese Heritage*. Somerville: Wisdom Publications, 2000.

Fields, Rick. *How the Swans Came to the Lake: A Narrative History of Buddhism in America*. Boston: Shambhala, 1992.

Finklestein, Dorothee. *Melville's Orienda*. New York: Octagon Books, 1971.

Franklin, H. Bruce. *The Wake of the Gods: Melville's Mythology*. Stanford: Stanford University Press, 1963.

Garfield, Jay L. *The Fundamental Wisdom of the Middle Way: Nagarjuna's Mulamadhyamakakarika*. New York: Oxford University Press, 1995.

Glassman, Bernie. *Infinite Circle: Teachings in Zen*. Boston: Shambhala, 2002.

Gretchko, John M.J. *Melvillean Loomings: Essays on Moby-Dick*. Cleveland, Falk & Bright Publishers, Inc, 1992.

Gupta, R.K. *The Great Encounter: A Study of Indo-American Literary and Cultural Relations*. New Delhi: Abhinav Publications, 1986.

Hagen, Steve. *Buddhism is Not What You Think*. San Francisco: Harper, 2003.

Harada, Sekkei. *The Essence of Zen.* Tokyo: Kodansha, 1993.

Hawthorne, Nathaniel. *The Portable Hawthorne.* Edited by Malcolm Cowley. New York: Viking Press, 1969.

Hicks, Granville. "The Meaning of Ishmael's Survival." Parker and Hayford, 1958, 265–266.

Hoare, Philip. *Leviathan, or The Whale.* London: Fourth Estate, 2008.

Hodgson, Brian Houghton. *Essays on the Languages, Literature, and Religion of Nepal and Tibet.* London: Trubner & Co, 1874.

The Holy Bible: New Revised Standard Version. New York: Oxford University Press, 1977.

Hongzhi Zhengue. *Cultivating the Empty Field: The Silent Illumination of Zen Master Hong-zhi.* Translated by Taigen Daniel Leighton with Yi Wu. Boston: Tuttle Publishing, 2000.

Hori, Victor Sogen. "The Nature of the Rinzai (Linji) Koan Practice." Loori, 117–130.

Huang Po. *The Zen Teaching of Huang Po: On the Transmission of Mind.* Translated by John Blofeld. London: Rider & Company, 1958.

Huc, Evariste Régis. *Recollections of a Journey through Tartary, Thibet, and China, during the Years 1844, 1845, and 1846.* New York: D. Appleton & Company, 1860.

Hui-Neng, Dajian. *The Sutra of Hui-Neng: Grand Master of Zen.* Translated by Thomas Cleary. Boston: Shambhala, 1998.

Huntington, C.W. Jr. *The Emptiness of Emptiness: An Introduction to Early Indian Madhyamika.* Honolulu: University of Hawaii Press, 1989.

Jacquemart, Albert. *History of the Ceramic Art: A Descriptive and Philosophical Study of the Pottery of All Ages and All Nations.* New York: Scirber, Armstrong & Co, 1877.

"Japan." *Putman's Monthly,* Volume 1, March 1853, no. 3, pp. 241–251.

Jones, Sir William. *A Grammar of the Persian Language.* London: W. Nicol, 1828.

Kaempfer, Englebert. *The History of Japan.* Richmond: Curzon Press, 1993.

Kapleau, Philip. *The Three Pillars of Zen.* Garden City: Anchor Books, 1980.

Keizan, Jokin. *The Record of Transmitting the Light: Zen Master Keizan's Denkoroku.* Translated by Francis Dojun Cook. Somerville: Wisdom Publications, 2003.

Kulkarni, H.B. *Moby-Dick: A Hindu Avatar: A Study of Hindu Myth and Thought in Moby-Dick.* Logan: Utah State University Press, 1970.

Ladislaus, I. Joseph. *The Quest for Spirituality in Herman Melville and Swami Vivekananda.* Bangalore: Asian Trading Corporation, 2001.

Leyda, Jay. *The Melville Log: A Documentary Life of Herman Melville, 1819–1891.* New York: Gordian Press, 1969.

Lin-chi. *The Zen Teachings of Master Lin-chi.* Translated by Burton Watson. Boston: Shambhala, 1993.

Loori, John Daido, ed. *Sitting with Koans.* Boston: Wisdom Publications, 2006.

Lopez, Donald S. Jr. "The Ambivalent Exigete: Hodgson's Contribution to the Study of Buddhism." *The Origins of Himalayan Studies: Brian Houghton Hodgson in Nepal and Darjeeling 1820–1858.* Edited by David M. Waterhouse. New York: Routledge, 2004, 49–76.

Maurice, Frederick Denison. *The Religions of the World and their Relations to Christianity.* Boston: Gould and Lincoln, 1854.

Maurice, Thomas. *The History of Hindostan: Its Arts, and Its Sciences, 2 Vols.* London: W. Bulmer and Co., 1795–1798.

Melville, Herman. "Billy Budd, Sailor." *Billy Budd, Sailor and Selected Tales.* New York: Oxford University Press, 1998, 279–362.

———. "Buddha." *Collected Poems of Herman Melville.* Edited by Howard P. Vincent. Chicago: Packard and Company, 1947, 232.

———. *Clarel: A Poem and Pilgrimage in the Holy Land.* Edited by Walter Bezanson. New York: Hendricks House, 1960.

———. "Hawthorne and His Mosses." *The Literary World* (1847–1853) 17–24 August 1850: American Periodicals Series Online, ProQuest. Web, 21 October 2010.

———. "Hawthorne and His Mosses." *Moby-Dick.* Edited by Hershel Parker and Harrison Hayford. New York: W.W. Norton and Co., 2002, 517–532.

———. *Journal of a Visit to London and the Continent, 1849–1850.* Edited by Eleanor Melville Metcalf. Cambridge, MA: Harvard University Press, 1948.

————. *Mardi: and a Voyage Thither*. Evanston and Chicago: Northwestern University Press and The Newberry Library, 1970.

————. *Moby-Dick*. Edited by Hershel Parker and Harrison Hayford. New York: W.W. Norton and Co., 2002.

————. *Moby-Dick*. Evanston and Chicago: Northwestern University Press and The Newberry Library, 1988.

————. *Pierre, or The Ambiguities*. Evanston and Chicago: Northwestern University Press and The Newberry Library, 1971.

————. "Rammon." *Collected Poems of Herman Melville*. Edited by Howard P. Vincent. Chicago: Packard and Company, 1947, 411–416.

————. *Redburn: His First Voyage*. Evanston and Chicago: Northwestern University Press and The Newberry Library, 1969.

————. "To Evert A. Duyckinck." 3 March 1849. *Correspondence: The Writings of Herman Melville, Volume 14*. Edited by Lynn Horth. Evanston and Chicago: Northwestern University Press and The Newberry Library, 1993, 120–122.

————. "To Evert A. Duyckinck." 5 April 1849. Horth, *Correspondence*, 126–129.

————. "To Evert A. Duyckinck." 13 December 1850. Horth, *Correspondence*, 171–174.

————. "To Lemuel Shaw." 6 October 1849. Horth, *Correspondence*, 137–139.

————. "To Nathaniel Hawthorne." 1 June 1851. Horth, *Correspondence*, 188–194.

————. "To Nathaniel Hawthorne." 16 April 1851. Horth, *Correspondence*, 184–187.

————. "To Nathaniel Hawthorne." 29 June 1851. Horth, *Correspondence*, 194–196.

————. "To Nathaniel Hawthorne." 17 November 1851. Horth, *Correspondence*, 210–214.

————. "To Richard Bentley." 26 June 1850. Horth, *Correspondence*, 162–165.

————. "To Sophia Hawthorne." 8 January 1852. Horth, *Correspondence*, 218–220.

————. *Typee: A Peep at Polynesian Life*. Evanston and Chicago: Northwestern Univeristy Press and The Newberry Library, 1968.

————. *White-Jacket or The World in a Man-of-War*. Evanston and Chicago: Northwestern University Press and The Newberry Library, 1970.

The Middle-Length Discourses of the Buddha: A Translation of the Majjhima Nikaya. Translated by Bhikku Nanamoli and Bikkhu Bodhi. Somerville: Wisdom Publications, 1995.

Mumford, Lewis. *Herman Melville*. London: Jonathan Cape, Ltd., 1929.

Mumon. *The Gateless Gate: The Classic Book of Zen Koans*. Translated by Koun Yamada. Boston, Wisdom Publications, 2004.

Nagashima, Andy. "*Walden*'s Cosmology." Web, 2 February 2010. http://wwww. thoreausociety.org/__activities/cs/global/AndyNagashima.pdf.

Ovid. *The Metamorphoses of Ovid*. Translated by David R. Slavitt. Baltimore: Johns Hopkins University Press, 1994.

Parker, Hershel and Harrison Hayford, eds. *Moby-Dick as Doubloon*. New York: Norton, 1970.

Parker, Hershel. *Herman Melville, A Biography*. 2 vols. Baltimore: The Johns Hopkins University Press, 1996–2002.

————. "*Moby-Dick* and Domesticity." Higgins and Parker, 545–562.

Porter, Carolyn. "Call Me Ishmael, or How to Make Double-Talk Speak." Bloom, 133–162.

Potter, William. *Melville's Clarel and the Intersympathy of Creeds*. Kent: Kent State University Press, 2004.

Powell, William F., trans. *Record of Tung-shan*. Honolulu: University of Hawaii Press, 1986.

Renker, Elizabeth. "Introduction." *Moby-Dick*, by Herman Melville. New York: Signet Classic, 1998, ix–xvii.

Rollyson, Carol and Lisa Paddock. *Herman Melville, A to Z: The Essential Reference to His Life and Work*. New York: Checkmark Books, 2001.

Salisbury, Edward E. "M. Burnouf on the History of Buddhism in India." *Journal of the American Oriental Society*. Boston: Published by the Society, 1849, 275–298.

————. "Memoir on the History of Buddhism." *Journal of the American Oriental Society*, 79–135.

Seng-Ts'an. *Hsin-Hsin Ming: Verses on the Faith-Mind*. Translated by Richard Clarke. Buffalo: White Pine Press, 2001.

Senzaki, Nyogen. *Like a Dream, Like a Fantasy: The Zen Teachings and Translations of Nyogen Senzaki.* Edited by Eido Shimano. Boston: Wisdom Publications, 2005.

Sharf, Robert. "The Zen of Japanese Nationalism." *Curators of the Buddha: The Study of Buddhism Under Colonialism.* Edited by Donald S. Lopez. Chicago: University of Chicago Press, 1995, 107–160.

Sullivan, J.W.N. "Melville's Lonely Journey." Parker and Hayford, 1923, 158–165.

Suzuki, Deisetz Teitaro. *Essays in Zen Buddhism, First Series.* Auckland: Rider and Co., 1970.

———. *Essays in Zen Buddhism, Third Series.* Auckland: Rider and Co. 1970.

———. *The Training of the Zen Buddhist Monk.* New York: University Books, 1965.

Suzuki, Shunryu. *Branching Streams Flow in the Darkness: Zen Talks on the Sandokai.* Edited by Mel Weitsman and Michael Wenger. University of California Press: Berkeley, 1999.

———. *Zen Mind, Beginner's Mind.* New York: Weatherhill, 1970.

Thoreau, Henry David. *A Week on the Concord and Merrimack Rivers.* Princeton: Princeton University Press, 1980.

———. *Journal.* 8 vols. Edited by Robert Sattelmeyer. Princeton: Princeton University Press, 1981–2002.

Tilton, Eleanor M. *Melville's "Rammon": A Text and Commentary.* Offprint from Harvard Library Bulletin Volume XIII, Number 1, Winter 1959.

Turner, Patricia and Charles Russell Coulter, eds. *Dictionary of Ancient Deities.* New York: Oxford University Press, 2000.

Tweed, Thomas A. *The American Encounter with Buddhism, 1844–1912.* Chapel Hill: University of North Carolina Press, 1992.

Vincent, Howard P. *The Trying-Out of Moby-Dick.* London: Southern Illinois University Press, 1967.

Wick, Gerry Shishin. *Book of Equanimity: Illuminating Classic Zen Koans.* Somerville: Wisdom Publications, 2005.

Wilber, Ken. *No Boundary.* Boston: Shambhala, 1979.

Wisdom of Buddha: The Samdhinirmocana Mahayana Sutra. Translated by John Powers. Berkeley: Dharma Publishing, 1995.

Wolf, William J. *Thoreau: Mystic, Prophet, Ecologist.* Philadelphia: United Church Press, 1974.

"Works in Press." *The Literary World* (1847–1853) 20 Nov. 1847: American Periodicals Series Online, ProQuest. Web, 21 October 2010.

Yamada, Mumon. *Lectures on the Ten Ox-Herding Pictures.* Honolulu: University of Hawai'i Press, 2004.

Young, Jennie J. *The Ceramic Art: A Compendium of the History and Manufacture of Pottery and Porcelain.* New York: Harper & Brothers, 1878.

Zen Flesh, Zen Bones. Compiled by Paul Reps and Nyogen Senzaki. Boston: Tuttle Publishing, 1998.

Index

Abe, Masao, 23
Ahab, x, 75, 110, 156; and ambiguity,
  xii–xiii, 21, 97; awakening of, xii,
  158–163, 162–163; and faith, 141;
  fixed view of, xiii, 48–49, 111, 156,
  166–167, 203n17; isolation of,
  131–134, 145, 156–158, 197n52; and
  language, 92–93; mind of, 125–127,
  155; suffering of, 21, 29–31, 47, 105,
  128–131, 156; and the whale, xii–xiii,
  48, 97–98, 105, 128–129, 132, 136,
  156, 166
Anderson, Tenshin Reb, 84, 153, 184n39,
  190n17
Arvin, Newton, xii

Baizhang, 57, 143
Batchelor, Stephen, 4, 154, 191n18
Bayle, Pierre. *See Dictionnaire Historique
  et Critique*
Blofeld, John, 152
Blue Cliff Record, 39
Blyth, R.H., xii, 109, 111, 112, 137, 161,
  162
Bodhidharma, 42, 73, 80, 86, 87, 90, 145,
  161; and facing the wall, 27, 41, 98
Book of Serenity, 110–111
Bryant, John, 51
Bulkington, 44, 118, 121
Burnouf, Eugene, 4–5, 182n9

Carpenter (of Pequod), 49, 61–62, 76, 126,
  130, 141, 155, 161
Chandrakirti, 108
China: American interest in, 10–11; Ch'an
  school of, xvi, 20, 35, 41, 57–58, 61,
  87; other Buddhist traditions in, 5,
  13–14, 16; other religious traditions of,
  4, 7, 179n18; Melville's sources
  regarding, 10–11, 25–28, 178n30
*The Chinese: A General Description of
  China and Its Inhabitants* (Davis), 11,
  26–28, 172, 182n9
Christianity, x, xii, 3, 10, 11, 15, 19, 23,
  28, 55, 70, 108, 136–137, 146, 152,
  182n25–183n26
Clark, Reverend Bryan, xvi, 175
Clarke, J.J., 11
Cleary, Thomas, xiii, 22, 43, 72, 143, 147,
  152
coffin life-buoy, 75, 77, 158, 160–162,
  167–168, 169, 172
compass (of the Pequod), 135, 157–158,
  161
Consular Cities of China (Smith), 58–59,
  61

Daggoo, 83, 135
dependent co-origination (aka dependent
  co-arising), xii–xiii, 76–77, 80–84, 99,
  110, 120, 129, 132–134, 151, 158–159,
  161–163, 166, 172

About the Author

Daniel Herman received his doctorate from Victoria University in Wellington, New Zealand, in 2011. He currently teaches American literature at the University of San Francisco and San Francisco State University. He lives in Berkeley, with his wife, daughter, and dog.

CPSIA information can be obtained at www.ICGtesting.com
Printed in the USA
BVOW02*1544220414

351103BV00004B/5/P